ON THE EDGE
David Jones
with Mike Dunn

**To my wife Ann, our children,
and my close friend, Phil Jones.**

Front cover picture by Martin Rickett, News Team Manchester

Published by Paper Plane Publishing Ltd.
© Copyright 1997
First edition August 1997
Printed by Stephens and George
ISBN 1-871-872-25-1
The rights of the author are asserted.

CHAPTER 1

Going Up With The Joneses

THEY'RE pouring out of pubs, waving and cheering, they're hanging out of cars, horns are beeping; and everywhere people are chanting the anthem only a chosen few get to sing each year: 'We're going up, we're going up...' Grown men and grown women who should know better, wealthy directors wise enough and old enough to know better — they've all abandoned restraint and commonsense. It doesn't matter who you are, what you are, where you're from — only one thing matters right now. Stockport are promoted. And right now, the man who made it happen — the man responsible for taking one of the nation's least glamorous clubs into the big time, is soaking up the unashamed joy. David Jones is sitting on the team bus — heading home after watching his team, the fans' heroes, win 1-0 at Chesterfield, and, therefore, clinch promotion to Division One.

The last time Stockport were in Division One was 1936 — and tonight the frustration of waiting for 60 years has finally exploded into one long party. As Jones recalls: "There was a convoy of cars and motorbikes in front of the coach for as far as you could see and it was like the fans were escorting us back home. Every time we went past a pub, the fans would come pouring out. They must have had a lookout or something, because people

Picture courtesy Manchester Evening News

Not so bitter....sweet promotion

just came bursting out of pub doors every time we approached. There were even fans hanging out of car windows — I don't know how someone didn't get killed. I remember, I couldn't take my eyes off one woman: I don't know how she was holding on, but I swear for at least half a mile she was hanging out of the side window, shouting and waving. If a big truck had come along she would have been decapitated — and I'm not joking. Everyone was beeping their horns and following us.... it was unbelievable."

The day Stockport County got promoted started for Jones like every other: a cup of tea for breakfast — nothing to eat — kiss the wife and kids goodbye and head off for work. But this really wasn't any ordinary day. Jones knew it, his wife and kids knew it, the players knew it, the chairman and directors knew it, the fans knew it — hell, everyone knew it. This was what an entire season had come down to. If County won tonight, they were up. Draw or lose and they went to Luton five days later needing a win to be sure of automatic promotion and avoid the lottery that is the dreaded play-offs. The problem was, they were up against Chesterfield. How ironic that these two teams should have been pitched together on this particular night. Soccer has a habit of throwing up fixtures that have their own little subplots like this. How many times does a player get transferred — only to find out his first game is against his old club? Leicester City may have won the Coca Cola Cup, and Chelsea the FA Cup, but the fairytale stories of both tournaments belonged to Stockport and Chesterfield. Both sides had risen above their station to thrill the nation with the most-talked about Cup exploits of the season — County reaching the semi-final of the Coca-Cola Cup and Chesterfield, led by their wily boss John Duncan, reaching the same stage in the FA Cup. Chesterfield had beaten Nottingham Forest and Wrexham to reach the Cup semi-final, and had then led 3-1 against Middlesbrough before finally drawing 3-3 in an epic battle at Old Trafford. All right, they lost the replay 3-0, but they were obviously no pushovers.

Now, here they were back in the real world, at home against Stockport with both sides desperately needing to win: County to go up automatically, Chesterfield to reach the play-offs. David Jones v John Duncan: the battle of the giantkillers. The other problem was that County were tired, desperately tired, and Jones knew it. So did his wife, Ann, who had shared the stresses and strains and the ups and downs of a phenomenal season — and who had become so engrossed in the club, she was now showing the tell-tale sign of fandom. "She was actually calling County 'us' and 'we'," Jones recalls. "I'm not a worrier... but Ann worries enough for everybody. Ann was really like a cat on a hot tin roof — she wanted to talk about it all the time over breakfast. I didn't want to talk about it. I just wanted to have my breakfast and get off to work — I knew what we had to do. Ann was telling me what I should say to the lads; and then she was asking me what I would say, and I was saying: 'I don't know, I don't know.'"

Jones stepped out of his house at 10.15am. The weather was lousy: murky, grey skies and the sort of persistent rain that dampens the spirit as much as the clothing. But Jones was delighted; the weather was his first break. "I knew the Chesterfield pitch was dry and bumpy and I didn't want the ball bobbling around all over the place," he said. "I knew if it kept raining, the pitch would soften up and the ball would be far more controllable." Perhaps God is a Stockport County fan, because it never stopped raining that day.

The gaffer, who lives in Southport, got into his car — a brand new Ford Probe he'd charmed County chairman, Brendan Elwood, into buying — and drove straight to neighbouring Birkdale to pick up the former Liverpool star, Gary Gillespie. Gillespie had joined County three months earlier from Coventry, who still paid his wages even though they no longer wanted him. Now he was one of Jones' trusted backroom team. Tall, calm, 'Mr Cool' Gary Gillespie. This bloke had seen it all before; had tasted the tension and excitement of far bigger games than this and knew how to take it all in his stride. They'd decided to head for the training ground, where County's youth team — the YTS lads who join the club dreaming of stardom — were being coached that day.

"We were talking and thinking about the game — what I was going to say to the lads and how we were going to approach it," recalls Jones. "Gary was calm. He's played in a lot of big games — big European games — and we both felt the most important thing was to be calm. I'm not an emotional person. A lot of people think that what makes you a good manager is running up and down the line, shouting and bawling at people. In some fans' eyes, that's what makes you a good manager — but that's not me."

After helping the kids, Jones and Gillespie eventually arrived at County's ground, Edgeley Park, at 1.30pm. Hanging on the main gate outside the ground was a good luck message, that simply read: 'Go for It'. "We got faxes and messages that day from all over the world," reveals Jones. "Some were from fans, from businesses, from sponsors, from my mates. There were faxes from as far off as Australia and America. This bloke in Australia hadn't been home for over 20 years, yet he'd been following us out there — he'd even seen our cup matches on Sky TV over there."

Jones and Gillespie read through the messages and were joined by Jones' most trusted ally at Edgeley Park; the man he made his number two, John Sainty. It was then that Jones named the men he had chosen for the battle ahead.

"To be honest, the team probably picked itself .... it was a question of who we had available that wasn't injured. I knew Chesterfield were going to come at us, because they had to win the game themselves, and that made me feel confident. When a team has to beat you, and you've got players up front that are very quick, you can defend a little deeper — and then break away. But that wasn't the main thing in my mind. The main thing was to get at 'em — it really was — and to get an early goal. Even at that stage in the day, I just knew we were going to go to Chesterfield and win. I knew, deep down, this was going to be our night."

County's players don't all live near the ground, and Jones had agreed that some of them could make their own way to Chesterfield that day. "We had thought about all travelling together in the morning," recalls Jones, "and having a bite to eat and a sleep at a hotel. But Chesterfield isn't that far away and I didn't think it warranted it this time. We picked up the majority of our team at Edgeley Park, except for 'Jonah', the keeper;

Gordon 'Sid' Cowans; 'Mazza' — that's Chris Marsden; Roger Wylde and Sean Connolly; they all went straight there."

It wasn't until an hour before the game that Jones got all his side together for the first time. There they were, huddled — almost squashed together — in the cramped Chesterfield dressing room. There couldn't have been a starker contrast: it wasn't that long ago that Jones was addressing the same players in the modern, clean, spacious — and comparatively opulent — dressing room of Middlesbrough's Riverside Stadium. Next door then were Ravanelli, Juninho and Emerson, and outside a 30,000 crowd excitedly waiting for the Coca Cola Cup semi-final to kick off. Next door now were Division Two 'journeymen' like Jamie Hewitt and Chris Beaumont — the latter a former County player himself. The stands were made of wood, the dingy corridors desperately needed a facelift and the chips on the decaying bathroom tiles had been there for God knows how long. Yes, this was the real world; not the fantasy-land of Middlesbrough or West Ham, Blackburn and Southampton where Jones' heroes had been seen and had conquered earlier in the season. The setting was strictly Division Two, but the match was far more important than the Coca Cola Cup semi-final. For the first time that night, Jones stood in front of the men who could take County to their greatest moment in 60 years, and carve his name permanently in the club's history. Or these same men could blow it all.

"Everyone in that changing room wanted First Division football," insisted Jones. "We had run our bollocks off for 65 games and we weren't going to throw it away now. Everything we'd worked for was up for grabs. They knew if they won the game they were in the First Division. I remember hearing Jim Gannon saying he'd waited seven years for this moment to come.

"I said to them that we had gone so close in the Coca Cola Cup — and the FA Cup and Auto Windscreen Shield — and that they couldn't throw all that away now. All those cup runs had been great — but this was the one we wanted."

The players are silent now; listening, listening. Jones knows the attention span of an average footballer isn't very long — "about 30 seconds," he quips — so he doesn't go in for long, drawn-out speeches: "I told 'em I'd rather lose this game than draw it, so let's go out all guns blazing. I really wanted us to go out and get at 'em; dictate the game ourselves, not let them push us back.

"I gave the team out, and then there really was nothing else I could say or do, so I let them go about their business. Some wanted to get changed straight away, others didn't. The likes of Sean and 'Kizza' — Kieron Durkan — and Tony Dinning wanted to get out on the pitch and kick a ball about. But the banter in the changing room was brilliant. Mazza's baby had just been born the previous Friday, a boy, so a lot of it was about that. Mazza's very, very close to Sean Connolly. Wherever Mazza is, Sean's following him! They room together, they're inseparable. So the lads wanted to know if Sean had been present at the birth as well.... and if there were any pictures!

"Gary Gillespie was taking the mickey, it was like if you stood up, you got the mickey taken out of you. It was all that sort of good-natured knock-about stuff. Brett Angell's good at it — we call him 'The Farmer' because of his accent, but he's very good at finding someone's Achilles Heel and going for it. It's not nasty. Everyone knows each other inside out and they're just having a laugh at each other's weaknesses."

The minutes were ticking away, and the little rituals and superstitions the players believe in, or go through, were coming to the fore. "They've got their little pecking order when they go out, for instance," reveals Jones. "Obviously Flynnie goes first, 'cos he's captain; but they seem to have worked out their own order after that — it's got nothing to do with me, it's something they've sorted between themselves. Alun Armstrong has to be out last, he will not go out until everyone else has."

Blond-haired Armstrong, just 24 years old, had come from Newcastle for £35,000 and had been an instant hit with County fans — forming the other half of County's strike force with the towering Brett Angell. He was County's baby-faced assassin; Edgeley Park's Ole Gunnar Solskjaer. But right now, 'Gunnar' Armstrong was causing a little concern. "Alun was really ill that day, he had a lot of stomach pains," says Jones. "He was very, very quiet and it took him a long time to put his socks on, an awful long time. I knew it was nerves; he's only young and he was very, very uptight — I think everyone could see that.

"That's when the banter really started. The hour before a game is the worst — there's nothing we can really do. The players know what we want and drumming the message over at this late stage isn't going to do any good." Cometh the hour, cometh the men, and suddenly the time had come to get on with the job.

"That's when all the players started shaking each other's hands and I stood at the door to shake their hands before they went out," recalls Jones. Outside, the rain was still lashing down, and the pitch was turning to mud — glorious mud, as far as Jones was concerned. The tiny ground was packed, the game was a sell-out, and the rain did nothing to dampen the fans' spirits. "It was a party atmosphere, the noise was tremendous," said Jones. "We walked out underneath the County fans, because they give away supporters half the main stand at Chesterfield. It's all wooden, and our fans were banging up and down with their feet. I've got a mate who used to travel all round the country — and even the world — with Liverpool, and he said the atmosphere was frightening. It reminded him of when Liverpool were playing away in Europe."

In that moment, Jones' thoughts flashed back to his wife, Ann, back at home in Southport looking after the kids. "I knew she'd be sat by the radio. Ann always feels that the tension's harder now I'm a manager than when I was playing — because when I played at least I could do something about it. If the ball was going into the net I could clear it. Now I'm manager she thinks it's all out of my control."

The County dug-out was full — with Sainty, Gillespie, County youth coach Joe Jakub and the man in charge of the club's School of Excellence, Austin Spate, squeezing in with the subs. They would share every kick of the ball — as if they were playing the game themselves. They would gasp and hold their breath together; they'd bawl and scream together, living on their nerves together for the following unbearable 96 minutes. Jones remained outwardly calm, unflappable. Within seconds he was standing on the sidelines, level with the players — kicking the ball in his mind, making the tackles, releasing the ball and building down the wings.

"We were frightening for the first 20 minutes," says Jones. "We had been doing that in last few games; starting like a house on fire and when we scored the goal, it was brilliant." That goal, the goal that put David Jones and Stockport into Division One, came after five minutes and is etched as clearly in his mind today as the moment he saw it happen.

"Our keeper, Jonah, picked the ball up in the box and threw it out to Toddy," he recalls. "Toddy's then done a great little shimmy down the line and Alun Armstrong's made a run out wide. Toddy hits it with the outside of his foot, into Alun's path. Armstrong checks back, crosses it and Brett — who's charged from the halfway line to get into the box — stoops to get his head to it.

"From where we were, we thought their keeper had got it at first — but once the ball hit the net, I was just punching the air for joy. Our fans erupted, the noise was phenomenal, and I was trying to yell at Flynnie: 'Go get the ball, they can't hit back if we've got it'."

County kept up the pressure throughout the half, with the Chesterfield keeper producing two good saves from Angell. "We were on fire, but I desperately wanted us to get a second," says Jones. Suddenly, it's half time, and Jones is back in the cramped changing room looking at eleven players who are 45 minutes from Division One.

"'Keep a clean sheet; keep a clean sheet and we win the game' — I kept saying it over and over," smiles Jones at the memory. "It was obvious really; but what else can you say — the adrenalin's pumping and it all comes down to that. We knew they would come out and bombard us with high balls in the second half and we had to stop their supply line.

"We knew the ball would come into the box from free kicks and long throws. Flynnie and Jim were going to be the key players, and Jonah of course, because they would bombard us. I was saying: 'Don't sit back and let them get on top of us. Try to keep the ball and we can dictate the pace, not them.'"

Exactly as predicted, Chesterfield started the second half like they were mounting a Second World War offensive. Over and over came the big bombs from every direction, indiscriminately trying to blow holes in the County defence. "Yep, they bombarded us," said Jones. On the County bench, the tension was getting unbearable: "I turned to Saint, and he couldn't watch the game — he didn't want to come out of our changing rooms because he knew we were so close. Everyone thinks Saint is calm but he's nervous as well, and all through that half he was on the sidelines clinging to a bar and looking up to the sky."

And then came the awful moment when despite all the praying, the not-daring-to-look, the screaming, the cajoling, the willing to win, County's dreams were almost blown away. "They caught us on the break and I turned to someone — no-one in particular — and said: 'We're in trouble here,'" recalls Jones. "They knocked a big ball across — it was Chrissy Beaumont who knocked it over — and their boy Ebdon ran in from midfield. We were holding our breath; I knew Saint wasn't looking, and I just remember Jonah coming out to make himself as big as possible. For a terrible moment I thought it had gone in but suddenly Jonah's size 12 boots have come out and he's actually kicked the ball away — even though he's diving the wrong way."

But that wasn't the end: if County were to go up tonight, Jones, the bench — and the fans — had to suffer more. They weren't going to do it the easy way. "Tom Bennett got injured," says Jones, "which I could have done without. But I had no hesitation in throwing Tony Dinning on, because I know he's strong and can handle the big crosses coming into the box." And, as fate would have it, it was super-sub Dinning who kept County in the game: "There was a big melee in our goalmouth; the ball's all over the place and suddenly I see Tony scrambling it away off the line. I guess it would have gone in if he hadn't been there."

Jones glanced up to the directors box, where, he recalls: "Two of them had their heads in their hands. I looked at Mr White, our vice chairman, who's been at the club an awful long time, and I don't think he's even watching the game. They looked totally drained."

And then the 90 minutes are up and Sainty's bawling at Jones: 'It's gone, it's gone'. But it's not over, and everyone who sleeps, eats, and drinks Stockport County are in for the longest six minutes of their lives. Six minutes! That's how much injury time the referee had determined there was to play out — and the fans are frozen to their watches, suffering the agony of every protracted second. One minute, two, three, four ... for God's sake, five!... and Brett Angell's losing it. He storms off to the ref, and demands to know what the 'effin' hell' is going on. Back home, Ann is hugging the radio — imagining the worst, as the minutes pile up and Chesterfield launch yet another offensive. Why won't he blow the bloody whistle?

Jones takes it in his stride: "I knew there would be a lot of extra-time. Our fans had kept hold of the ball when someone blasted it into the stands — and I was thinking: 'For Christ's sake throw it back, the ref will just pile on the minutes'. I brought Brett off — he'd run himself into the ground — and I sent on Ken Charlery telling him to keep the ball. He did it brilliantly. I remember one incident in the corner and they couldn't get the ball off him. It seemed like ages — although it was probably only about ten seconds; but it seemed an awful long time.

"They were throwing men forward to get the equaliser, and I kept stepping on to the pitch because I couldn't see past their manager, John Duncan. I remember when I turned back, there seemed to be 20-odd cameramen —and a TV crew — sticking cameras up my nose; watching every movement I made. I wanted to swear but I couldn't because I knew I was on TV — and I remember that it went through my mind not to say something abusive on the telly."

Blow the whistle, blow the whistle, blow the bloody whistle ref! There wasn't a blue and white supporter alive right then not thinking the same thing. All around the ground everyone was looking at their watches. Ann was at home, staring at the clock; and across Stockport and Manchester thousands of fans and wellwishers were battling to survive the heart-stopping tension. And then it's over. The wait, the 96 minutes, the 60 years, it's all over.

"I jumped up and punched the air and then turned to John Duncan. He shook my hand, and I remember he said: 'You deserve it — you've deserved it all season, you've been the best team'. That meant a lot to me at that moment."

Then, in a split second, Jones thinks of all the people who really do deserve this moment: his wife and kids; his close friends; the girls in the office; the man who cleans the stands, the fans — and the chairman. "I turned and headed straight for the directors' box," he continues. "The chairman looked emotionally drained, absolutely shattered — normally he's immaculate; but his hair was all over the place. I just gave him — and Mrs Elwood — a big hug. I just felt that after everything he had done for the club it was right that he was the first person I went to. He had taken a gamble on me — because he'd given an unknown quantity the job — and I wanted to repay him; because he'd given me everything I'd asked for. I was indebted to him for giving me the opportunity. I'd promised him I'd get the club up and I'd kept my promise."

By now, County's ecstatic players were dancing and jigging in front of their delirious fans — and Jones battled through the crowds of wellwishers to get back on to the pitch: "The first person who came to me, when I came down, was Brett and he gave me a big hug. He's played for Everton and Sunderland, but this night meant a lot to him as well.

"It meant a lot to everyone — to everyone in that changing room and the football club. I suddenly remembered the girls in the office before we left for the match: Linda, Joanne, Andrea and Amy — it meant so much to them. Everyone was willing the club to go up. The players were down the bottom end with the fans. They were everywhere, all over the show. I went looking to shake their hands. Saint gave me a big kiss — he looked even more exhausted than the players, he was shattered.

Picture courtesy Manchester Evening News

Flynn-tastic....County's captain Mike Flynn

"The players walked over to us; Flynnie, with his shirt off, wrapped around his head, gave us a big hug. There was Mutchy and Mazza — and big Jonah just engulfed me. Then it was just a case of going round shaking hands with them all. The look on Jim Gannon's face was a joy to see, because he had been at the club a long time. It was party time, and the players were jumping up and down on the pitch.

"The fans were just chanting my name and it felt great, really great. My body was tingling, it really was, and I just felt immensely proud. We were on the pitch for a good 20 minutes, and the fans were dancing up and down, singing: 'Going up, going up... Stockport's going up'. That sounded good. Every step I took, there was a cameraman — or a mike being shoved up my nose — and it was still raining and I was getting wet and I wanted to get in.

"It was then that I noticed the chairman charging down the pitch, in his suit, in the mud. He looked so happy, he didn't care about the rain. I looked around, and I could pick out the fans I'd got to recognise week in, week out. Their faces were just ..... well, I wish I'd had a camera myself to capture that. There were fans crying — men and women — and when we went back under the stand, to get to the changing room, everyone was leaning across to pat us on the back. Grown men in suits were shouting: 'You've done it, you've done it.' We all eventually got back in, and I closed the dressing room off to say a few bits and bobs. I just said this moment was their reward for all their endeavour and hard work; they should savour it, go and wet Mazza's baby's head — and then go for the championship at Luton."

What followed next was one of the two most poignant moments of that night. Jones went for a quiet drink with the man he had just outfoxed — John Duncan. Jones and Duncan, alone in a room with a can of lager each. The two men who had filled the back pages of every national newspaper in the country with their cup heroics, and who had turned Chesterfield and Stockport — as unlikely as it seems — into household names.

"John was down in the dumps," recalls Jones. "He was very sad, and I apologised that it was us, of all people, that had destroyed his chances of reaching the play-offs. We reflected on the season, on our cup runs, and on the crippling number of games our teams had played. I have a lot of time for John. It's nice to speak to an experienced manager — and he's one of them — and you try to learn from their good points. I had no feelings for Chesterfield whatsoever during the match but after the game my feelings were for John — we had been down that road of playing so many games. His team looked tired — they'd given it their all, but it didn't happen for them."

Jones then headed for the directors room — and more plaudits. He was standing in front of the Ceefax, relishing the sight of the league table that confirmed Stockport were promoted, when Sainty appeared from nowhere to say: "It's time to go home boss."

"It was really quite quiet going back on the bus," recalled Jones. "There were a few beers, and little bit of champagne — but it was relaxed and quiet, with just a bit of music on the radio. I phoned Ann then for the first time, and she was shouting and screaming down the phone: 'We've done it! We're up! We're up!' I told her I wouldn't be coming home — I'd already had some beer and a couple of glasses of champagne, and I don't drink and drive.

"There were loads of people outside the ground when we arrived back in Stockport. My son, Lee, was on the bus with us and he told me the following day that he'd wanted to ask me something as we got off the bus —

but I was just lost in a sea of supporters. We got into the ground, got all the kit and boots off and four of us — me, Sainty, Gary and Joe — sat in the office and opened champagne.

"After half an hour there was a knock on the door and a fella walked in and asked when all the coaches were due back — because he was waiting for his son. We just said he'd be waiting a long time because all the coaches were stopping off at the pubs on their way back."

Then came the second poignant moment of the night. Jones decided to walk to a local pub, the Fingerpost, where a party was already in full swing. It was there he saw the man who had missed out on the night's dramas; a man who had helped make it all possible. Luis Cavaco was the exciting winger that Jones had bought in the pre-season from Portugal — and his goals and skills had made him an instant hit with the County fans. He gave County width, stretching defences until they didn't know which way to turn. But his season had been cruelly destroyed by a seemingly innocuous tackle at Wycombe, two weeks earlier, that left him with a broken leg.

"The first person I saw in the pub was Luis," said Jones. "Someone had phoned him at home from the pub and he could hear people chanting his name in the background over the phone. As soon as he heard that, he said: 'Come and pick me up' and so a couple of supporters went to get him. When I walked in, he was sitting at the bar. I shook his hand and gave him and his missus a hug. I wanted to make him feel part of it — he's been a part of the success."

Jones was deluged by fans, eager for his autograph on any scraps of paper and beer-mats they could find. But the night was taking its toll, and desperate for some sleep, he decided to head back to his room at the Britannia hotel. "I must have been floating," he recalled. "I must have walked 100 yards past the hotel when I suddenly got a panic attack because I didn't know where I was. I mean, how the hell can you miss the bloody hotel — it's enormous!"

Jones slept well that night, and returned to Edgeley Park the next morning to open the congratulatory faxes and letters, and to give the girls in the office a big hug.

"I bumped into Arthur Collister," he recalls now, "who cleans the stands for us, and gets all the stuff ready for the first team and the reserves. He does the half time teas, and blows the match ball up for the first team.

He must be 60-odd and he's been at the club a long time. It had been his birthday on the Saturday, and he said it was best present he'd ever had."

Jones then had a few moments to himself in his office and started to reflect on the last 24 hours: "My abiding memories of that night? Seeing the chairman running down the pitch in the mud. I was trying to get out of the rain and he's running back down the pitch into it. Saint's face during the game — looking up at the sky, unable to watch any more — also sticks in my mind. Then there was the cameras stuck up my nose with six minutes to go; and, also, the fans escorting us home after the game. I guess those are the things I remember the most."

CHAPTER 2

Singing The Blues

DAVID Jones is surrounded by kids — youngsters nobody wants. Rejects at the tender ages of 12,13,14,15; in danger of plunging, almost before his eyes into lives of crime, drugs, prostitution and prison. Some of these kids are from broken homes; some have been sexually abused; some have been kicked out of mainstream school because they are too disruptive, too unruly. It's Jones' job to put them back on the straight and narrow — to stretch out a hand and stop their fall, to repair the damage and hurt that has blighted their lives.

But nobody can see the damage and hurt that Jones is feeling right now. This is a professional footballer who was up there with the greats; a player who once walked out at Wembley, proudly wearing the shirt of Everton; a tough, tenacious and talented defender who had started dreaming of playing for England after being pencilled in for one of Don Revie's squads. And now here he was, surrounded by tormented, tearaway teenagers, desperately trying to become a social worker and loathing every minute of it.

"It killed me, it absolutely killed me," confessed Jones. "I was surrounded by kids from all over the place — from the Isle of Man to the Isle of Wight — and they were from broken homes; they'd been abused, some of them didn't even know how to hold a knife and fork. And I couldn't honestly tell you how on earth I'd ended up there...."

Jones spent two and a half years training to be a social worker; after his brilliant career as a professional footballer was snuffed out by one vicious tackle on a bleak night in 1981. He had gone into football — like every young, talented player — full of hopes and dreams of making it to the top. The difference for Jones was that the dreams turned into reality.

He was born in Liverpool's most notorious district, Toxteth, in August 1956. Like all the kids in that soccer-crazy city, football rapidly became a passion for him; and not surprisingly, Jones supported the team his dad followed — Everton.

Recalls Jones: "My mum always reminds me of the day I was bought my first pair of football boots and kit. It was in the early hours of the morning when my parents were woken by a noise. They rushed downstairs, thinking there had been a break-in or something, and there I am sleep-walking in my boots and kit. I must only have been four years old."

David has two brothers; Billy is the eldest, and works for a chemical firm; and younger brother Mark, who also played professional football before going into local government. When Jones was five years old, parents Pat and Bill moved the family to Halewood, an area which spawned great players like Steve McMahon, Archie Stevens and Brian Kettle. Jones attended Halewood Grange School, and throughout this period religiously went to all Everton's home games — and some of the away matches, when they were local enough.

This was the era of the formidable Everton team that included such soccer legends as Alan Ball, Joe Harvey and Howard Kendall — "they were my idols," says Jones — and it was then that the youngster started playing for Woolton Boys Club.

"Ironically, it was Liverpool who spotted me to begin with. I was invited to go to Mellwood on Tuesday and Thursday nights — I would have been 14 at the time. I'd been knocked back as a schoolboy —because you had to show you could kick the ball across the pitch from one touchline to the other, and I couldn't do it. They just wanted the biggest and strongest players at that time."

Jones left school when he was 15, without taking any exams, after his dad got him a job as an apprentice motor mechanic. He was still part of the Liverpool set-up when he received a phone call that would — suddenly —

make all his wildest dreams come true. "An old gentleman called Tommy Fairfoul phoned me up and asked if I would play for Everton," he recalls. "As if I needed asking after supporting them for so long! On the day I signed pro for them, Bill Shankly offered me terms at Liverpool — but there was no way I would have changed my mind. Signing for Everton meant an awful lot to me — and to my dad. He used to take me everywhere to all the games; and when I actually joined them, he'd take me there every day on the way to work. Mum and dad were my biggest help — if I wanted to go down that road then they were all for it."

David Jones signed professional terms with the legendary Billy Bingham — who went on to manage Northern Ireland — and suddenly, instead of watching his idols, Jones was training alongside them. That is something he will cherish for ever:

"As a fan, my heroes were Ball, Harvey and Kendall, and they were still playing for Everton when I signed. I idolised them and all of a sudden I'm training with them. I'll never forget Big Joe Royle. I was 16 and he took me into what they called the Cowshed at Bellfield. He used to practice crosses there and I was asked one day to mark him. Well, I was beating him in the air, winning every ball, when all of a sudden he sticks an elbow on the end of my nose. He turned round to me and he said: 'Son, you've got to watch these big hairy-arsed centre forwards, they'll always do that to you!'

"It took me seven years to get even. Joe was playing at Bristol City and I went through the back of him and said: 'Hey Joe, you've got to watch these big hairy-arsed centre halves!' Seven years and I never forgot it."

Jones played around 180 games for Everton and became a favourite with the fans. He modestly describes himself as a 'bread-and-butter' player; a no-nonsense defender who made up for what he might have lacked in finesse with sheer effort and willpower. "I was a good defender, solid, I could pass, " he said. "I think the Everton supporters would always take to someone who would give 100 per cent — and that's what I always tried to give. I think they would put up with you having a bad game, because they knew you were always out there trying your best."

Looking back, Jones is intensely proud of his international achievements. He was selected for both the England youth and Under 21 sides, and knew he was close, very close, to breaking into the full international squad.

"The England youth side was formidable when I was playing," he said. "There was the Wolves goalkeeper, Paul Bradshaw, then Bryan Robson and me at centre-back, and then the likes of Steve Wicks, Alan Curbishley, Peter Barnes, Gary Owen, and Ray 'Butch' Wilkins — it really was one hell of a side. Obviously it was players like Ray Wilkins and Bryan Robson who went all the way, but when I moved up to the Under 21s, I was playing alongside Glenn Hoddle. Frightening when you look back at it."

Goodison Park was Jones' entire life at this period; he literally slept, ate and drank Everton, and was willing to do anything for them. Even get married. He met his future wife, Ann, on a blind date — "yes," he smiles, "we were childhood sweethearts, she had long blond hair" — when he was just 15. The pair had been at the same school for four years, but hadn't plucked up the courage to talk to each other once during that period.

According to Jones: "It was a case of knocking around with one another; although when I left school, I didn't see her again for another six or seven months. Ann still wanted to go out with me and she asked my mate if I would meet her in the pub. I agreed, so we met at the Baby Elephant in Woolton Village. I was starting my football career and then my best mate at the time arranged for us to meet again in this pub and it went on from there."

Everton obviously approved of Ann because it took one of the most famous names in soccer to push Jones into popping the question. "It was Billy Bingham who told me to get married," confessed Jones. "He said it would settle me down; a good family life would be best for me as a player."

The first of their four children, Lee, was born in 1977 and Jones admits: "It's Ann who keeps all the family together. She does virtually everything. Family life is very important to me — but she looks after all the financial side. She pays the bills, she's 95 per cent of the house."

Gordon Lee was Everton manager when Jones experienced his greatest moment as a player — stepping out at Wembley for the club he'd supported ever since he was a boy. What a strange game fate can play — twisting and turning as swiftly as it takes a George Best or a Gianfranco Zola to send a defender spinning with just the slightest jink of the body.

When Jones went to Wembley, all that time ago, it was for the League Cup Final. How ironic that, 17 years later, Jones would achieve one of his greatest moments as a manager in the same competition — now known as the Coca Cola Cup — when he miraculously guided County to the semi-finals. But it was the moment when he actually stepped out of the players' tunnel — the moment when, right before his eyes, Wembley was awash with blue and white, and the deafening roar was coming from thousands of adoring Everton supporters — that has stuck the most. That was the greatest thrill soccer could give a player who had been besotted with this club all his life. A player who had spent his childhood dreaming of such a moment.

"That was my first time playing at Wembley," he revealed. "For me to run out in an Everton shirt, when two or three years earlier I had been stood on the terraces watching them, was unbelievable."

Everton were up against Aston Villa — and the match ended in a barren 0-0 draw. The sides drew again in the replay at Hillsborough — 2-2 this time — and then disaster struck for Jones. An injury ruled him out of the third, and ultimately conclusive, clash between the two sides. Having hit the the dizzy heights of playing at Wembley, he now sat a frustrated and forlorn figure as Everton desperately grappled to win the coveted prize. The inconsistencies of soccer were cruelly underlined for Jones. He was reduced to the role of spectator — a role he had thought was behind him now — and watched, helpless, as his team-mates lost and the dream was shattered. "We got beat by a Brian Little goal," he recalled. "I didn't play, because I had a knee injury. It was as if I'd gone from the greatest moment in my career to the most disappointing in one quick step."

Jones' love affair with Everton remains just as passionate today, but, in 1981, the time came for separation. Still at the height of his playing career, Jones decided the time had come to move — even though it meant tearing himself away from his beloved club. He explains: "I wanted to play centre half at Everton, but by then we had too many top-class centre halves at the club. Gordon Lee promised me I'd always play full-back for him, but he couldn't promise me the position I really wanted."

Two clubs came in for him — Ipswich, managed by Bobby Robson, and Coventry, led by Gordon Milne. Jones didn't know it then, but he was about to make one of the worst decisions of his professional career — a decision that would ultimately lead to misery, heartache, and, in the darkest depths of his despair, tears.

"Bobby Robson tried to sign me at Ipswich — I spoke to him on the phone but I didn't go down," recalled Jones. "They wanted me to play alongside Kevin Beattie — but I chose Coventry because, being a naive lad, I thought Ipswich was too far to go. Being a Liverpool lad, Coventry seemed a little bit nearer and closer to my family. It's strange that three and half years later I moved to Hong Kong without thinking twice about the distance! It's just one of the little lessons you learn, I suppose."

David Jones' Dugout Delight

David Jones rapidly realised he had made a disastrous move when the little guarantees he understood Milne and Lee had agreed never materialised. They seem petty, minor things now; but at the time they meant a lot to a player who was in demand, and expected to be rewarded accordingly. He'd been transferred for £260,000 — which was considered a big fee at the time — and knew that England boss Don Revie was ready to include him in the full international squad. But the rot was setting in — and worse was round the corner.

"The Coventry boss, Gordon Milne, promised me things and then didn't deliver," insisted Jones. "I never got things written in my contract that I should have done. For example, when I moved he promised Coventry would buy me a car — I used to lease a car off Everton. I was told they would buy it — but they never did. They told me we'd have a house with carpets; but again, we never did. I was only a young lad, I wasn't very experienced, and I never got these things in my contract. In the end I stopped playing for them. At the time I totally blamed the management — but looking back now, I've got to say it was probably six of one and half a dozen of the other. I did do my best for Coventry to start with, but it just seemed it was never enough."

Emotionally, Jones was on a down. But, the niggling misery the dissatisfaction with his contract was causing faded into insignificance one bleak night in 1981 — the night his world caved in.

****

David Jones doesn't like talking about the scything tackle that destroyed his career as a professional footballer. Even though it was 16 years ago, the pain is too close; the anguish too fresh in his mind. Even though his short career as a manager has brought him rapid success with County, that reward can't erase the wounds that one, brutal challenge caused. And nor can he rid his mind of the resentment he still feels towards the 'nobody' player, who, in one moment of violent stupidity, snuffed out a brilliant career.

Remember, Jones was still at the pinnacle: his stages were Old Trafford, Anfield, Highbury, White Hart Lane. He took it all for granted until the night he faced Derby County, in — of all things — a reserve game. Talking as though the incident had happened last night, Jones recalls: "I'd just cleared the ball and, as I was swivelling, this young lad came across and decided he wanted to take my livelihood away. I felt a sharp pain straight away and heard something snap — it was the cruciates. I wanted to throttle him there and then because I knew something serious had gone."

Jones claims he can't remember the name of the man who ended his career, although one suspects he could if he really tried. One thing's for certain though — he's never forgotten the face: "Yes, I still feel bitter towards him because I was really on the crest of a wave — I was really flying at the time, I seemed to be going right to the top. He was nothing — he never made it — and all of a sudden one reckless challenge takes my career away. I can still feel that challenge; but the one thing that I realise now, later on in life, is that if I hadn't have had that then, I wouldn't be down the road that I'm on now."

Jones hobbled off the pitch — "they iced me and put me in plaster" — and then set out on the long, agonising haul back to recovery. But once again, he found himself at loggerheads with Coventry; and to this day accuses them of not giving him the proper medical diagnosis he so badly needed. Despairing of the treatment he was getting at Highfield Road, Jones went to see his own specialist — who finally diagnosed exactly what was wrong.

"I didn't feel Coventry were doing enough for me," he remembers. "My specialist confirmed my cruciates had been torn; but when I went back and told Coventry, one of their specialists told me I might never have had one. Can you believe it! That's how much they hadn't checked my cruciates properly. Again, I wasn't happy with the way Coventry were treating me; it was just another unsavoury and unhappy experience."

It was another six months before Jones was back playing first-team football but, in his own words: "I didn't have an operation and I never felt 100 per cent with it, I knew I'd lost something. I played first-team football again but it just wasn't right."

Neither the physical nor the emotional scars that came with the injury have faded. Jones still winces at the memories of that tackle, and the way he was frozen out by an uncaring and unsympathetic Coventry management. At least Jones has wisdom on his side, and — as he approaches his 41st birthday — the maturity to learn from this harrowing period in his life. Yes, he is still bitter; yes, he wonders whether England caps were round the corner if he had been able to carry on playing free of injury. But now, as he learns about management and enjoys the first flushes of success, he is turning the bad experiences to his favour — and to Stockport's.

"After all that happened to me — and I try to emphasise this to my staff at County as well — I know that when a player has a bad, long-term injury, the worse thing that can happen is for his manager or coaching staff to stop speaking to him. I got that at Coventry. You're, like, cold shouldered. There's not a great deal the manager can do except to come in and say: 'Hallo, how are you, how's your family?' — but that goes a long way. I do try and do that because it is a period in a footballer's life when you can't do anything. You're stuck in plaster, you see the lads running round, and then you're lonely. It's a very, very lonely track back when you've had a long-term injury."

That understanding, that insight, helped Jones deal with County's Portuguese winger Luis Cavaco, who, agonisingly, broke a leg against Wycombe — just as County were within grasping distance of promotion. "As soon as Luis broke his leg, yes, my mind flashed back to what had happened to me — although his was a nothing challenge, he was just unfortunate that his leg was caught; a one in a million chance," said Jones."Luis is now going through it; he's starting it because he'll be in plaster for a few months — and then his hard work begins. When he's training, and all the other lads are having a laugh or have gone home, he'll suffer in those moments. It's a very, very lonely way back.

"When one of our YTS youngsters, Danny Youngo, did his cruciates, I went and sat with him in hospital and I think that goes a long way — if it's genuine feeling, then it goes even further. I told him it was a lonely life coming back, and sometimes you think it isn't worth it; but it is, because, once you are back playing again, it's the best feeling in the world."

****

David Jones was back playing football — fooling everyone except himself. He knew, deep down, he hadn't recovered fully from his atrocious injury and he feared for the future. From the height of playing at Wembley, he was facing the low of redundancy, of signing on at the Job Centre and scouring the small ads for work. And then, just when he needed it most, fate twisted once again; this time in the unlikely shape of an Oriental gentleman — with the equally unlikely name of Mr Wong. No, it wasn't the owner of a nearby Chinese takeaway; although Mr Wong was certainly in the takeaway business. He was in Britain recruiting players for the rapidly-expanding, and highly-lucrative, soccer leagues in Hong Kong — and he wanted David Jones.

Explained Jones: "I'd been bombed out at Coventry, I knew they didn't want me, and then suddenly the opportunity to go abroad arose. It was a fella called Mr Wong — honest that was his name — and he wanted me to play for three months for Seiko, the watch company, out in Hong Kong. I said yes — just to get out of Coventry really.

"Besides, the money was good and that was another big reason for going. I wasn't prepared to traipse half way round the world if the money wasn't any good. And I did well for them; we never lost a game in three months and won all the cup competitions. I was playing alongside Dutch internationals — that was a good experience — and there were players like Alan Ball, Trevor Brooking, and even Bobby Moore, playing in other teams out there. It really was very competitive; there were five or six teams that would have held their own in the bottom half of the First Division at the time."

Jones returned to England and heard that both Stoke City and Oxford United were interested in signing him: "I remember speaking to Jim Smith at Oxford, but deep down in my heart I knew my knee wasn't 100 per cent. And then Seiko offered me the chance to go back again — so I took it and went there for 16 months."

He was back on good money — about £50,000 for the season — and was playing for Hong Kong's most-successful team: "We won virtually everything that was going in Hong Kong; and I played all over the world with them, against national teams and the like. We were so good, we used to keep the score down to 0-0 at half-time — just so the boss would panic and come in and offer us more bonuses! We were streets ahead."

But there was a price to be paid. Playing week in, week out, on the dry, hard grounds out in Hong Kong was putting an unbearable strain on his knee and Jones knew time was running out. "I came back and didn't know what I was going to do," he recalls. "And then Gordon Lee phoned me up from Preston and asked me if I would play for him for a couple of weeks. I said yes — and ended up staying for two seasons."

But once again, fate was waiting patiently to twist the knife...

****

When Bryan Robson brought Ravanelli and Co. to Edgeley Park for the semi-finals of the Coca-Cola Cup, these men — used to the riches of Premier League life — probably experienced a small culture shock, a tremor. If that was so, then the shock Jones suffered when he first played at Preston was far beyond anything the Richter Scale could measure. He'd plummeted from Wembley to Deepdale in the time it takes one brutal tackle to erase a player's career — and a fall never seemed so steep.

He'd crashed from the bright lights to the dim lights — quite literally. "I remember playing my first night match and I couldn't believe it — they hadn't switched all the lights on," he recalled. "You know, I'd been used to playing at Old Trafford and Goodison and Anfield, and now I was wondering if my eyesight was damaged, as well as my knee."

The Preston team included Jones' younger brother Mark, and the former Manchester City centre-half Tommy Booth — who helped ease Jones into life at the bottom: life in the Third Division, facing the likes of Wigan and Halifax, where once Manchester United and Tottenham had stood. "Out on the pitch everyone was just turning and running away from you. It was a big culture shock but Tommy warned me what to expect," explains Jones.

But Jones was delaying the inevitable, making himself play football rather than face the harsh reality that his career was, effectively, over. He couldn't train day-in, day-out, with the team — because of the wear and tear on his knee — and increasingly he relied on cortisone injections to help get him through games. "In one way I was lucky because I was strong-legged, and I had strong hamstrings, so they took the brunt of it really," he said. "But I never had the operations that Paul Gascoigne and all them lot had — it wasn't around then. Each day, each match, was a grind and I was in pain. But it was just the fact that I wanted to play. I'd go in on a Monday and ice it, and then the physio at Preston, who was quite good, would get to work."

In the end, nature had the final say. For Jones there would be no gentle way out of the game; no money-spinning testimonial in front of thousands of adoring fans. Nothing to cushion the blow, but tears. And Jones isn't afraid to admit he cried the day his career ended. He recalls: "My knee went on me on the last kick of the ball, in the last game of the season, against Lincoln. I was just swivelling on the ball and the whole thing just collapsed. It was like my whole body had rotated on my knee. I just felt the sharp pain again and I knew it wasn't right."

Jones went home that night and broke down: "Yes, I was crying. I was only 29 and I was finished. You don't know what you've got until it's taken away; and that's the same in football. Playing football had been my life — and all of a sudden I wasn't in it. Believe me, that's hard, that's very hard. I was resentful of the bloke who was to blame — I'd probably run him over now if I saw him because I do feel he took half my career away. He's never been in touch — and he never went on and made it. I was a hard-working, bread and butter player, a good defender close to playing for England — so yes, I felt very hard done by."

What does an ex-pro do once the game's up. Jones hadn't a clue; perhaps he'd be a HGV driver; perhaps he'd buy a pub; perhaps he'd just scout around for jobs. Anything. The future looked bleak, the dreams were shattered, there were no prospects, no hope.

****

The next two-and-a-half years of David Jones' life would be the toughest and most harrowing he had faced. As unbelievable as it now seems, he spent that time training to be a social worker — trying to help kids nobody wanted — when all the time he was silently screaming to get back, somehow, into soccer. Jones isn't entirely sure how he drifted into social work, other than he was desperate, and fate was up to its usual tricks again. Out of the blue, he received a call from a gentleman called Adrian Esmat, who Jones had met during his schoolboy soccer days. Esmat now ran a home for problem kids — Clarence House — in Formby, Lancashire. And he wanted Jones' help.

Jones is still uncomfortable talking about this period in his life: "It's something in the past that I don't want to go back to. It was just a job. I don't know how I got into it, why I got into it, I just landed up in it.

"Clarence House was for kids from all walks of life; mainly kids that ordinary schools couldn't control. These were children that had been abused; that came from broken homes. There was such a broad spectrum of different problems there. I was a care officer and I helped look after the kids. I'd go to court with them — things like that. What you were doing was trying to put them back on the right road.

"The barriers were broken because everyone associated me with Everton. If they were Liverpool supporters, they hated me — and if they

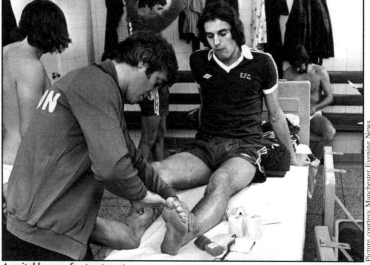

A suitable case for treatment

Picture courtesy Manchester Evening News

were Everton they loved me. So, all of a sudden the contact had been made. I dealt with such a variety of people that sometimes I just couldn't believe some of the things I was being told. Kids were coming who didn't even know how to eat with a knife and fork.

"They were given everything at Clarence House, they were probably better off than my kids; they got holidays and all sorts — and they had their clothes and food paid for. They'd been through a lot in their lives, so maybe they deserved it — although some of them didn't want it, and some did."

After the £50,000 a season he earned in Hong Kong, Jones was now on £9,000 a year and spending his free time ploughing through social work courses at colleges in Liverpool and Chorley. He gave it two-and-a-half years; he gave it the best he could, and hated every moment of it: "One of my best friends, my accountant Phil Jones, said he couldn't believe how low I was. He said it was terrible thing to watch me sinking and sinking."

Jones couldn't let go of football; it was in his blood, it was all he had known, it was his way of life. And, when he needed it most, football, in its non-league guise, came to the rescue. Brian Griffiths, the manager of Southport, wanted an assistant — and Jones fitted the bill. "I'd given everything to the social work; but having the non-league, that was my saviour," admitted Jones. "It was the non-league that kept me alive. I played a few games, but mostly I was coaching; and that's where I really got the bug to become a manager. And we did well. Andy Mutch was there; we sold Mutchy and Shaun Teale — it was a very good side, and we did well in the FA Cup."

The Griffiths/Jones partnership then moved on to more success with, first, Mossley and then Morecambe. Jones admits: "I owe a big debt to Brian because I would probably have just slipped out of the game without him. He got me back among players again — it was a good crack, and it opened my eyes a little bit. I was seeing, for the first time, how tough life in the non-league is; how players were getting up at six in the morning for work, and then coming to play for us at half past seven the same night. And I had to combine my social work with the football as well. In fact, I'd take the kids at Clarence House to training as an outing for them. It was good education for them, because they were getting out and about in the real world.

"I was gradually working my way into the non-league scene, hoping I'd get on. I applied for jobs all over the place. Whatever full-time job was in the paper, or on the grapevine, I would apply for."

In the end, it was Stockport who would throw Jones the lifeline he so sorely needed; although County nearly lost their man to one of his former Everton team-mates. "I had an opportunity to go with Bruce Rioch at Millwall," reveals Jones. "We had played together, and I phoned him up looking for a job. I was going to go down for an interview — for youth coach — when John Higgins phoned me from Stockport and asked me if I would fancy being youth coach there. So I went along for the interview and a couple of days later was offered the job."

Danny Bergara was Stockport manager then, and Jones clearly recalls their first conversation together: "Danny asked me what did I want to do in the future, what was my ambition? I looked straight at him and said I wanted to be a manager. That was the first time I met him."

Jones had no idea just how ominous that reply would prove to be. Little did he expect the controversial course of events that would leave him sitting in the seat occupied by the man who had just quizzed him. Jones gladly accepted the £180-a-week position, but very quickly found himself frustrated in his new role. "I found it very difficult, because — to be honest — Danny didn't really want a youth policy," he said. "The kids I was dealing with weren't of the quality that I liked. It was very hard for me at first, because it seemed such a dead-end job. I began wondering whether I had made the right decision, because it really was hard work. I was travelling up and down the motorway in my own car — I didn't have a club car then, and I was paying my own petrol — and I was driving 100 miles a day. It was hard going."

But the new man had made an impression with Bergara, and when County's first team started to struggle, the Uruguayan made Jones his assistant. "It was nice to work with quality again," said Jones. "It was like a big release valve for me. I'd already been working with the pros after training had finished; you know, kicking balls and stuff like that, but now I was back with them full-time."

Even so, Jones had no idea what he had let himself in for. Like the rest of Stockport, he looked upon Bergara as a legend; a great man who knew his football, and had a magical way of catapulting little clubs like County into the big time.

However — he very quickly learned the truth....

CHAPTER **3**

Laying The Ghost

THE shockwaves that shuddered through Stockport on the day Danny Bergara was sacked as County manager were almost audible. If you listened closely, you could hear the disbelief; the stunned dismay and the angry backlash as fans took in the shocking news — and then spread the word. How could they do this to Danny? County was, after all, Danny Bergara's 'Blue and White Army.' It was Bergara who got County promoted in 1991, after 20-odd barren years. It was Danny who took them to Wembley — think of it, County at Wembley! — for two play-off finals, and two Autoglass Trophy finals. OK, they lost the lot — but County at Wembley? That was magical, that was unthinkable, and it had actually happened — thanks to Danny.

No loyal fan doubted Bergara. He was the little Uruguayan with the big knowledge of football; who, when he talked in his beguiling South American dialect, spoke about "butterflies-in-dee-belly" — and everyone loved it. And behind the scenes? Surely everyone at County loved Danny just as much as the fans. Surely? But, the indigestible truth was that things weren't quite what they seemed. As hard as it is to understand, loveable Danny wasn't quite the hero he was made out to be. Hidden from the fans,

from the public gaze, was a side of his nature that Jones found unaccept-
able. The the single-minded obstinacy, the despotic style of management,
the abusive phone calls in the middle of the night when tempers were
fuelled by the destructive influence of drink — they all drove the men who
had to work alongside Bergara to breaking point. And that included David
Jones. The brutal truth is that had Danny Bergara stayed at Edgeley Park a
moment longer, then Jones — and his assistant John Sainty — would have
quit of their own accord. They couldn't stand working with Bergara any
longer.

"I was looking round for another job — and Saint was as well," confirms Jones. "If another one had come, I would have gone without hesitation. I'd already contacted my friends at the PFA, and they were looking
out for work for me. The time had come for me to go."

That's how close County came to losing the greatest manager in their
history. Jones is hesitant over talking about Bergara; he knows there is still
great affection for the man among Stockport fans — and he is acutely
aware of the debt he owes Bergara, for lifting him out of non-league football and bringing him to Edgeley Park. He is desperate not to betray Danny,
but at the same time Jones is desperate to lay the ghost. Indeed, that was
the title Jones would have chosen for this book: 'Laying the Ghost'. Ever
since Jones became County manager, the spectre of Bergara has haunted
him. In the background he's heard the voices whispering: 'It's Danny's
team really'. Winning promotion to Division One — the one thing Bergara
couldn't do — is the way Jones has finally laid that ghost.

Bergara's reign as County manager ended in The Belgrade Hotel, after
a notorious bust-up with chairman Brendan Elwood. Two days later,
County held an emergency board meeting and Bergara was on his way out
— and Jones was on his way in.

But what had gone wrong, why had it come down to this? "In the end,
Danny thought he was God," said Jones. "That's what it all boiled down to.
If he said a player couldn't get any better, then absolutely no-one could
ever improve him. He wanted to be compared to the likes of Bill Shankly
and the other greats — but, in the last two years, I never saw him at a single training session."

Jones wanted his number two, John Sainty, to be involved in this sec-
tion of the book. They have both experienced the real Bergara, they both
have first-hand knowledge of the tempers and mood swings.

Picture courtesy Manchester Evening News

England Expects. Jones, Hoddle, Wilkins, etc., in the U-21 squad

And Sainty offers his assessment: "Danny even said he was one page short from being a genius. He'd actually read a book about geniuses, and firmly believed he was one page short of being one himself. For me, his biggest single downfall was that he wouldn't listen to advice." Jones nods his head in agreement, adding: "In the four years I worked with him, I don't think he trusted my opinion once."

Sainty and Jones were increasingly frustrated at the style of play Bergara wanted. They knew it had been successful up to a point — but it was also obvious that point wasn't enough. Danny couldn't lift Stockport to the one place they had come so agonisingly close to in the play-offs: Division One. Perhaps he was paying the price for his own success; expectations were high now at County, and people were demanding Division One.

"Danny always talked about first building foundations, and then adding a storey and then another storey," said Sainty. "But then the building stopped and he didn't know how to add any more. His style of play was the long ball, and it wasn't our style of play. We were surprised; we never imagined that was how a South American, of all people, would play the game. But that's how Danny wanted it; and gradually it became the long ball — and then the even longer ball. There was no build up — no play — there was no quality in our style. Whenever we got a new player, it was to cover for a player we already had — it was never to improve on the squad we had."

Every time Jones and Sainty tried to talk to Bergara, they hit a brick wall. "I think he was fearful of change — of changing something that had worked well so far," said Jones. "But once teams had worked out how to play against the long ball, it became robotic — and we needed players with a little bit of flair to break the opposition down. The trouble was, we didn't have any."

And the trouble was, Bergara wasn't willing to tolerate anyone questioning his methods. "He wasn't a person you could bend or talk to," notes Sainty. "If he wanted to make cheese on toast, there is a way — the Danny Bergara way of making cheese on toast; and no other way would do."

The Bergara/Jones/Sainty relationship came under intolerable stress when Stockport made the long, exhausting trip to Plymouth for a league game. It had been a disappointing season, and County needed three points to be absolutely safe from relegation. Recalled Jones: "The Plymouth thing all centred around Peter Ward. He'd been out for a few games, and we'd been playing Bound in midfield — who, to be fair, had done well. But now Wardy was fit. Danny asked us who did we think should play — Wardy or Bound? Sainty and I said Ward, Danny said: 'What about Bound?' — and this went on right up until an hour before kick off and he still hadn't decided. In the end I said: 'Look Danny, whatever you do, we'll back you on it'.

"But he got that frustrated, he just crumpled up the team sheet and said: 'Right, you get on with it'. So we picked Wardy — and we won the game. And it kept us safe from relegation. I realised then that I'd stopped learning from Danny. Instead of learning what to do, I was starting to learn what not to do."

The tension, the frustration, was bubbling over into training sessions as well — where Jones and Sainty could barely comprehend Bergara's bizarre philosophy. As Jones points out: "Last season, we played 67 matches — more than any other team in the entire Football League — but that's not half of what we were doing under Danny. We were doing four practice matches a week — and we're talking hour, hour-and-a-half matches. We would even play a full-scale practice match, split into three 20-minutes sessions, every Friday before a game.

"Each session served a purpose: in case the opposition played 4-2-4; in case they played 3-5-2; in case they played any other way — we'd rehearse how we would cope with it on the Saturday. And that was his way. Sainty and I were stunned; we'd never seen this kind of management anywhere before. It seemed that we were always more concerned about what the opposition were going to do with us — rather than what we were going to do with them. The players were never allowed to express themselves."

By now, Danny Bergara's team was focused around one man: the bean-pole striker, Kevin Francis. 'Get it to Francis, and we'll score' was the philosophy — and Stockport's players were reduced to satellites, desperately trying to beam the ball towards their towering transmitter. Explained Jones: "It had got to the stage where our players were automatically playing balls into corners when there was no-one there. The players were told that if you are in this position, then this is where you must play the ball. There might not be anyone in that position to play the ball to, but the ball still had to go there."

Francis could score goals, his menacing height spread panic in Second Division defences, but Jones and Sainty were bemused by Bergara's reluctance to make the most of this height advantage.

According to Sainty: "We wanted to play with two wingers but Danny wouldn't do it. We kept pestering and pestering him and in the end he relented — and we won six games on the trot. The seventh game we lost — and Danny changed it straight back there and then. We then went to York, won with the old system and that was it, he stuck with it. He was definitely a systems person."

Jones and Sainty were sinking under Bergara's despotic style of managment; a style where only one man could be king — and his servants were merely underlings obeying his every command. "We might all be at a training session, and he'd turn to one of us and say: 'Right, you do the warm up — but I want two minutes of this, three minutes of that!' In other words, you were never, ever given your head," revealed Sainty. "Danny wanted to cloak you; you couldn't do anything unless you had his approval. He would always say if you want a divorce then get rid of someone — but at the end of the day we wanted a divorce from him."

Jones and Sainty kept their feelings a closely guarded secret. The one thing they weren't prepared to do was stab Bergara in the back; not the man who had brought them both into league managment. But that cast-iron bond of loyalty was stretched to its limits when Begara, his day's work completed, turned to drink for relaxation.

Even today, in this post-Bergara era of success, the loyalties still run deep; and both Jones and Sainty will always keep the intimate details a closely-guarded secret. They knew Bergara enjoyed a whiskey in the evenings, but they steadfastly refuse to say how much, or how often. They will not make a value judgement and perhaps unfairly say things like: 'He sometimes drank too much for his own good.' Instead they say: 'Yes, he had a drink; but what may be a lot for one man, can be absolutely nothing for another.' They will not break the confidence or cast aspersions. Insisted Sainty: "You couldn't cover for him but we would protect his back. We would never have got him out of the job; we would never have stabbed him in the back. Certain parties told us afterwards we should have made them aware; but we wouldn't do that while he was in the job."

But Jones and Sainty knew Bergara would have a drink after a game, and then their problems would begin.

"I don't think the players knew, but certainly after games — when it was more like a release thing — we would have many arguments that I would say were drink related, " said Jones. "But then the following day, the subject would never be brought up again — he would never hold any grudges against you."

The Bergara inquests would drag on into the night, and Jones would get late phone calls at home to hear Danny's voice on the other end of the line: "He'd phone up some evenings and just go over the same old ground. He'd go over stuff you'd talked about three hours before — and that became the norm. Everyone feels pressure; and Danny would have a drink after the game. But he could also have a day off and then phone me, and I would know he'd had a drink — it didn't matter, he would drink at home, and he would drink at work, once he'd finished his day. You couldn't knock him for that. We would never know how much he was drinking. If we left him at seven o'clock at night, and he'd been having a drink then, we didn't know how much longer he was going to go on for.

"But if he phoned you late in the evening it sounded like he'd been drinking. Sometimes you need a release valve and his release valve was probably a combination of having a drink and us. But he'd only drink in private, never in social circles. You'd never see him drunk at a sports dinner or anything like that. That's not his way. He never disgraced himself, or the club, through having a drink when he shouldn't do. He never drank at at training, or before matches — it was nothing like that. He always behaved correctly and properly then."

According to Sainty: "The drinking would begin after a game — good or bad, it didn't matter if it was a good result or a bad result. It was like you had to analyse a game — but he had to ram his opinion home. And he would always be right; unless we lost — then it was someone else's fault."

Danny Bergara's sacking stunned County fans everywhere, but the dismissal came as no shock to Jones and Sainty. They knew the truth, the reality behind the legend. In fact, they knew more than most of County's directors, but had never revealed to anyone the intimacies of what life was really like under Bergara. But the County board were increasingly frustrated with Bergara for their own reasons: for four years they had pleaded with him to move from his home in Sheffield, and live closer to Edgeley Park. He steadfastly refused, only using the digs he had been provided with by the ground when it suited his own purposes.

However, the wounds that had festered for so long finally burst open one Wednesday night at The Belgrade Hotel, when Bergara was involved in an ugly exchange with County chairman, Brendan Elwood. Explained Sainty: "For four years, Danny had been given a food allowance; he'd been given four years of digs, and suddenly the directors felt: 'Right, you earn enough money now, we're not going to pay any more'. So they knocked off his expenses — the whole lot — and he'd been stewing over it for 36 hours. He saw it as a curtailment of his privileges. They wanted to stop drink going to the players — and he took it personally. We used to have a couple of cases of beer on the coach coming home from matches and they stopped that. It was all mainly to try to help Danny, but he didn't see it that way." Suddenly, the writing was on the wall — although, even then, Danny couldn't read the words.

Two days after his bust-up with Elwood, an emergency board meeting was convened and, as Jones explains: "It was an accumulation of things for the board: Danny wouldn't move from Sheffield; the results weren't going well; he was phoning people up all hours of the night — I think they'd just had a bellyful of him. Saint and I had this all the time, so we were used to it. But I don't think the board could see which direction the club was going in any more. It was a build up of various things — but, in the end, it all boiled down to the expenses.

"Even when the board meeting was in progress, Danny was very blasé about it all, and, at about one o'clock, he even suggested that perhaps he should apologise! All in all, it took him two days just to realise that it was him who should say sorry. But it had gone too far by then — although I honestly think that Danny believed that the club would never get rid of him. He thought he was invincible."

But Bergara wasn't invincible, and the drama of the emotional day when he was sacked will be etched onto Jones' memory for a long, long time. He will never forget the look on Bergara's face as he came out of the board meeting — bewildered and crushed — and the heart-rending minutes when he helped Danny pack up his belongings and leave Edgeley Park for the last time. This was Bergara at his lowest ebb, stripped of his title, no longer the master, no longer the genius.

Even for Jones, it was an intensely sad moment. Word had rapidly spread around Edgeley Park that the directors had convened an emergency meeting and Jones recalls: "I was training the lads out on the pitch, and everyone's asking: 'What's going on?' Suddenly Danny comes out and says to me: 'I think they're going to send me on a fortnight's holiday — give me a break, so when I come back everything will be all right.' But, to be honest, I just couldn't see that happening."

Bergara was then summoned to the Board room, and returned ten minutes later to his office. Continued Jones: "Danny called me in and said: 'They've sacked me.' I felt very, very sad for him because he couldn't believe it, he didn't want to go — he wasn't going to go. He just didn't want to leave the office — he kept repeating: 'I can't believe it, I can't believe it.' But he'd been given only so long to get his stuff and get out.

"Saint came in, and we started helping Danny pack — and it was just so sad. He was taking his time, slowly taking pictures down off the wall and recalling those special moments, saying: 'Do you remember this, do you remember that?' I don't think he knew what to do with himself. We told him to go away and we'd pack the stuff."

But there was more drama to come. The fraught tension in Bergara's office was broken by a telephone call, this time summoning Jones up to the Board room. The Stockport boardroom fits the archetypal picture of an old-fashioned room where great servants of the club have made monumental decisions over the years. Jones walked in to find the entire board sat round the great big antique table that dominates the room, with every old chair occupied — bar one.

"I remember everyone looking very down, very dejected," recalls Jones. "They told me to take a seat and then said they'd just sacked Danny, which I already knew. I thought they were going to ask me and Saint to take over until they found someone they wanted, but then the chairman looked at me and said: 'We'd like you to become manager.'"

The words shot through Jones' brain like an electric current, but before he could reply, the chairman continued: "But we don't know how you feel about it. What we'd like to do is give you until the end of the season, and see whether you want it and whether you're capable of doing it."

Now it was Jones' moment to speak, and he seized the opportunity — without hesitation, without doubt: "I told them I wanted it. They asked me who I wanted as number two, and I said Saint. It all took a matter of seconds." So that was it: the King was dead, long live the King. It had been a bloodless coup — not orchestrated by Jones, or Sainty, but one the deposed monarch had brought upon himself. Deep down, Jones had been waiting for a moment like this ever since Brian Griffiths had given him the chance to be assistant at non-league Southport. That's when he got the management bug, and, although he would have wished the circumstances to be different, he knew his life was back on course for the first time since that desperate night when one reckless tackle ended his playing career.

But there was no time to relish the moment, no desire to gloat. The first thought that raced through Jones mind was: 'How do I tell Danny?' "I just went back down to the office," he says. "I went over to him and shook his hand and said: 'Danny, they've offered me the job and I've taken it'. He replied: 'Well, they were grooming you all along, all the best, you'll need it!' And then he walked out."

Jones stood staring at the walls of Danny Bergara's office — only now it was David Jones' office — looking at the discoloured squares and rectangles punctuating the plaster, where moments earlier Bergara's treasured pictures and photographs had hung: "I must confess, the first thing I thought was: 'Bloody hell! What do I do now?'"

There was still no feeling of triumph, or elation; but most of all there was no feeling of betrayal or guilt. "I think Danny felt Saint and I should have gone with him," says Jones. "But it never crossed our minds, because his sacking wasn't over football. If it had been something that was going on on the football side — something that we all believed in — then by all means; but we needed a job as well, and the sacking had nothing to do with football matters. If Danny had stayed, I would still have been looking round for other jobs. I felt very sorry for him, especially after seeing him gather all his stuff up in his office, but I didn't see how it could have gone on any longer."

Jones picked up the phone, his phone, and called Ann to tell her the news: "She asked me how long had I got the job for; and I told her it was a case of see how it goes. I think she was worried. We'd discussed that I wanted to be a manager — but never County manager."

The new boss was plunged straight into the deep end. County had a tricky away match at Shrewsbury the next day, and already the knives were out. Obviously, there was no time to tinker with the team. Jones was left holding Bergara's baby, and he had to make the most of it. And he knew that whatever else happened, this was a game County must not lose. He was on trial, and the jury wouldn't be springing to his defence. Bergara's sacking had stunned the disbelieving fans who worshipped the Uruguayan, and each week devotedly chanted: 'Danny Bergara's Blue and White Army'. It would take something special to turn that into 'David Jones Blue and White Army' — and Jones knew he would have to face a lot of anger and resentment.

"I believe there was fighting on the terraces at Shrewsbury because some fans wanted Danny out, and some didn't," said Jones. "Half the fans were chanting his name, half were chanting mine. It was very hairy. It wasn't a nice situation to be in, but we just had to get on with it."

Fate twisted Jones' way again that day, and to his immense relief County got a 1-1 draw — thanks to a Deniol Graham goal: "It was very important for me not to lose that one because it would have given the fans more ammunition. Even at the following home game the fans were chanting: 'Board Out' and all sorts. They still thought it should be Danny Bergara's 'Blue and White Army'."

But the reality was that County didn't lose another match that season, and — to coin one of Bergara's favourite sayings — the foundations had been laid, and a new storey was about to be built.

****

Tonight, David Jones is in exalted company. Sitting alongside him is Alex Ferguson and, for once, the Manchester United manager is not the centre of attention. Tonight, the spotlight is shining directly on Jones — the Division Two Manager of the Year. The man who had brilliantly master-minded the most talked about giant killings of the year in the Coca-Cola Cup — and who had lifted little Stockport County to the lofty heights of Division One — was getting the recognition his exceptional management skills deserved.

And the people who were paying him this accolade, the people who had decided he should be named Division Two manager of the year, were the people who knew best of all. Not the fans, not the press, but his peers. The managers of all the other Football League clubs who have one thing in common with each other — they all know just how excruciatingly difficult their jobs are. And tonight they had decided that Jones was the best of their profession in Division Two. The David Jones who had only been in this management game two years, but in that short space of time had proved his pedigree. Indeed, he'd done in 24 months what many of them would never achieve in an entire career.

As ever, Jones took it all in his stride — although when he arrived at the glittering awards dinner, he'd no idea he had won. He assumed the divi-sional award would automatically go to the manager of the champions — Bury's Stan Ternent. "I was supposed to be going away on a golfing holi-day to Spain, when I got a phone call from John Barnwell, who looks after the League Managers' Association. He told me I'd got to get to the dinner — although he didn't tell me why."

Jones abandoned his travel plans and drove down to London with Sainty, arriving at their hotel at 3pm. "I got my knuckles rapped as soon as we arrived because we'd missed the AGM," chuckled Jones, who on his arrival was still blissfully unaware of what was to come. "We then got a lift to the awards dinner off John Duncan — the Chesterfield boss — and he asked me whether I knew who'd won it. I said no, and he didn't tell me — even though he's on the committee!

"When we got there, I was standing at the bar, having a drink with a couple of managers, and the next thing I know a fella from the Nationwide League comes up and says: 'Dave, we need you for photographs'. I asked why, and he replied: 'You've won the Division Two award'. And that was the first I knew about it."

So Jones took his place at the top table — and no-one could argue that he hadn't earned the right to be there. Sitting with him was Alex Ferguson,

Picture courtesy Manchester Evening News

'Corporal' Jones on the Preston front

the Premier Manager of the Year, and all the other managers who were being honoured that night: Bolton's Colin Todd; Fulham's Micky Adams; and the overall Manager of the Year, Barnsley's Danny Wilson.

"As I said in my speech," recalls Jones, "I really felt very proud and honoured to receive the award — especially when it's your own peers who are voting for you. It meant a lot, but I also said I was picking it up on behalf of my staff as well, because they play such a big part at the football club with me."

But it was rubbing shoulders with the biggest and the best that made the lasting impression on Jones. Now he was one of them — one of the elite — and while he still has higher rungs to climb, he could be treated with respect. "I felt very proud sitting on the same table as Alex Ferguson," he continued. "At the start of the season Alex invited me to United's training ground, and I went and had a cup of tea with him and sat with him for an hour and had a chat. I wanted to go down and have a look at their facilities, and talk to him about a player. He was very relaxed; you see a completely different Alex Ferguson then, very calm, very chatty.

"And then at the awards night, I spoke to him again and he seemed to have time for me. It's not just a handshake or a 'Hello' and then he buggers off — he'll always stop and have a talk with you. He told me how well we'd done, wished us all the best and said: 'Long may it continue'. That meant a lot to me, because it's nice when people who have won everything in the game still find the time for young managers. The managers I admire most are the obvious ones: Alex; Dalglish; and the likes of Bill Shankly and Brian Clough. It's what they have achieved in the game, and how they went about it, that impresses me. Shanks started Liverpool from virtually nothing, didn't he, and went on to be a great manager. The same was true with Clough. I just like the way they conducted themselves."

Whether Jones is from the same mould, only time will tell. But one thing is for sure — that's what his sights are set on.

****

When Stockport chose David Jones as their manager they were taking a gamble. Nobody could know for sure whether he was really up to the job; whether he could handle the pressure; whether the calm, unflappable personna would crack now the buck stopped with him. He came untried and untested. Would he have the strength to rebuild, to make decisions; would he be ruthless when he needed to be and charitable when the situation demanded?

Who, and what, was the real David Jones? County were about to find out and, in the process, Jones would discover things about himself he never knew existed. That's what management does to you. Whether you manage a football club, or a factory, it's the ability to deal with people and problems — and not turn into some Jekyll and Hyde aberration in the process — that will determine whether you can do the job or not.

The management game pushes you to the limits. David Jones is essentially a nice man: open; sociable; easy to get on with. The kind of person you want to be friends with. Would the job change him, or make him?

One of the first things Jones did when he took over, was kick out the man whose precious goal had spared him an ugly baptism from County's incensed fans. It was Deniol Graham who had scored the critical goal which earned County a 1-1 draw against Shrewsbury in Jones' first game in charge — a game Jones dared not lose. Out on the terraces, the fans were fighting among themselves; livid that their hero, Danny Bergara, had been sacked just 24 hours earlier — and Jones put in charge. Graham had thrown Jones a lifeline with that goal, but now there was no place for sentiment. The new manager of Stockport County was on a mission from which he would not waver: to rebuild Danny Bergara's 'Blue and White Army' — and Graham had to be the first casualty.

"I knew I had to dismantle Danny's team, because I knew it wasn't good enough," said Jones. "The optimism going into my first full season was still very high; but, deep down, I knew it was going to be a rebuilding job.

"So Jones' first priority was to weed out the players he didn't think would make the grade — the deadwood— and that included Graham. "Deniol was the first senior player I let go," recalls Jones. "I just called him down and said I wanted to make changes, and he took it like a pro. There is a saying that if the players aren't doing it, get them out before they get you out. I can't play any more, I can't have an influence out on the pitch. The only way I can have an influence on the pitch is to bring in the players who are going to do it for me. If I've got players who can't do it, or who don't want to do it, then I have no hesitation in getting rid of them. They're not benefiting me, and they're certainly not benefiting the football club.

"Football is dog-eat-dog. My son, Mark, is at the club now, but if I didn't feel he was good enough, then I wouldn't sign him."

So beneath the amiable exterior lies the tough streak, although Jones distinguishes between this and ruthlessness. He firmly believes he's only been ruthless once, and he takes no pride in recalling that incident: "I'll be ruthless if I need to be. I would never, ever stab anybody in the back. I don't think you have to do that to get on. I believe if you do things the right way, then things will happen for you. It takes an awful lot for me to reach boiling point. I think I'm a very calm, placid fella, but once you've breached that, you've had it with me. I've been ruthless with players when I've had to leave them out, even though they've been playing well, but the most ruthless I've been so far was with the boy Michael Oliver.

"Someone told Oliver he was going to be the new Paul Gascoigne. Yes, he had a lot of ability, but the only comparison with Gascoigne was that he looked like him — and he probably drank like him as well. Playing wise, the kid wasn't prepared to work at it. I remember we were down at Wycombe the season before last and lost 4-1. I was having trouble with the lad; he was passing comments which I could hear down on the touchline. He was talking about his own team-mates, saying: 'He's useless, and he's rubbish — why doesn't the manager put me on.' So I dug my heels in and thought 'Right, you can sit there and suffer.'

"Then, as the final whistle went, we're walking off and Oliver's shouting: 'Taxi for the manager; call a taxi for the manager, he won't be here

ing: 'Taxi for the manager; call a taxi for the manager, he won't be here long'. So I thought; 'That's it.' I went to the chairman and I told him I wanted Oliver out of the door. The club had paid money for him, but the chairman said fine, if I felt it was the right decision, then I could go ahead with it.

"So I called the lad in and told him I was letting him go and if he wanted I'd get a taxi outside for him. And that's the only time when I've really felt I've been ruthless with a player. I think everyone else has been treated in the right way.

"I didn't like doing it, but Oliver had become a bad apple and you've got to get them out of the dressing room. We don't have any bad apples in this football club. Of course, you have the moaners and groaners. The worst players to have in a football club are first-team players who aren't being picked. If they're good pros, they get on with it; if they're bad, they will moan and there will be a lot of undercurrents — and then you start to get cliques.

"The good thing about our club, I can honestly say, is we don't have that. That's all been weeded out. I always say to a player when he comes to the club: 'You've only got two ways to go in football. You either play well and get in the first team, or you play well to go and find a better club'. I've never known anybody play crap, mess about and go on to better things."

So Jones was proving he had the strength to carry out the tough decisions, the ones that effectively end players' careers. But there were many aspects to that part of the job that took some getting used to. Especially when he had to look a youngster in the eye and say: 'Sorry son, you're not going to make it.' "That's the hardest part of my job — letting the kids go. You've just got to be honest with them. And you honestly hope that they go on to prove you wrong. Football is based on opinions — and just because I think a player might not be right for Stockport County, doesn't mean I wouldn't love him to go elsewhere and make it."

One of the problems Jones hadn't anticipated when he took over was getting the players to accept him in a new light. For the last four years he'd been coaching them day-in, day-out, and, in the process, he'd become one of the lads; enjoying the banter and having a laugh.

Now that had to stop. "I always remember an incident with Sean Connolly during the first pre-season I took," recalled Jones. "We were play-ing a five-a-side match and Sean's team should have had a corner, but I did-

playing a five-a-side match and Sean's team should have had a corner, but I didn't give it. I gave a goal-kick instead and we broke away and scored.

"Sean then ran the length of the pitch to shout at me: 'You cheating bastard!' The lads looked back in amazement and were saying: 'You can't call the gaffer that, you can't call the gaffer that'. I called Sean in later on and said: 'Look, I can't have that; I'm going to have to fine you. I don't mind you calling me a bastard, but don't call me a cheat!' He apologised and we made him buy mine and Saint's dinner. I knew it hadn't been said in the wrong spirit, but there were little things like that to cope with. It was just as hard for the players as it was for me.

"We'd all been friends for two or three years. I was the buffer between them and Danny; and all of a sudden there isn't that buffer any more. One minute they're calling me Dave, or Jonesy, and then they've got to call me boss. It gradually changed, especially when I started getting players out and bringing in my own. The new ones called me boss straight away because I was the one who had signed them."

The new, young, ambitious manager also had to learn about all the mundane little tasks that go with management. The boring things that someone else always deals with — only now, he was that someone else. The in-trays barely able to hold the mountains of paperwork; the phone calls from directors, sponsors, even fans who've somehow got hold of the number; players' domestic problems, their coughs and splutters; and the never-ending demands of the press.

"When you've got big games coming up, a lot of your time is taken up talking to reporters," said Jones. "I don't mind, but I'd rather be out on the training ground — out with the players, running around, joining in.

"Then there's all the letters you've got to answer — and we've had tons this year from all around the world, because of the Coca-Cola Cup run. And we reply to them all. You get invitations to lots of things. I would love to go to everything but you just can't. There's always dinners, functions and presentations. It would be great to attend more, because I think the people deserve it. But over the last 12 months in particular, it's like everyone wants a slice of me — and, although I'm a big fella, there's just not enough to go round.

"I don't do after-dinner speeches, but if I'm asked to do a presentation or something, then I'll try and do it. It's become easier the more I've done. I found that part of the job hard at first because I'm naturally a quiet person off the field — I'm not quiet on it, or in football — and I used to feel very embarrassed sometimes. With being at Everton and Coventry as a player, I got used to the TV attention, so when that came round again during our Coca-Cola Cup run, I slipped straight back into that."

But Jones would, ultimately, be judged by what went on out on the pitch — and that was where he imposed his foobailing beliefs. Both he and Sainty were determined to boot out the abhorred long-ball game — the trademark of the Bergara era — and they were sharply focused on what they wanted and had no problem defining the style of play they were after. "The main thing was that we wanted every player at the football club, no matter where they were on the pitch, to be comfortable with the ball," said Jones. "I wanted players that could play and be strong, and possessed everything you need to be a player. It's not just all about being skilful; you need to want to be a winner; you need a big heart; you have to be determined to do something. I just wanted players, throughout the club, that were like that. Players that would express themselves, and do something out of the ordinary."

It sounds easy. Many theories *sound* easy. By now, Jones had proved he could be a dismantler, a butcher of sides; but could he be a creator, an innovator? Could he practise what he preached — could he unearth the players which his theory, his vision, required? And more to the point, could he actually persuade them to come to Edgeley Park?

****

Jones knew exactly what sort of player he wanted: players from a higher division, who'd tasted life nearer the top and wanted more of it. Players that were still hungry for the game, who craved first team football, but for whatever reason were being wasted by their current clubs. And he found them. Brett Angell, formerly of Everton and Sunderland (not to mention County); Chris Marsden (Coventry); Paul Jones (Wolves); Tom Bennett (Aston Villa). They all had the same thing in common — they'd known better days and they all wanted to get back to them. But identifying them was one thing — persuading them to join one of the country's least-glamorous clubs was quite another. How do you sell Stockport? How do you make the jump from Villa Park to Edgeley Park not feel like leaping off a cliff? The first thing Jones didn't do was take them into his office!

"Yes, Stockport did have a bad image among players — mainly because of where the club had been over the years," agreed Jones. "The changing rooms, I mean, phhhew, you've just got to close your eyes! I have an office that's like a dungeon. I don't sit in the office, I can't, there's no windows. You are under the main stand — and I still had the big iron girders going through the office when I took over. It's a 100 times better now than the way it used to be — honest to God! — it's all been refurbished, with cupboards and a false ceiling put in.

"I never interview new players down there — I'll take them up into the new part of the ground, the executive lounge. I'll get them looking out of the windows, out on to the pitch. You come down to my room and you feel like you are in a dungeon. I call it 'the pit' because that's what it is."

Thanks to chairman Brendan Elwood and his board, Jones was able to show prospective new players tangible proof that the club was heading in the right direction. "I remember signing Tom Bennett and he's looking at the big new stand behind the goal, the pitch being re-laid and the ground looking absolutely fantastic," said Jones. "And that was a big selling point for Tom, because he knew he was coming to a club that had a pitch he would be confident that he could play on. The new stand proved to him that he was coming to a place that was progressing. And, naturally, I told him about our plans to build more new stands. That's how I sold Stockport to Tom.

"You've got to sell the club to them — but the main thing is to be honest, not to lie. You tell them it's a young club — I know the club is over 100 years old, but it has young players, young managers, a young board. And you sell it to them by saying we're going places. When Paul Jones and Brett Angell were thinking of signing, I promised them I would get them into the First Division. That's how I sold Stockport to them."

The Jones sales pitch was obviously convincing but solving County's image problem wasn't the bottom line. As ever, the bottom line was money. If Jones wanted better players, he needed to pay them better money — and yet the club obviously couldn't sustain a crippling wages bill. At the start of last season, basic wages for County's first team players were between £25,000 and £60,000 a year; according to seniority. That's average for most Second Division clubs, but hardly the sort of money that would bring better quality players to Edgeley Park. When Jones started the season he was on a basic salary of £50,000 — considerably less than the £92,000 Danny

Bergara picked up in his last year at the club. Money's always the bottom line, and no matter how much players may crave first team football, they still have the mortgage to worry about and the monthly savings schemes to pay into.

Jones and Elwood overcame the problem with an ingenious bonus scheme that worked on one simple principle: the more County won, the more the players would earn. "The biggest carrot is first team football, and a lot of players will give up money for that. All the players I brought into the club from the First Division had to take a big cut in basic wages — about 30 per cent each," revealed Jones. "But they can earn it all back, and more, through bonuses."

County's bonus scheme works like this:

• All players receive appearance money, with players on the lowest basic wages earning the most — about £100 a game.

• Each player is also guaranteed an additional £20 for every League point the side wins.

• Once County have amassed 25 points, this bonus increases to £30.

• When they've got 35 points, it rises again to £40.

• This principle then continues until the side have 65 points, when players can then earn a maximum of £65 for every additional point the team wins.

For example, if County had won the last game of the season at Luton, each player would have earned an additional £195. On top of this, County introduced a 'roll-on' incentive scheme. Players are guaranteed an additional bonus for the number of consecutive games they win, but this is rolled back if they suddenly lose or draw.

Explained Jones, who is on the same bonus structure as his players: "Players might get £10 extra for winning two consecutive games, £15 for three; £20 for four, and so on. If, for example, we won six games, but then lost one, we'd be knocked back to the fourth bonus amount. If we drew, we'd go back to the fifth.

"The chairman's philosophy is this: he'll pay it if you earn it. He doesn't mind paying out extra for success; and, as far as I'm concerned, that's where he's put his money where his mouth is.

"When I get players in, I can show them that if they play 50 games they will earn so much, and if the team start winning games on the trot they'll earn even more. If someone came here from a First Division club and they were on, say, £80,000 a year, they wouldn't be offered that by us. They might get £50,000 basic but then they'd have to earn the remainder — and that's up to them."

Jones decided against bonuses for goals or clean-sheets — "Because you defend as a team and you attack as a team," — but there are bonuses for players who are not expected to score. "Brett Angell doesn't get paid any extra for scoring a goal," he said. "But a midfield player might get £1000 if he gets 10 goals, just as an incentive."

Lack of money is the trap most managers fall into in football. How many times do we read about a manager who has moved to a new club, thinking he will have millions to spend on new players, only to find the reverse is true. Steve Coppell at Manchester City comes to mind; Ray Harford at West Brom — and even George Graham at Leeds. But Jones is a pragmatist. He accepts clubs like County can't pluck money from thin air, and has set about making the best of that situation.

"I'm not given a budget, but what I'll do is identify a player I want, within reason, and then go to the chairman," he says. "Up until this season, I wouldn't go and look at a £250,000 player, because I knew we couldn't afford it. It's not just the £250,000, it's the wages that go with it. If you buy a player for £250,000 you're probably looking at £100,000-a-year wages — plus you've got to put them on a three-year contract. So, suddenly, you're spending over half a million pounds on one player."

What Jones and Elwood have done is find other ways of rewarding players, through their ingenious bonus scheme, and through the security of long contracts. Says Jones: "If a player comes in and does well, one thing I can guarantee is that the chairman will call them in and give them a better contract. If a player starts the season off well, he'll be given a new contract by Christmas."

The system works, and the proof is in the number of County players who have already committed themselves to extended contracts at Edgeley Park. While most clubs can have up to 20 players out of contract at any one time, nearly every County player accepted new two or three year deals long before the end of last season. That's a remarkable compliment for Jones, and a fitting testament to the way County's finances are structured.

"The vast majority of our players signed their contracts three months before the end of the season, when we were flying in the Coca-Cola Cup, and in with a shout of promotion," said Jones. "They all knew that at the end of the season they'd be out of contract and could have gone elsewhere, but they all signed. That's a good sign. It means we must be doing things right and the club must be heading in the right direction."

****

Drink. Every footballer likes a pint — just ask Paul Gascoigne. Jones isn't a party-pooper, but his thirst for success was more potent than for a bottle of scotch. He wasn't going to let his hopes and dreams sink beneath a crate of empty lager cans.

One of the first radical initiatives Jones introduced when he took over was to bring a dietician to the club, who would talk to the players about the foods they were eating — and make them question their drinking habits. He was taking the lead from clubs like Manchester United — who had made the connection between diet and performance years ago, and employed their own full-time chef to prepare specially-balanced meals for the players.

"I just felt that was the way the game was moving. If anything gives you an advantage, then look at it," said Jones. "We wanted to educate the players on what they were drinking after the game — and during the week. Traditionally, in English football, every player likes a pint. But you've got to do it in moderation. We weren't saying this is what you must do, we just gave them the advice so they could decide for themselves."

And it wasn't long before Jones and Sainty noticed the message was sinking in. "We used to take a couple of cases of Budweiser on the coach for after matches — especially if we were at somewhere like Millwall and faced a long journey home," said Jones. "In the past, that would have been drunk by the time we'd got out of London. But this year we've noticed that we're not even doing half a crate. So we now know the lads are thinking about what they're drinking — they're looking after their bodies.

"You try to do everything for them — but if they don't want to do it, they won't. Treat them like kids, they'll act like kids, treat them like men, then they'll be men. There's no blanket ban on booze. Of course they still like a drink, but over the season they've been spot on."

The dietician devised individual menus for players struggling with their weight, and bars of chocolate suddenly disappeared from the dressing room — replaced by bowls of fresh fruit. "We now have pineapples, bananas and other fruit in the dressing room before and during matches," reveals Jones. "And players like Matthew Bound and Alun Armstrong got their own diets drawn up. Alun always felt tired during games — so it was a case of correcting his intake and getting him to eat at the right times. We advised the players about what to drink after games; suggested they drank as much water as possible and replaced lost energy with the right foods."

Personal appearance was another facet of team life that Jones wanted to tackle. Stockport players used to be provided with club suits for matches, but the new manager thought this was going too far. "I don't want the players coming in looking like tramps; and for home games everyone has to wear a shirt, tie and suit — for away games it's a tracksuit," said Jones. "But I felt they needed to think more for themselves — or else you're literally doing everything for them, even how they dress.

"And it's fun seeing what they turn up in. Some of the lads are outgoing and come in with the most outrageous gear. Alun Armstrong will wear velvet suits, silks shirts, things like that. It adds a little bit of spice."

Jones isn't a disciplinarian; there are no draconian orders that must be obeyed. Players are expected to turn up for training on time, 11am, and ensure they bring with them the right gear — the tracksuits, sweat shirts, shorts and socks, which are provided by sponsors Adidas. Under Bergara, training sessions were dominated by energy-sapping eleven-a-side practice matches, even on the Friday before a game. Jones and Sainty put an immediate stop to that, concentrating instead on short, five-a-side games.

"We always start with half-an-hour warm ups — stretches and stride-outs, to get the body warm," revealed Jones. "Then we switch to whatever

Picture courtesy Manchester Evening News

Hong Kong Heroes

it is we want to concentrate on; if, say, the quality of crosses hadn't been right in our previous game, then we'll on work on that. Most of our training is geared to the ball, passing and movement. I think we only played one full-scale practice match last year, and that was at the start of the season. We play an awful lot of small-sided games, where the emphasis is on passing and movement and creating space — either for yourself or someone else."

This is the Jones/Sainty philosophy; making players feel confident on the ball, encouraging them to be aware of options — the exact opposite of Danny Bergara's long-ball strategy. When Todd feeds the ball out of defence to Marsden, and he deftly flicks the ball down the wing for Cavaco to latch on to, that swift, flowing movement is the nucleus of what Jones believes in: encouraging the craftsmanship of football and not insulting the game with an almighty hoof up the park.

"The smaller the games, and the tighter the areas you train in, then the more comfortable you should be when you get out on to a full-sized pitch," explains Jones. "We deliberately set out to play a lot of small-sided games and everything we do is done with the ball. Even the majority of our running is done with the ball. Players don't feel they're doing a lot of running if they've got a ball with them — even if they're just carrying it."

Training sessions normally last an hour and a half — ie, the length of a game — and Jones reveals: "We'll work on moves down the flanks and when we do crossing and finishing we'll work on little exercises. Basically, we're trying to give the players three or four options, maybe more. But hopefully, they might ignore all that and do something completely different. Now that's what I really want. Players who can think for themselves."

The bulk of County's stamina work is done pre-season, when Jones will take the players on hour-long runs —two or three times a week, morning and afternoons. Last year they went to Portugal to do that; this season they'll be slogging their way across Tatton Park, close to their new training ground at Knutsford. "You start with the long runs and then, as the days count down to the new season, you shorten it down to sharp stuff," explained Jones. "The good trainers are the Flynnies, the bad ones are the Alun Armstrongs. We normally find the worst trainers are the forwards — they don't like running!"

If County face a long-distance away match, they will stay overnight at a hotel. "We'll train on the Friday morning, and the coach will pick everyone up at about 1 o'clock. We'll all have an evening dinner, then it's off to bed," said Jones. "In the morning, we'll got for a walk at about half eleven, have a pre-match meal at mid-day, and then the countdown begins for the game in the afternoon. We normally send someone to watch the opposition, usually a couple of weeks before. We only study them to see what formation they play — we're not really bothered about what they do. Danny used to worry about the opposition too much; we've known him change the system three or four times during a game because the other team were swapping and changing."

Slowly, but surely, the Bergara legacy was fading. Jones was bringing in his own players, his own training methods, his own style of play. There was a new professionalism emerging at Edgeley Park; players were learning to take pride in themselves and in the way they played the game. But there was another arm of the club Jones felt had been badly neglected during the Bergara years. The club's youth policy — or, to be frank, the complete lack of one.....

****

Danny Bergara spoke about building foundations at Edgeley Park, and yet, paradoxically, he bulldozed the very structure that would have put the club on a sound footing. The Uruguayan thought youth policies were a waste of time; he couldn't understand how, or why, County would benefit from one. All his attention was directed towards the first team — at the expense of everything else. This rankled with Jones, who felt County were wasting a golden opportunity to invest in the future. While other clubs were seizing the initiative, and getting the best kids on board at an early age, County were stuck at the bottom of the class. Jones brought in former Wigan manager, Dave Philpott, to begin with — and he introduced a school of excellence. Philpott left for Tranmere a year later, and was replaced by the man who has now become the headmaster: Joe Jakub.

"Joe used to play for Burnley, in the days when they were a First Division side and were famed for grooming young players. So he had a good grounding, and I took him from Preston where he was assistant youth coach," said Jones. "He's been with us 12 months and we're already reaping the benefits. We're now taking kids that would have normally signed for Manchester United or City — but they're coming to us instead. The success with the first team breeds that as well — kids don't want to be associated with a crappy club.

"But this year we have taken on five YTS kids — last year we took on two. As far as I'm concerned, a youth policy is the foundation of the club — whereas before, our only foundation was the first team."

And unlike Bergara, Jones finds the time to encourage and watch the kids: "If we're at home, and the kids are at home on a Saturday morning, then all the staff will go through and watch them. I think it's important for the youngsters to see that we take an interest. "

County now have 20 YTS kids on the books. They come into the club at 16, and serve a two-year apprenticeship. "The first two, three, four months you might as well not look at them, because they're just schoolboys coming into a man's world," said Jones. "Footballers don't distinguish between a senior pro and a junior once a youngster starts training with the first team. They know these kids are coming to take their job away. That's an education for the kids in itself because all of a sudden they're being thrown into a man's world and it's all about how quickly they'll grow up in that world."

Below the YTS lads, are the 12, 13, 14 and 15-year olds; who play on Sundays, and train twice a week. Jakub has a staff of ten under him, all fully-qualified part-time coaches. "Joe's like a manager, father and uncle to all these kids. He's not just teaching them about football, he's helping them learn about life," said Jones. "Crewe will spend £250,000 a year on their youth policy, we spend about £35,000. But it's a vital part of a club's structure. The chairman always wanted it — and we felt it was a must to set into action. When I took over I was determined to do this. Although we had a youth policy, the standard wasn't very high — and our scouting system was poor. It's still in its infancy really...."

CHAPTER 4

Please Don't Let My Girls Die...

DAVID Jones is in the accident and emergency ward at Southport infirmary; staring in disbelief at the broken body of his five-year-old daughter, Chloe. Her tiny arms and legs are buried underneath an avalanche of wires and traction devices — and the irregular bleep of the heart monitor sends an icy shiver through his own body. Chloe is barely conscious as she tries to understand what's going on. Jones turns to his distraught wife, Ann, and the pair clutch hands thinking — but not daring to utter — the appalling words: 'Is she going to live?' This terrifying scene would be enough for any parent to suffer once in their lifetime — but, horrifically, Ann and David would be back five years later, barely able to grasp the fact that their other daughter, Georgia, was lying prone in the same ward, in the same bed, also fighting for life.

The dramas that have developed on the pitch this season are nothing to the dramas Jones and his wife have experienced in their private life. On two separate occasions, they have been confronted with the fear that their daughters were going to die. That's when football takes a backseat, when the worries and stresses of a manager's job become irrelevant. If Jones had been forced to surrender County's promotion this season to guarantee Chloe or Georgia's health, then there would have been no contest.

The Jones' have four children: Lee, at 19, is the eldest and has just signed professional terms with County, hoping to follow in dad's footsteps as a successful footballer; Danielle, 17, is the eldest daughter and studying at college; she is followed by Chloe — who is now 12 — and Georgia, at two-and-a-half, still affectionately called the 'baby'.

While Jones can remember with pride the day each one of them was born, the date August 2, 1990, will also be etched on his mind for a far more sinister reason. Jones had not long accepted the job of youth coach at County, and had gone that day to Manchester where the team was playing in a youth tournament. He knew that his wife Ann was going with her sister, her niece — and Chloe — to the annual funfair held at the RAF base in Wood Vale, Southport.

"I drove home from Manchester and pulled up outside our house, totally unaware anything was wrong," he recalled. "Lee was playing in the road and he ran over, shouting: 'Dad, dad, you've got to get to the hospital quickly — Chloe's been in an accident at the funfair'. Even then, Jones had no idea just how appalling the accident had been — although something made him drive in a frenzied rush to the hospital: "I just put my foot down there and then. I remember deliberately going round the roundabout by the police station the wrong way round, because it was the quickest way of getting to the hospital.

"When I got there, Ann was in a right state. I asked how Chloe was and Ann kept repeating: 'I don't know, I don't know'. I still didn't really know what had happened — there wasn't time to find out, everything seemed a rush. I just went behind the curtain where Chloe was — and I couldn't believe what I saw. She was lying there, with all sorts of monitors and tractions on her to keep her still. I didn't know what to think — I suppose I was in shock really; and Ann certainly was. The doctor then appeared and told us there were no head injuries but that Chloe had broken the neck of her femur."

That was the news Jones did not want to hear. His experiences in football had given him a better than average understanding of the human body, and he understood the doctor all too well.

"I knew it was the main growing bone in the body and when I started asking the doctor important questions, he got a bit stroppy; asking me whether I was a doctor myself, and whether I knew what I was talking about. I explained I was in football and knew a bit about the body — but he seemed to take offence at that. I guess I was putting him on the spot."

Chloe's pelvic bone was also broken, and she had severe lacerations on the back of her knee. 'She was just a baby,' said Jones. "She was lying there, looking so small and helpless, moaning and groaning."

It was then that he slowly pieced together the full horror of what had occurred at the funfair — the moment when a high-speed ride turned sickeningly into a high-speed nightmare. Chloe and her cousin had been spellbound by the Cyclone Twist; and had stood mesmerised as the cars shot in front of each other, flinging their screaming passengers from one side of the ride to the other. Chloe was like any normal child at the fairground, and the speed and the thrill of the twisting ride proved irresistible. As soon as the cars came to a standstill, and the laughing, dizzy passengers climbed off, in jumped Chloe and her cousin — while Ann and her sister sat in the car behind. Amid the laughter and the excitement at what was to come, nobody realised that the iron bar that was meant to keep them safely in hadn't been locked properly — and that tragedy was just seconds away.

According to Jones: "The ride started, and the next thing Ann sees is Chloe hanging on to the bar of her car." The force and speed of the ride had flung Chloe forward, and the bar had shot open as she was pushed against it. "My niece bravely held on for some time, but in the end, if she'd held on any longer she'd have come out as well.

"Chloe's still desperately hanging on, and my wife is screaming to stop the ride but no-one takes any notice. Then, as it's going into the second rotation, our Chloe's flung about 30 feet up in the air."

Ann is sat paralysed with fear, watching the tiny body of her daughter plummet through the air like a dead weight. And the infernal ride keeps on twisting round and round and round. Added Jones: "As the cars crossed in front of each other, Chloe just falls right between them. It was then, at that moment, that Ann thought our Chloe had been decapitated."

Incredibly, the ride kept going, until one of the fairground operators from another ride rushed over and literally pulled the plug. "The bloke whose ride it was never switched it off," said Jones. "Ann says he seemed to be too busy eyeing up the girls, you know. To this day, he's never, never made any contact to find out how Chloe is — which I find totally unbelievable."

Picture courtesy Manchester Evening News

The Jones gang....early days

Barely able to comprehend the full horrific story, Jones channelled his mind back to Chloe's appalling injuries. He listened anxiously as frantic doctors phoned specialists around the country, seeking immediate advice: "They didn't know what to do with it — they didn't know whether to pin the bone or not because of her age. It wasn't their fault, they weren't doing anything wrong, it's just she was so young and that was the problem."

Chloe was eventually put into a Thomas Splint, and remained in that hospital for three long, agonising months: "She was in so much pain for the first ten days afterwards, and Ann lived in the hospital morning, noon and night for the first month. It was terrible to see. There's Chloe, stuck in this bed in hospital, the poor girl can't move because of all the tractions and everything — she's just flat on her back, motionless.

"I think Ann was really scared at this time. Chloe was getting high temperatures and she would go into convulsions because of the pain. I was just so relieved she didn't have a head injury — anything else I could cope with. If she couldn't have talked to us, or her neck was broken, well, I don't know how I would have coped with that. The worst thing really was not knowing what the consequences were going to be for her.

"The doctors were waiting for the blood supply to return to see if the bone would still grow. If that didn't happen, Chloe could have lost a leg or something."

While the tragedy was devastating for Chloe, it also had a devastating impact on the Joneses family life, with things never really getting back to normal. "We didn't sit down as a family again for ages," explained Jones. "We sent our other kids all over the place — Lee went to Newcastle to stay with friends and Danielle stayed with Ann's sister. I had just started the new job with County, so I couldn't take time off. I used to get up really early, go to hospital first thing in the morning, go to work, and then after training in the afternoon shoot back home — which is about an hour's journey. You can't say to a five year old that you can't come to the hospital to see them but the miles I clocked up were phenomenal. And, by now, Ann was literally living in the hospital. We only ever saw each other when I visited, and the only time Ann came home was to get a quick shower and change when Chloe dropped off to sleep.

"Really, the strain and stress on our family was awful. We always used to make sure we all sat down for a meal together but we haven't done that for so long now."

Slowly, painfully slowly, Chloe started to show signs of improvement, and after 12 excruciating weeks, she was allowed home. That was a momentous day for the entire family, but the Jones still faced a long, hard battle in the months ahead. Chloe needed full-time care and Ann had to give up her job as a child care officer at a special school. Jones was on poor money at County — barely £170 a week — and the couple had to dip into their savings to make sure their daughter got all the care and attention she needed.

"She was on crutches for months and then she was in a wheelchair after that," recalled Jones. "It was a full-time job for Ann, carrying her up the stairs and everything. Ann held it all together. With me starting the new job, it wasn't as though I could take the time off — especially as the season was starting and we had two or three games a week."

It was another four months before Chloe could return to school, Farnborough Road, and even then she needed a specially constructed seat because she couldn't sit down properly for long lessons. She constantly needed medication to ease the shooting pains that would never go away — and to this day still come unannounced to rack her body. "She missed a lot of her childhood really," reflected Jones. "Her quality of life was affected — hell, our quality of life was affected."

Still barely six years old, Chloe was then pushed through endless programmes of physiotherapy and hydrotherapy — anything to get her mobile again. But her anxious parents were also concerned about the psychological impact on their tiny daughter, and were alarmed when they noticed her starting to draw strange, sinister pictures. Explained Jones: "It was about a year after the accident when we first noticed odd little signs. If we drove past the site of the fair, the RAF base, she would turn her head away — it affected her like that — and then she would draw pictures of funfairs and all the rides were mangled up and broken. It was things like that. It was really horrendous for her — and for Ann."

Chloe's 12 years old now, and looks as healthy and fit as any normal child approaching her teenage years. But the pain hasn't gone away and she still cringes if she ever passes a fairground. She still does special exercises, and when the pain attacks get too bad, she returns to hospital, sometimes for weeks on end, to get bed-rest and medication. Admits Jones: "Even now, we still don't know what the outcome will be. She still gets bouts of really bad pain. Every so often her hip just seizes up and the pain shoots down her back. Then she goes back to hospital. Last year she was in for three months because the pain was that bad. It just reappears from nowhere, although we seem to think it's worse in the winter time. If she wants to go and play on a bike, and she over-exerts herself, the pain will come back."

The pain for Jones has also translated into the thousands of pounds he has lost seeking compensation — and a secure future for his daughter. A protracted legal battle with the fairground owner has still failed to produce a penny, although Jones is suing for negligence and loss of earnings: "I don't want any money for me or Ann but we want it for Chloe — in case she ever needs any medical treatment in the years to come. We don't know, because of the injury, what her life will be in the future — we don't know what sort of job she can have, for instance.

"She might need a new hip, or something like that, nobody knows. She looks fine now, but all I want is to set up a trust or something so there is money there if she needs it. This tragedy has cost us a lot of money — Ann had to give her job up which was a big blow; it meant that an important income was no longer coming into the house. I was on a low income at Stockport anyway, so we had to start dipping into our savings to pay for solicitors and medical things. It just snowballed, and it put the whole family under a lot of pressure."

How much trauma can one family take? Five years later, just when the Jones felt they had turned the corner, and that surely life couldn't have any more cruel tricks in store, those horrific feelings of fear and desperation came charging back. Those five years had been punctuated with one joyous event at least — the birth of their third daughter, Georgia. But it was Georgia who would have them living on the edge once again. Again the timing stank. The family were desperately looking forward to a holiday in Florida — naturally, to see Disney World and enjoy the sunshine. They needed this break so much, the waiting almost hurt. It was as if they were all pinning their hopes on this holiday — it was a trip that would signal, finally, a return to proper family life; and mean all the stresses and strains of Chloe's injuries would be swept away at last. Hell, everyone needs a good holiday. Jones' first full season in charge at Edgeley Park was coming to an end. The team still had vague hopes of reaching the play-offs (in the end it went down to the last match of the campaign) and the stress was enormous.

The night the world would come tumbling in again, County — and Jones — were in London preparing for their game with Brentford the next day. Fate always seems to dictate that Jones is many miles away when a crisis strikes. He recalls that it was late at night when the ringing of the phone shattered the silence in his bedroom, and he wearily fought off sleep to take the call.

As he remembers: "It was Ann saying our baby was just lifeless, moaning and groaning in the bed, and she was very worried about her. We talked it through over the phone, and decided it was probably just a high temperature — like all babies get. But Ann couldn't sleep that night through worry, and eventually went back into Georgia's room in the early hours of the morning to check she was OK. Ann says Georgia just couldn't stand up — there was nothing there — so she grabbed her out of the cot, put her in the car and rushed her down to the hospital. Ann knew, there and then, something was not right"

The emergency doctors that night admitted little Georgia straight away, and as fate would have it, put her in the same ward, in the same bed, where Chloe had been struggling against her horrific injuries five years earlier. "It really was like deja vu," said Jones. "We knew all the nurses and doctors and everything." Again the Joneses faced a tortuous wait while the doctors tried to work out what was wrong with their baby. But it wasn't until the surgeons carried out the dreaded lumber test that Jones tasted real fear.

"I knew then that they were testing for meningitis, and that was an horrific moment," he says. "They jab in a big needle — a lumber puncture — right into the spine. I was there, holding the poor little baby down, Ann just couldn't face it. Georgia was screaming the place down. She was lifeless, she couldn't lift her head, she couldn't lift her little arms, and if you so much as touched her, or tried to lift her, she'd just go hysterical. I think we both thought we were losing her that night."

Again, the Joneses family life was plunged into turmoil. Ann was back living in the hospital full time, and friends and family were shipped in to look after the other kids. According to Jones: "Ann was like on duty, she used to help out around the place. It's only a small children's ward and the people in there are dead friendly. They rolled out Ann's chair-cum-bed and she lived there again for a month. To be honest, we got very friendly with them, and Ann ended up helping out with all the other kids."

The days turned into weeks as baffled doctors battled to find out what was wrong. Explains Jones: "Georgia went through days of tests, only having painkillers to see her through. They didn't dare give her drugs straight away for fear of masking what was really wrong." And then came the breakthrough, when one of the doctors — ironically a next-door neighbour of the Joneses — said they were testing for ostemylititis. Jones explains the condition: "It actually effects footballers, when they get a cut or a gash. It's like a virus that gets into your joints, but it's very rare for it to happen to a baby. They started checking her knees and elbows, and all the places it normally attacks, but Georgia's had actually attacked the pelvic area. Once they found what it was, they could then bombard the body with the antibiotics that were needed."

Treatment was immediate, and it wasn't long before the Joneses started wondering whether they could go on that dream holiday to America after all. "We'd cancelled the one we had arranged but we all still badly wanted to go away," said Jones. "The specialist said we would be OK taking Georgia to America because the medical facilities are so good over there."

Desperate for the holiday they had surely deserved, the Joneses flew off into the Florida sunshine — and another stack of problems: "The first problem was we had to take all Georgia's medication with us. We had to declare going through customs that we were taking all these drugs — and explain what each one was, and what they were for.

"The second problem was actually giving the drugs to her. The medicine she had to take stank — and you had to put it in a syringe and then open her mouth and squirt the stuff in. Now when you are away on holiday, and you're trying to hold down a baby who doesn't want to keep still so you can force this stuff down her throat — well, it's not very easy. There I am, desperately trying to keep her still, squirting this syringe full of horrible looking liquid down her, and everyone's looking at you wondering what on earth's going on. It seems funny now, but believe me it wasn't at the time, because it was vital Georgia kept up her medication."

Despite the setbacks, the holiday proved a lifesaver for the family. "Yes, it did us all the world of good," reflected Jones. "The weather was great and the kids saw all their favourite Disney characters — and Ann and I could see both Georgia and Chloe growing stronger and stronger with each day."

And as the relieved parents enjoyed the break their bodies yearned for so much, Jones saw their children in a new light: "The two scares made them more precious to us. You don't appreciate what you've got until it suddenly hits you that you might lose it."

CHAPTER **5**

In The Land Of
The Giants

IN February 1950, a club record 27,833 fans packed into Edgeley Park for what many that day would say was Stockport County's greatest cup adventure. The supporters were wedged together so tightly that their every breath, their every movement, was executed as one great mass of humanity. Breathe in, breathe out — together. Eat football, sleep football — breathe football. Together.

Some fled the ground, terrified of the crush; terrified there was no space to raise an arm, move a leg. Parents were anxious for their children, but at the same time they were hypnotised by the drama unfolding on the pitch. It was a match you dared not miss.

County were facing the mighty Liverpool in the FA Cup fifth round; a Liverpool that included Bob Paisley and Joe Fagan in their team.

In the Stockport side was the legendary Alec Herd, whose son David went on to unforgettable glory with Manchester United. And it was Herd who was at the centre of the controversial incident that will never be forgotten by those present that day. He had given County a deserved lead with a powerful header. The roar that had erupted from Edgeley Park was so ferocious, it mushroomed out across

Stockport like an atomic cloud — the fall-out littering the area for miles around.

And then, when Herd was sent crashing to the mud in the 56th minute, at least 20,000 blue and white fans gulped in the air and bellowed 'penalty' with a single voice. All eyes turned to the referee, expecting to see the movement of the arm, the clenched fist edging toward the mouth, the whistle.... blow the whistle.

Nothing. County's players rushed towards the static figure in black, appealing, protesting — and in that one kamikaze moment, Liverpool seized their chance. Breaking clear, Paisley released the ball to Fagan, who crashed the ball past County's stricken keeper, Tiger Bowles.

All that drama inside one minute, but worse was to come. Entirely against the run of play, Stubbins took off on a solo run into the County half, and fired a thundering shot towards Bowles. The ball thudded against the keeper's leg, but — as the crowd breathed a collective sigh of relief — it cruelly ricocheted back towards the Liverpool striker, who lashed the rebound into the net.

Brave Third Division Stockport had been robbed and every blue and white fan knew it. To this day, all those present still fondly remember the day County terrified Liverpool.

But it wasn't as good as this........

This is Liverpool again. Now it's January, 1965, and County are bottom of Division Four, the Reds top of Division One. The two sides are drawn together in the fourth round of the FA Cup, at Anfield, but everybody has written off Stockport. The epic struggle of 1950 is recalled, when County went so close, but the task facing them this time seemed Herculean.

The Liverpool team is a who's-who of international football: Ian St John, Ian Callaghan, Roger Hunt, Tommy Smith, Chris Lawler; County's team a who-the-hell-are-they from Fourth Division domestic football. But it is the no-hopers who silence the Kop; when Len White, freshly signed from Huddersfield, heads the ball home to give brave County the lead. Against all the odds, they weather the storm, and although Liverpool equalised, they hang on for a replay at Edgeley Park....

But it wasn't as good as this.....

This was the double whammy of 1972/73 season; when County took on and beat Crystal Palace and a star-studded West Ham United in the League Cup. A Hughie Ryden header had taken care of Palace, and then came The Hammers. Edgeley Park was full again, the expectant crowd anxious to see English soccer's greatest captain, Bobby Moore, lead his glamorous team out on to the pitch.

And, in the grand tradition of Cup giantkilling, the First Division boys were Hammered 2-1; thanks to goals from Malcolm Russell and a Tommy Spratt penalty. The crowd held their breath when a Clyde Best shot powered against a post, but County had done it again — and their reward was a home tie against Arsenal.

But it wasn't as good as this....

Eight years later, and it's the League Cup again. It's the second round and County are away at First Division Sunderland, after drawing 1-1 in the first leg at Edgeley Park. Nobody expects Fourth Division strugglers Stockport to win — Sunderland are fourth from top of the old First Division, and they soar into the lead through Stan Cummins. But this time it's the Roker roar that is silenced, as Dave Sunley's explosive equaliser and Tommy Sword's nerve-jangling penalty clinch an historic 2-1 triumph.

But it wasn't as good as this.....

Old Trafford, August 1978, and County's famous player/manager, Mike Summerbee, saunters over to a corner flag in front of the Stretford End — and blows his nose on it! Thousands of snarling United fans hurl abuse at the man they still hate from his Manchester City days — but it doesn't matter. County are in the middle of another epic cup adventure.

Again, it's the League Cup, second round. Stockport have been given the draw every fan dreams of — Manchester United. It should have been played at Edgeley Park, but County switch to The Theatre of Dreams so as not to miss out on a massive pay day. And what a pay day it was, with 41,761 packing Old Trafford and paying £56,527 to witness a night to remember.

United, whose side included Martin Buchan, Joe Jordan, Gordon McQueen, Brian Greenhoff and Arthur Albiston, took a flattering 1-0 lead through a Jordan header. But battling County stunned the Old Trafford crowd after the break, levelling with an Alan Thompson penalty — and then deservedly taking the lead after a magnificent Terry Parkes solo goal.

It was unthinkable, it was unbearable; County were 15 minutes from pulling off one of the biggest shocks in soccer. The news was so phenomenal it was flashed out on BBC television.

And then, as had happened 28 years earlier against Liverpool, the referee turned the tide. United equalised from a free-kick after County's keeper, Mike Rogan, was cruelly adjudged to have stepped outside his area as he punted the ball up field; and, with seconds left, the Reds were awarded a controversial penalty — which Jimmy Greenhoff gratefully crashed home to pull off a heartbreaking escape.

But the night had belonged to Stockport and everybody knew it. Led by Summerbee, County's weary heroes did a lap of honour and 41,000 appreciative fans — including United's — rose as one to salute the little men from Division Four.

But it wasn't as good as this.......

This was Wembley, and County go there an incredible four times between 1991-1994; twice for the play-off finals and twice for the Autoglass Trophy.

Once at Wembley would have been enough — but four times was, and will always be, unbelievable. To see County walk out of that famous tunnel, where the Manchester Uniteds, Liverpools and Arsenals of this world had gone before, was to be lifted into fantasy-land.

Each time, the cry was: 'Danny Bergara's Blue and White Army', and each time the fans made the trip down to Wembley praying for just one thing — victory.

And they were so close. Hanging in the bar areas underneath the Wembley stands are the flags of all the clubs that have come to Wembley — and left as victors. If you stretch with all your might, and raise your finger up to the ceiling, you can almost touch the proud emblems. Almost, but not quite. And that was the story of Stockport's Wembley adventure.

Every pilgrimage down the motorway, which began full of hope and dreams, ended with the harrowing sight of County's forlorn players slumped on the Wembley turf; drained, exhausted, burying their heads in their hands as another defeat — always by one goal — took its agonising toll.

Going to Wembley was great, but losing there was shattering. It definitely wasn't as good as this.......

****

Eat football, sleep football, drink as much Coca-Cola as you can stomach. And David Jones could have stomached gallons of it after masterminding an astonishing cup run that sparkled more than the black stuff itself.

As well as being remembered for promotion, season 1996-97 will be recorded in Edgeley Park history as the year of the greatest cup adventure of them all. This was when going to Wembley would have been different, because the prize was more glittering than ever before. This was when Stockport County fans dreamt of not only going to Wembley, but — having won there — moving on to the San Siro, or the Nou Camp, next season for the UEFA Cup. That's how close the dreams were — so close, you could almost stretch out and touch them. Just like those flags.....

And, to be fair, the dreams weren't based on fantasy. County became the toast of the nation as they reached the semi-finals of the Coca-Cola Cup — felling with contemptuous ease Premier League giants Blackburn, West Ham and Southampton en route. Was there anybody the David Jones' Blue and White Army couldn't beat?

County fans had to pinch themselves just to make sure it really was happening. Was it really Stockport on the back pages of every national newspaper in the country? Was it really Edgeley Park where, suddenly, TV cameras — and the likes of Andy Gray and Big Ron Atkinson — were converging for the big-match shows?

And, excuse me, wasn't that Ravanelli who just walked in through the players' door. Look, look over there... that's Graeme Souness, isn't it, and there's the West Ham boss, what's his name? Harry, that's it — Harry Redknapp!

In the final analysis, season 1996-97 will be celebrated for promotion, the single most important objective to David Jones and Stockport County. But every time a County player, director, fan looks at one of those little red cans full of that black, gaseous, drink, there'll be one or two other cherished memories that come flooding back....

****

Stockport County 2, Chesterfield 1
Chesterfield 1, Stockport County 2
(County win 4-2 on aggregate)

David Jones will never forget the menacing words a County director whispered to him, as the greatest cup adventure in the club's history began its magical course back in August.

To this day they have stuck in his mind; words of pressure when he least needed to hear them, carrying a punch that struck well below the belt.

County's great cup adventure began with a home match against Chesterfield; first-round ties being staged over two legs. The irony of the fixture would only become apparent as the dramatic season that lay ahead began to unfold.

County would go on to dominate the Coca-Cola Cup, Chesterfield the FA Cup; and it would be Chesterfield who would later stand between Stockport and automatic promotion in the penultimate game of the season.

Jones was desperate for victory over Chesterfield, to build up County's flagging morale. They'd lost the opening league match of the season, 1-0 at Crewe, and needed a quick pick-me-up.

It came via Andy Mutch, who fired home two goals as County raced into a comfortable 2-0 lead in the first leg at Edgeley Park. But the nerves crept in when Matthew Bound was harshly sent off — and Chesterfield clawed back a vital away goal with a Tom Lormor penalty.

Recalls Jones: "We won 2-1 but we felt hard done by. We were coasting at 2-0 up and then had a player dismissed — and we didn't feel it warranted a sending off. That let them back in. Suddenly everyone was feeling a little apprehensive about the second leg, because we all knew Chesterfield were a good, solid side and it would be a difficult game. We all feared that a one goal lead wouldn't be enough."

And that's when the pressure cascaded in on David Jones' shoulders. By the time the second leg came round, County's league form had gone into freefall — and they were now a humiliating 22nd place in the table.

Nobody fully understood why County were performing so badly, including Jones, but a depressing air of pessimism was sweeping Edgeley Park.

And, like every other lower division club, County were desperate to stay in the cup; praying the next-round draw would pitch them against an Arsenal or Manchester United — and the prospect of a bumper pay-day to fill the club's coffers.

The money men aren't dreaming of Wembley when cup runs begin, and nor was Jones. He was astute enough to realise his job at this stage was to earn County some badly needed pennies. And that was when one of County's directors, Dave Jolly, gave Jones the benefit of his advice — with one of the most crass statements a director could ever make to his manager.

County had arrived for their showdown at Chesterfield when Jolly seized his moment. "I'll never forget it," confessed Jones. "Dave Jolly came up to me, and his very words were: 'Dave, we've GOT to win this.'"

Jones stared at his director in disbelief. Disbelief that anyone could think they needed to utter such a stupid statement to the manager; as if they really thought that the sentiment had never dawned on Jones.

"I just looked at him and said: 'Well Dave, I sort of know that. I actually want to win it as well — believe me, we're not going out there to lose.'"

Deep down Jones knew what Jolly was getting at. The director helps to look after the club's finances, which were in a parlous state. Anything County could do to bring in the cash would help appease the bank manager. Said Jones: "I knew how important it was to get into the next round. I knew everyone wanted a big club to generate money, because that's what all small clubs survive on. But it was doubly important for me; because we hadn't had a good start to the league season, and the side badly needed a confidence builder."

But Jolly's words came thundering back when Chesterfield took the lead, pulling the tie back to all-square on aggregate: 'We've GOT to win, we've GOT to win' — and here they were, struggling again; victory looking as far away as the famous twin towers of Wembley themselves.

But victory was just around the corner: Paul Ware swinging the tie back in County's favour with a brilliant free-kick, and Andy Mutch wrapping up a battling 2-1 triumph. Eat football, sleep football, drink Coca-Cola — stick that down your throat and swallow it, Jolly!

"That was a big relief; but then we got Sheffield United in the next round and, in all honesty, people were a bit disappointed — because it wasn't a big enough club," said Jones. "Again, one or two of the directors weren't that impressed — you can't win! It wasn't going to be a full house at our place and Sheffield United had absolutely tonked us at home two years earlier; so everyone automatically thought: 'Here we go again'. Plus, Sheffield weren't doing particularly well at the time themselves, so it didn't seem to be a good draw for us."

****

Stockport County 2, Sheffield United 1
Sheffield United 2, Stockport County 5
(County win 7-3 on agg)

The total annihilation of First Division Sheffield United will be treasured by David Jones for one deeply personal reason. As ecstatic scenes of jubilation exploded around United's Bramall Lane, something private, something intimate, happened to Jones that gave him the biggest boost of his brief managerial career.

Once again, this stage of the Coca-Cola Cup was over two legs, with Sheffield, managed by the legendary Howard Kendall, due at Edgeley Park for the first encounter.

In the league, County's wretched start had gone from bad to abysmal. They'd crashed to 23rd in the table, picking up a miserly two points from their first six games. The only ray of hope had come on the Saturday before the Sheffield United tie — when County had pulverised Plymouth at home 3-1, with their best performance of a so far inept season.

The crowd for the home leg against Sheffield reflected the level of optimism around Stockport at this time: a spartan 4,000, battling without success to make the Edgeley Park terraces look full. But out on the pitch, County's sorely needed revival was continuing, and they pulled off a richly-deserved 2-1 victory with goals from Tom Bennett and Mike Flynn.

"We would have won by a lot more if it hadn't been for their keeper, my mate Alan Kelly," insisted Jones. "It was the best display of goalkeeping I had ever seen at Edgeley Park — different class, absolutely superb. The only thing that annoyed me was the way they scored their goal. Before the game,

Picture courtesy Manchester Evening News

Rover and out. Blackburn bite the bullet

we had spoken about where the danger was in their side, and warned our players they would use set-pieces to get round the back of our defence.

"When you speak to your players about something like that — warn them about it — and then it goes and happens, you get annoyed. That's exactly how they scored — a free kick and the boy Michael Vonk's come round the back and put it in. I wasn't terribly happy with that!"

Although County's league form was picking up — they won their next game 2-1 at York — the doubters were still having a field day. Jones could hear the whispers: '2-1 ain't enough... they won't win at Sheffield... we're out of it now.'

"A lot of people thought it wasn't enough," he confessed. "We went to Sheffield, and the one thing we didn't want to do was give them an early goal because they are a good side. It was a case of getting at them first."

What happened next would leave Jones spellbound. He watched in stunned disbelief as everything he'd dreamt about, every move he'd meticulously planned with Sainty in training, every twist and turn, flick and intricacy, came breathtakingly to life.

County were rampant — destroying Sheffield 5-2, with Armstrong (two), Bennett, Gannon and Angell bagging the goals that left Jones purring: "Never in my wildest dreams did I imagine we'd end up winning like that. When we scored the fourth, I remember asking Saint how many have they got to score. I was still trying to work out how many they needed to pull back level. I just couldn't believe it.

"It was just a display of attacking football that was unbelievable. It was like everything you've done in practice comes true — comes right for you. Everything we seemed to hit, or head, went in."

Victory was especially sweet for Jones, because he'd got the better of one of his footballing idols: Howard Kendall. "I used to clean his boots and everything at Everton!" said Jones. "When I was a lad, supporting Everton, it was the era of Ball, Harvey and Kendall. When I went to Goodison, I played a couple of first-team games with Howard — although he was on the way out by then — and to pit myself against him was an honour really.

"The biggest compliment Howard gave me on the night was that he felt we were a good footballing side, and I was going about it the right way. That was nice to hear."

But that wasn't the only thrill Jones would receive that momentous night. While County's heroes were dancing and waving in front of the delirious travelling fans, Stockport chairman Brendan Elwood sought out his young manager.

Jones had been in the job for over a year now, and was acutely aware of the debt he owed Elwood for giving him the break into management. Tonight, he was to realise, was the moment he started to repay that debt. Revealed Jones: "The chairman came up to me after the game, and he gave me a big hug. It's just my own personal view, but I felt that hug — and all the things he was saying — showed he was very proud of me. I think he felt then he had made the right decision about me — and that gave me great confidence.

"I would say that game was really the start of a relationship with the chairman that grew and grew. He's Sheffield based, he was a Sheffield United supporter and it was just such a big thrill for him to be going up into their boardroom with all his feathers up. I think he was so proud of the way we had won, and it was as if I had repaid him after the poor start as well."

Suddenly the pessimism that had insidiously crept into Edgeley Park — like a stranger in the night — and spread its poisonous despondency across the terraces, was starting to lift. And the antidote was the cup. Through their cup exploits, County started to re-discover their league form. The side that everyone felt had the ability to do it, were at last doing it.

"I always felt if the team played to their potential they were capable of beating anyone," insisted Jones. "The cup run was probably the start of us doing well in the league. Through the cup the players found their form in the league."

Eat football, sleep football — drink Coca-Cola. County were now in the third round and surely due the dream draw that the directors, the players, the fans and the manager were thirsting for....

****

Blackburn Rovers 0, Stockport County 1

David Jones is pushed on to a stage and microphones are thrust aggressively towards him. The spotlight is on: in front of him are hoards of pressmen, hungry for quotes; television cameras trained directly on his face, ready to record in microscopic detail his every expression. Suddenly a voice rises above the assembled throng, and rivets Jones right to the spot: "David, would you say you've just put the final nail in Ray Harford's coffin?"

Everybody had wanted Manchester United. The memory of that heroic night back in 1978 — when County came so close to winning at Old Trafford — still lingered. Just imagine Eric Cantona walking out at Edgeley Park; just imagine Fergie storming off the pitch, furious after watching his side turned inside out by rampant Stockport. Just imagine...

Instead, County got Blackburn, and people STILL weren't happy! "Blackburn weren't doing well and it seemed a bad draw," said Jones, chuckling at the memory. "Although we were going to a Premiership side, people didn't feel we would be going to a full house. Everyone was hawking for Man United or Liverpool, an Arsenal, someone like that.

"Blackburn was also a bit of a disappointment, because you have to count the pennies, you know. We thought they'd get a crowd of about 14,000. OK, you'll make a few bob but not as much as you would have liked."

County prepared for their first encounter with Premiership opposition in the same way as they'd prepared for every other game. The players trained together on the morning of the match, then travelled to a hotel in Blackburn

— where they had lunch from a carvery — and then off to bed for an afternoon nap.

Although they were up against millionaire Jack Walker's side, Jones was making no special allowances. Rovers were now a shadow of the side that Kenny Dalglish took to championship glory. Alan Shearer had gone, but there were still plenty of big names at the club, including skipper Tim Sherwood and England's number three goalkeeper, Tim Flowers. And they would prove to be the two leading characters in the drama that was to follow.

Jones recalled: "I told our players to go out and be us — to put on a Stockport County show. The players were starting to believe in themselves — they were beginning to think we couldn't be beaten. A big lift was getting Alun Armstrong back, because he'd been injured against Preston — a bad ankle injury — and nobody really expected him to be fit in time. That was a big lift to the camp.

"Whoever you play, no matter what level you're at, you've always got to think you've got a chance, otherwise don't bother turning up — you're beaten before you go out. The one thing I've instilled into the players is the belief that, whoever they play, they're always in with a chance."

So suddenly Stockport are in the big time, and Jones and the players are relishing it. The plush Ewood Park stadium provided a stark contrast to back home: beautifully-appointed changing rooms and a maze of corridors, that led to plush conference suites and executive boxes. Everywhere opulence, money, big time.

"It was all set up for us," said Jones. "There was a brilliant atmosphere on the night, a beautiful stadium and a beautiful pitch. Our supporters were setting off firecrackers — it was a carnival — and there was a confidence growing within the side that we could get a result."

Blackburn themselves were having a torrid time in the Premiership. Ray Harford, who'd been Dalglish's right-hand man during their championship year, was struggling to follow in the master's footsteps — and the pressure on him to beat Stockport was immense.

Jones had far less to lose, he'd survived his early-season managerial crisis, and he came to Blackburn relaxed and buoyant. In fact, one of his biggest concerns that night was how to keep the colour of County's kit a closely guarded secret.

Blackburn are famous for their trademark blue and white shirts; which ruled out County playing in their first-choice colours. The problem was,

County's black and white away kit also clashed, so sponsors Adidas had to come up with a third strip for the night.

"We were laughing because we couldn't wear our away shirts, or our home shirts, so Adidas went and got us the Romanian national shirt — the yellow one — as a one off," said Jones. "Everyone was asking what colour shirts were we going to wear, but we were under orders not to tell because Adidas couldn't market it as our shirt. Our away kit is usually black and white, the same as Germany's national team, so the fans guessed we'd be wearing green — which is the Germans second strip.

"It was meant to be the best kept secret in football. We had 4,000 fans at Ewood Park that night and when we walked out there's a fella sat in the front row with a Romanian shirt on. God knows how he found out!"

County followed Jones' instructions to the letter that night, tearing into Blackburn straight away, never letting the Premier giants get into their stride; dictating the game, pushing them back.

It was exhilarating stuff, and Jones and the fans could sense a shock was on the cards. The noise was coming from the Blue and White Army — but where was the goal coming from?

Enter Captain Fantastic, the man with the most explosive throw-in in soccer, Mike Flynn. He casually picked up the ball, ambled back towards the perimeter fence, and then charged forward, hurling the ball high into the night sky.

All eyes shot upwards, waiting for the rapid descent, waiting for the bomb to come down and explode God knows where. The ball reached its peak, arching downward in mid-flight, its trajectory and target suddenly clear — the towering bulk of Brett Angell.

Still the ball is coming down, gathering pace and force as it plummets towards the Blackburn goal. And in that moment, one of England's finest keepers panics. Tim Flowers, understudy to David Seaman in the national team, a player of immense talent and experience, races off his line and desperately tries to punch the ball away from the predatory figure of Angell.

Flowers' clenched fist connects with the ball, but only to smack it straight on to the back of Blackburn skipper Tim Sherwood's head. The ball ricochets out of control, and spins straight back into the empty Blackburn net. 1-0 Stockport, and the County fans erupt.

"You could see the Blackburn players' heads drop there and then, you could feel it — you could sense it," said Jones. "They were having a terri-

could feel it — you could sense it," said Jones. "They were having a terrible time in the league and the fear-factor set in at that moment. Their players were just passing the ball, they'd get it and then get rid of it immediately — because they didn't want the crowd to boo them. They were just playing safety football."

County dominated most of the second half; Flowers redeeming himself with a string of magnificent saves that kept Blackburn in with a shout. But at the other end, Paul Jones was proving himself equal to the task, guaranteeing County hung on to the lead they so richly deserved.

"Jonesy pulled off a magnificent save when Sherwood burst through and blasted it towards the net. He went down to his left and pulled off a great save," recalled the boss. "But we had a spell in the second half when we could have scored three or four more goals — and to see the way we were knocking it around, and the applause we were getting off Blackburn's own fans at the end, was a huge satisfaction for me.

"I was very proud to go to a Premiership side and play good football and win it in the way we did, and I think everyone there that night knew we deserved it."

The scenes at the County end, when the final whistle went, were bewitching, and Jones could only watch and let it all sink in. Ewood Park, where Kenny Dalglish had proudly displayed the gleaming Premiership trophy to his adoring fans, now belonged to Stockport. The players rushed over, and someone, somewhere, let off a firecracker — casting an eerie red glow over the cock-a-hoop supporters. This wasn't Second Division football, this truly was Roy of the Rovers.

"It was the first time as a manager that I'd beaten a Premiership team, and to go there and win was unbelievable," said Jones. "Before the game, the best I'd really hoped for was a draw and to get them back to Edgeley Park."

Jones was still floating when he was ushered into the Ewood Park press room to face the baying reporters. "All of a sudden I'm on a stage with all these mikes stuffed up my nose. It was an awesome room," he recalled. "And then one of the reporters asked me if I thought I'd put the final nail in Ray Harford's coffin? What a thing to ask! I thought it was totally out of order and I just fobbed the question off. But, truth be known, I probably had — although, at end of the day, it wasn't just my result that drove him out."

Jones never got a chance to talk to Harford that night, although he did seek out Alan Irvine and Terry Darracott: "I knew them because my son,

Lee, had been at Blackburn as a kid; and when I drove him there for training I got to know some of their people."

The following morning saw Stockport County plastered over the back
pages of every national newspaper. "What pleased me," continued Jones,
"was the way all the reports acknowledged the way we had beaten
Blackburn. It wasn't just that we'd beaten them — it was how well we had
played."

Eat football, sleep football, drink Coca-Cola. Now it's getting serious,
and Sky TV want to come to Edgeley Park to televise County's reaction
when they hear the fourth-round draw. And what a draw it was....

****

West Ham United 1, Stockport County 1
Stockport County 2, West Ham United 1

It was one of the great goals; one of the most superbly-executed headers
ever seen at Edgeley Park in the club's 114-year history. The ball rocketed
high into the net — an unstoppable projectile, placed with a precision only
a draughtsman could comprehend. No goalkeeper in the world could have
blocked that header — and it kept Stockport County in the Coca-Cola Cup.

Thank God for Iain Dowie.

West Ham United was the name out of the hat, and memories of that
heroic night in 1972, when County beat Bobby Moore's team 2-1, came
flooding back. That was in the League Cup as well. "Yes, it was a great
draw for us — except that it was away from home so we couldn't take that
many supporters with us," said Jones.

But County had an enemy within the camp, and this was no time for
divided loyalties. David Jones had become friends with Les Sealey — the
famous goalkeeper who kept on playing for top clubs despite his advancing
years — when they were at Coventry together. Jones had persuaded Sealey
to bring his goalkeeping acumen to Edgeley Park, and, through the course
of the season, Sealey had attended training sessions once a week to help
turn Paul Jones into the finished article.

Sealey was officially with Orient at the time, and as Jones explains:
"He'd come over once a week, on his day off. He'd come in and advise,
and things like that, and concentrate on Jonesy. But then he went back to

West Ham — and here we were playing them in the cup. So his visits to us had to stop because he didn't think it was right to be coaching us when we were playing them.

"His loyalties were with West Ham, though, and he warned their boss, Harry Redknapp, not to take us lightly. Les had been to our training sessions, he'd walked round our ground and watched us train, so he knew how strong we were."

West Ham — who, like Blackburn, were having a wretched season — had a line-up of international stars that read more like the United Nations than a Premiership football team.

There were the Romanians, Ilie Dumitrescu and Florin Radaciou; Slaven Bilic, the Croat who's now joined Everton; Portugal's Hugo Porfirio; the Czech keeper Ludek Miklosko — and then there was Northern Ireland's Iain Dowie.

None of them fazed Jones, who was determined to prepare for this trip to London in the same way he had for Millwall or Brentford. "We went down the night before and stayed in a good hotel. Just because we're poor old Stockport, it doesn't mean we stay at boarding houses — we do stay at top hotels," said Jones. "Overnight stays for league games cost anything from £800-£1200."

County usually take a squad of around 20 to away matches — 16 players and a staff of four — so it's not exactly a cheap night out.

Tottenham boss Gerry Francis had given permission for County to use the Spurs training ground on the morning of the match. "We trained there and had a really good build up," said Jones. "Everything felt right, we had a meal, and then went to bed at about one-thirty in the afternoon for a nap. Then the players came down for tea and toast at around quarter past five. That's how we always prepare."

By now, County were the focus of intense media attention. Sky TV were coming to Edgeley Park to film Jones getting in and out of his car, speaking on the phone in his office; the players were being asked for quotes by reporters hungry for a story.

"The club was starting to grow, and the attention we got from the media was superb," recalled Jones. "The players were starting to get a taste of what it could be like at a higher level, and they liked it. The spin-off for me was that it made them push harder for promotion."

As the County coach wended its way through the congested streets of east London, the memories started to return for Jones — who had played at Upton Park many times during his Everton and Coventry days. "Some of our players had never been there, but the first thing that struck me was that it hadn't changed that much," he said.

In the ground, the 1,500 travelling County fans were in full voice behind the goal directly opposite the Bobby Moore stand. If ever a name served as a reminder that this was the big time, it was that one.

The match was a sell-out, with over 20,000 fans packing the ground. The two teams were one step from the quarter-finals — and West Ham's success-starved fans knew this was their most realistic chance of glory this season.

Recalled Jones: "When we walked out on to the pitch, you could feel the atmosphere — it made you tingle. And the pitch looked superb."

County got off to a bright start, with a couple of speculative shots; but then West Ham pressed forward, taking the lead when Radaciou skipped through the defence to rifle the ball past Jones.

It should have been over then — remember this is Premier League versus Second Division — but County kept their shape and their composure and, as Jones recalls: "I turned to Saint and said if we can get in at half-time just 1-0 down, we've got a chance here. And we did. I needed to sort out one or two things because we were getting over-run a little bit.

"I felt we were defending a little bit too deeply and giving them too much respect. We needed to close them down a little bit quicker on the ball. We weren't moving the ball quickly enough, we were getting caught on it, and when they got the ball we weren't closing them down.

"It doesn't matter how good a player is, if you close him down you'll always find the weak spot. They'll give it away sooner or later.

"We were giving them too much space and time, and when you do that with top players they'll run rings round you. I thought we felt inferior to them but it was just a case of closing them down as soon as they received the ball. But I really believed we weren't out of it yet, I knew we could score goals, and I told them to believe in what we'd been doing."

Jones also made a tactical switch that would alter the entire course of the match. He replaced the struggling John Jeffers with his brilliant Portuguese winger, Luis Cavaco: "I had to change it, because 'JJ' was carrying a knock — and he wasn't having the best of games anyway. The fact that he had a knock made my decision a little bit easier."

And it was a breathtaking moment of Portuguese skill that turned the game, Cavaco seizing on a mistake by Julian Dicks on the halfway line to race clear and fire the ball home past Miklosko's despairing reach.

It was fitting that this tiny, unknown player — who had come to County for nothing at the start of the season — was now showing the multi-million pound foreigners at West Ham how to play the game.

"It was such a relief to see the ball go in the net," admitted Jones. "I turned round and looked at Harry Redknapp and Frank Burrows and their heads just sunk. We got stronger and stronger after that and, again, the fear factor seemed to set in with their lads. They started playing a little bit of safety and that let us back in."

By now the tension is building all around the ground. County don't deserve to lose — but, as the minutes tick by, the fear that West Ham will grab a cruel winner starts to spread. "With ten minutes to go, you don't want to lose it," said Jones. "So I threw Tony Dinning on and virtually closed up shop. I didn't want to lose the game because I knew getting them back to Edgeley was a guaranteed full house.

"Then the whistle went — and, again, it's a brilliant night because we've taken on a Premiership side, on their turf, and proved we could play some good stuff. The players were doing things that I'd always hoped they were capable of doing: Jonesy was confident in goal; Tom Bennett and Mazza were brilliant in midfield; Flynnie and Jim were big and strong at the back; and Brett and Alun were a menace up front. We were really playing as a team.

"It was such a good feeling that we could play football and do it in the right way. We were showing we could do a lot of good things — and the players were proving to me what they were capable of.

"I think the fans could see it as well — that was the pleasing thing. We went a goal down but we stayed very calm; and, again, that's a credit to the coaching staff. If we'd panicked, then the players would panic."

County's heroes rushed to salute the delirious fans, and then returned in high spirits to the changing room, where Jones was waiting to say a few words. "I like a couple of minutes after the game to say well done, or you were crap or whatever, and the players are good at it because they'll go quiet and listen to what I've got to say," he said. "Then we opened the door and everyone started pouring in."

Jones left the players to it, and went for a drink with the man he'd just outfoxed, West Ham boss Harry Redknapp: "We had a beer and, again, Harry thought we'd played well — although he reckoned we'd got away with it a bit in the first half. But you need that luck in football.

"He was disappointed with the result — but I think he still felt quietly confident coming up to Stockport."

Once again, the nation's press turned its attention to Stockport the next morning. "We weren't just on the back pages, we were getting on the front pages as well," said Jones. "I even had Radio Five phoning every minute of the day — it was all good publicity, good for the club, and, again, it helped us in the league with our home gates starting to go up."

Jones was also pleased that County weren't suffering a hangover from their cup exploits. In previous years, when they'd battled valiantly against Everton and Aston Villa, the following league games had been the classic case of After the Lord Mayor's Show.

"Invariably we'd lose the game immediately before a big match, and then lose the one immediately after," said Jones. "What really pleased me was that we were winning those games now. The cup was lifting us, not distracting us."

He was particularly enjoying Sky TV's coverage of County, although he was reluctant to perform for the cameras: "They were following us everywhere, they wanted to watch us train, they wanted me to get out of my car and walk over and sit in the office. That was the only thing I didn't take to — I didn't mind them following me about, but I couldn't act for them; I couldn't pretend to be doing something I wouldn't normally do."

Jones also drew the line at the cameramen coming to his home to film his wife and family. "My home is private, it's where I go to switch off, and Ann shies away from all that sort of attention," he explained.

But Sky were giving County the sort of coverage the local terrestrial television companies were failing to provide — and, in particular, Granada television's football coverage, hosted by Elton Welsby.

"The biggest bugbear for Stockport is Welsby," says Jones. "Other teams in the area were also doing well so he wasn't really mentioning us on the local programme. It was a case of: 'Oh, and Stockport got a draw at West Ham' — something like that — nobody was taking much notice of us, or giving us much chance.

"But the Sky coverage was spot-on and what really struck me was the attitude of their front men, Andy Gray and Alan Parry. I think they fell in love with the club. We were the underdogs and they wanted us to win, and I think they got a bit carried away with it all. I remember West Ham arriving for the replay, and going out to look at the pitch — and the pitch was awful. But Andy Gray was saying: 'Never mind the ground hindering West Ham, it'll hinder Stockport just as much'. Now in the past, commentators would have said the exact opposite: they'd have said the bad pitch would benefit the smaller side, it'd be a leveller. But here was Andy Gray saying it would harm us just as much as West Ham and I took that as a great compliment."

The replay day arrived, and the biggest home crowd of the season so far packed into Edgeley Park, believing they were coming to witness a formality. "I was more nervous than ever before," confessed Jones. "Everyone expected us to win. The expectation from the supporters was getting bigger and bigger and it was like we'd done the hard bit at West Ham, and now we were going to win — as easy as that. But far as I was concerned, we'd done the easy bit at West Ham; the hard bit was still to come."

Not for the first time, Jones was determined to treat this like any other home game. The players trained the day before as normal, and reported to Edgeley Park on the night of the match in the usual way.

"We didn't study videos or anything like that," said Jones. "If you start delving too much into Premiership sides they'll put the fear of God up you, because of all the internationals they've got. The goals don't move, the

Southampton surrender. John Jeffers, Andy Mutch and Brett Angell celebrate

pitch stays the same, you're only competing against one another — and the belief in the camp was still growing and growing. The players honestly thought they could do it. There was no need for videos."

West Ham's line up included the brilliant Portuguese international, Hugo Porfirio, who had missed the first game. His presence made an instant impact, and The Hammers started strongly. It wasn't that surprising when Julian Dicks made amends for his blunder in the first leg to power home a scorching header, and give West Ham the lead.

Jones remembers thinking: 'Aye, aye, here we go again'. County had fallen into a habit of going a goal behind, of making life that little bit more difficult; but each time they'd bounced back.

"Even the fans didn't seem too worried," he added. "In fact, they were becoming blasé about it, as if it was the norm. Even I was thinking: 'Bloody hell, here we go again'. Because of what we'd done in the past, I still felt confident. It was disappointing to go a goal down but I still felt we were capable of scoring at that time.

"We'd had a couple of chances ourselves before their goal, but we had to keep Porfirio quiet. He hadn't played in the first game, but oooh, he looked magnificent! We couldn't get near him to begin with."

Jones' optimism proved well founded, although he could never have foreseen the astonishing goal that would set County up for one of the greatest nights in the club's history.

As well as the magical skills of Porfirio, the West Ham side also included the less-than-magical skills of Northern Ireland's Iain Dowie. The big, lumbering striker is a brute of a player — finesse and skill are not terms he is familiar with; his fierce, none too handsome face could send more shivers through a defender than his footballing prowess could ever manage.

County pressed forward straight from the kick off, eager to redress the balance, and a menacing cross was sent curling high into the West Ham area. Suddenly, the predator in Dowie came to the fore, and, with the instinct of a deadly striker, planted his head firmly on the ball.

It was probably the greatest header he'll ever send goalbound, and it soared straight into West Ham's net before he'd hit the ground.

As own goals go, it was goal of the season; probably the decade. Dowie stood frozen in horrified disbelief at what he had just done; while the rest of Edgeley Park didn't know whether to laugh or cry — but, in the main, they laughed.

"It was a good ball into the box, and a great header; an unbelievable header. In fact, it was an absolute screamer of a header and I don't think he could have placed it any better if he'd been attacking," says Jones, barely able to contain just the slightest hint of Scouse mirth. "He was in the right place at the right time for us — it's as simple as that. Sometimes you need that little bit of luck."

There was nothing lucky, however, about what happened next. The West Ham fans — drenched from the torrential rain that kept relentlessly driving across the sodden ground — barely had time to recover from the shock of seeing their own player score in his own net, when Brett Angell compounded their misery.

It was almost a copycat goal, Angell directing a brilliant header high above the despairing lunge of keeper Miklosko. The ground erupted; County had turned the game on its head in a handful of breathtaking seconds. Recalls Jones: "To kick off and then score the goal we scored — and it was a good goal, a quality goal — to score it straight away like that completely took the wind out of them. And the fans — the noise around the ground, was deafening.

"When I watched the video of the match afterwards, I remember hearing Andy Gray and Alan Parry screaming: 'We're back in it!' They weren't saying Stockport are back in it, they were using words like 'we' and 'us' — as if they were part of our club. I think they got carried away as well."

Jones got the players in at half-time, and kept repeating the one, simple instruction: 'Keep a clean sheet and we're through.' But it's never as easy as that, and Jones had to suffer the second half scares, and near misses just like every other Blue and White fan. "I couldn't wait for the whistle to blow," he confessed. "We had a few scares but we could have scored goals as well. The nearer it got to 90 minutes the quicker I wanted it to end because we were so close.

"Every ball they kicked, I'm kicking. The thing that annoyed me most was that we were 2-1 up, with two minutes to go, and we're still wanting to attack, and get forward, and I'm just wanting them to hang on to the ball.

"I was bawling and shouting at them to keep the ball, but the players were flying by then and they couldn't stop themselves. When the whistle finally went, it was an unbelievable night. The fans came racing on to the pitch and it was just superb.

"Everyone was bubbling in the changing room, but straight away I knew I had to calm them down. It was a case of: 'Yes, that's a brilliant result but I'm going to be the old fart now, the party pooper, because we've got a game on Saturday in the league — and that's our priority.'"

And that sums up how Jones felt about the West Ham triumph. It was a wonderful bonus, a sideshow, but it wasn't the main attraction. "I told them to enjoy the night, not to go daft, and to remember it was back to work on Saturday. It was a case of bringing them right back down to earth. I didn't like doing it but it was the league we wanted."

Jones will never forget the tortured look on Harry Redknapp's face after the game. Redknapp had blown millions on his fancy foreigners, and now they'd been made to look worthless by a team of bargain-basement nobodies.

"Harry was shattered, he was absolutely gutted," revealed Jones. "There's not a great deal you can say; I don't want people to say things to me after we've lost a game. But I think it was devastating for him."

Jones knew what to expect the next morning, he was getting used to it now. "The radio people wanted to speak to me at seven in the morning and, believe me, the days of me getting up that early are long gone! It was brilliant; I'm on Sky, doing their football show — it was amazing."

And the more he appeared on television, and on the back pages of the newspapers, the more recognition Jones received. Suddenly heads were starting to turn when he walked down the street, strangers were recognising him and wanting to shake hands, to share the success.

"I normally take my staff out for lunch to get away from it all, but now we couldn't get away from it," he recollects. "We were going ten miles out of Stockport and waiters and people were coming up to congratulate us. With the coverage we were getting on TV, our faces were starting to get well known."

This wasn't an ego trip for Jones, he's not the sort of person to go broadcasting his achievements to anyone who cares to listen. He doesn't need to see his face on a television screen to underline his success.

Jones had been used to television attention during his playing days, and slipped back into the familiar routine comfortably, answering and fielding questions with ease. But he also realised he was now a buffer between the cameras and the players. So long as he was deflecting all the media attention, it wouldn't distract the players from the single most important objective — promotion.

"It was a case of making sure they kept their feet on the ground and keeping their sights focused on the one target we wanted, the league," he asserts.

Eat football, sleep football, drink Coca-Cola. Who'd have thought it; Stockport are in the quarter-finals — and the way everyone is feeling, they're on their way to Wembley....

****

Stockport County 2, Southampton 2
Southampton 1, Stockport County 2

Matthew Le Tissier casually saunters over to the corner flag, barely able to contain a broad grin, as he provocatively glances up at the County fans squeezed into their allotted corner of The Dell. He has just given Southampton the lead, and choruses of: 'You're French and you know you are' bellow out at the England international, as Stockport's frustrated supporters try desperately to get even. 'Le Tiss' takes it in his stride, acknowledging the sarcastic humour with another wry smile.

But it's County who will have the last laugh....

****

The quarter-final draw of what was rapidly becoming the greatest cup competition in the universe for Stockport fans, pitched County against another Premier League force — Southampton, managed by former Liverpool boss, Graeme Souness.

The level of expectation around Edgeley Park, around Stockport, had spiralled out of control. Directors, fans, media; everybody was losing sight of the fact that County were still a Second Division side.

In a way, that was understandable. Out on the pitch, County were playing a standard of football that belied their lowly status; they were beating Premiership sides, and it was easy to forget the reality of their place in the scheme of things: a Second Division club, on the fringes of the play-off zone.

"The way we looked at it," said Jones, "West Ham was our final. All of a sudden, Southampton becomes our final. It was great to finally be handed a home draw but, in all honesty, we've beaten two Premiership sides and you would expect the third to be well warned by now. On the day, if they performed to the best of their ability — and even if we performed to the best of ours — they should come out on top. But the fans had become blasé, and a lot of the press were talking as though we were on a par with the Premiership clubs. I remember we went to Bury after the West Ham victory and got a really good draw, but people were disappointed because we hadn't beaten them. It was as if beating a top Second Division side should have been easy for us."

County's exploits were the talk of the nation, but now they were discovering sides were trying that little bit harder to beat them in the league. "Every other team were up for us — they wanted to do what West Ham and Blackburn couldn't," claimed Jones. "I didn't mind that because I knew that meant we had to be at our best all the time. It was good for us."

The fan-mail was pouring into Edgeley Park now. Jones was receiving letters from old school pals and acquaintances he'd long since lost touch with; there were letters from as far away as Australia and America — emigrants who'd left Stockport years ago, but had been reminded of their old home as news of County's exploits spread across the world.

"Then a girl phoned us up and asked us if we'd model some clothes," laughs Jones. "She knew nothing about football — she'd never even heard of Oldham Athletic — but she knew Stockport had got a team.

"That's the way it was going. The press were constantly hanging around but it's part and parcel of the job; you put yourself up there, and you've got to be prepared to take it all. And it was promoting the football club, which was important, and it wasn't doing me any harm."

Like Blackburn and West Ham before them, Southampton were another side struggling to stay in the Premier League. But they were a strong side. Souness had bought in powerful players; the Dutch international, Ulrich Van Gobbell; the blond Norwegian, Egil Ostenstad; and the Israeli international Eyal Berkovic (now at West Ham).

And, of course, there was also the irrepressible Matthew Le Tissier. This man could swing a game with the slightest feint of the foot; on his day, he was George Best and Ryan Giggs rolled into one. But, like many supremely talented footballers, he blew hot and cold. Against a Second Division side, you'd expect him to be hot.

Said Jones: "People kept asking me about Le Tissier, but I said if I worry about Le Tissier then what do I do about the other quality players they've got? Yes, he's a world-class player, and of course it's worrying to watch him, but if I man-mark him, then we'll end up man-marking all of them. And if we did that, it would stop us playing the way we like to play."

A rock-hard Edgeley Park pitch meant the game had to be re-scheduled and once again the rain came lashing down on the night the match went ahead.

County prepared exactly as before, training the day before the game and meeting at the ground an hour and a half before the game. "We felt they wouldn't have relished the conditions — it was pouring down with rain, just like it was against West Ham, and the pitch wasn't the best; in fact, it was bloody awful," said Jones. "With our fans on top of them, generating a lot of noise, it was all set up for another kill."

Again, it was another full-house — and as was now becoming usual, County fell a goal behind when Ostenstad slotted the ball underneath Jones' body. "We'd had a good start and then when that happened I thought: 'Here we go again'," said Jones. "But this time, even I thought it must be coming to an end now. But what happens? The same thing that happened against West Ham. It was unbelievable; and again, when you watch the Sky video, Alan Parry and Andy Gray say: 'Don't write off Stockport; they might be a goal down, but don't dismiss them'. And what happens? We go and score the two goals!"

If ever the expression déjà vu was meant to define a case of history repeating itself, then this was it. Just as they'd done against West Ham, County came storming back — swiftly equalising when Angell powered the ball home.

And then, in the blink of an eye, little Luis Cavaco flew through the air to send a diving header straight into the far corner of Southampton's net. 2-1 to Stockport — and the fans are pinching themselves, waiting for someone to say: 'Wake up, it's all a dream, it's not really happening'. It was beyond their wildest expectations.

"When we scored the second virtually straight after the equaliser, I couldn't believe it," admitted Jones. "The fans were just dancing up and down. I was looking around and seeing grown men and women going berserk — they were loving every minute of it."

County were comfortably in control when the half-time whistle went, but Jones still warned his players not to relax; not to give Southampton the space to get back into the game.

And they carried out his orders to the full for another 25 minutes; Armstrong even missing two good chances to make the game safe. But County were up against a far stronger side this time, and the sheer physical effort of dictating the game for so long started to take its toll. The tell-tale sight of rolled-down socks told its own story.

"In the end, it was like Souness had 12 or 13 players out on the pitch. I'm sure when he brought on substitutes he never took any players off, because we were just getting over-run! We couldn't get the ball out. It wasn't that we weren't trying, we just couldn't get out," recalled Jones.

"We had chances to kill them off and if we'd have been playing anyone other than a Premiership side we'd have won the game 4-1. But because of the quality of players they had — and the pace they had at the back — we just couldn't get that third goal."

Tension gripped the terraces, anxious fans spent more time looking at watches than at the almost unbearable drama on the pitch. The Southampton raids came thicker and faster, the seconds crawled by; and with barely five minutes to play, County cracked.

Again, Ostenstad somehow managed to trickle the ball through a mass of legs and bodies into the County net — and thousands of blue and white hearts were broken.

"It was a poxy goal, bad defending by us, an awful goal to give away," says Jones bluntly. "But it was frightening because they were looking stronger and stronger and you could feel it."

And then came a last, final drama — when for one chilling moment, County's heroic cup adventure looked doomed.

Matthew Le Tissier, of all the people, was in the clear with a gaping County goal directly in front of him. It was easy; and he was going to score. The Southampton fans were already celebrating as Le Tiss casually chipped the ball towards the empty net. There is absolutely no doubt the ball was going in, and County were about to be KO'd by a sickening sucker punch.

All eyes were glued to the ball as it agonisingly inched towards the goal. Some fans turned away, unable to bear the injustice of it all. And then, in what seemed like a blur, County's skipper — Mike Flynn — appeared from nowhere to hurl himself across the goalmouth and deflect the ball from its almost magnetic path and out for a corner. The relief that exploded around Edgeley Park in that moment was louder than the roar that had erupted when County took the lead.

They were still in it.

"When Le Tissier went through I honestly thought that was it, we're out, because it was the last seconds," said Jones. "And then, all of a sudden, Flynnie appears. I actually thought he'd handled it — I half expected the referee to blow the whistle. At end of the day, Southampton deserved the draw but it would have been a travesty if we had lost."

The replay meant yet another bumper pay day. By now Stockport were starting to pay off long-standing bills. The cup run would generate a massive £1.3million windfall through gate receipts and Sky television revenue — and that had enormous benefits for Jones.

"It meant the club was generating money without having to sell players, which had always been the traditional way of surviving," he said. "Now the football was bringing in the revenue and that meant I could keep the better players at the club."

Few now believed County would stay in the cup. They'd given it their best shot, earned the right to a replay; but winning at The Dell was not a realistic proposition. Jones, however, was one of the few: "We've always got a sting in our tail and I felt if Southampton thought it was all over, then we were in with a chance."

County travelled down the day before the match, staying at the infamous hotel where disgraced goalkeeper Bruce Grobbelaar allegedly accepted a 'bung' for throwing a football game.

They trained on a patch of grass on the seafront in the morning: ate the usual pre-match meal; slept in the afternoon and woke up at 5pm for tea and toast. Again, it was the tried-and-tested routine.

Jones told his players to go out and be calm; not to be in awe and to stick to the style of play that had brought them so much success so far. But instead, County came out to a packed Dell and froze. The nerves were so evident, you could see the players shaking as they desperately tried to scramble the ball away from their Premier League opponents.

Le Tissier was in his element; teasing and toying with County as he sent two awkward shots hurtling towards keeper Jones — the second looking even more menacing than the first. Somehow you knew he was teeing himself up for a third effort, and sure enough it came, this time crashing into

County's net, sending choruses of: 'When the Saints go marching in' soaring into the night air.

"We were in awe of them," confessed Jones. "It was the worst start to any of our cup games, we were dreadfully nervous. Right from the start, our defending was awful. Toddy got caught on the wrong side; Flynnie gave the ball away; Jim was making mistakes. We looked very, very nervy."

But nerves are a peculiar affliction. Strangely, Le Tissier's goal had a calming effect on County — as though the players were saying: 'We might as well just get on with it now.' And that's just what they did; sticking to what they knew best, working their way down the wings, passing the ball intelligently, refusing to panic. "When Le Tissier scored, it was a case of: 'It's happened now, we've got nothing to lose'," confirms Jones. "The worst thing they did was score, because it settled us down and the players started to play."

Suddenly there was confidence where there'd been fear; movement where there'd been clumsiness — and when the half-time whistle blew, the game was clearly not over. "That's what I told them at half-time — push the ball around, stay calm, get the ball in behind them, because they're not the strongest at the back," says Jones.

The nerves had gone now, the fans could sense it, and County came out after the interval and pressed forward. "Then we got the break," continued Jones, "some great individual skill by Alun, a good little flick into their box and a great finish from Brett."

Ah, the old Angell/Armstrong one-two! It was a stunning goal, thoroughly deserved and it lifted every County fan to their feet. Victory was in the air.

Now it was Jones' turn to make a contribution. To the surprise of the fans, he substituted the man who had just pulled County level, and brought on the experienced Andy Mutch. "It's 1-1, and Brett's run himself into the ground," explained the County boss. "He had been out for so long with injuries, and now he was back playing two games a week — every week. He was starting to look a bit tired. On top of that, I thought the game was going into extra time, so I decided to bring Mutchy on. I'll never forget it, because Mutchy turned round to me and said: 'Put me on boss and I'll get you a goal.' I'd just picked up my new car by then, the Probe, and I said to him, laughing: 'Get me the winner Andy and I'll give you a ride in my car'.

It was just chit-chat before he went on — and then he goes and does it! Unbelievable."

Mutch's goal was a formality; a mere tap-in after more brilliant work from Armstrong — but that didn't matter in the slightest.

Eat football, sleep football, drink Coca-Cola: Stockport County were heading for the semi-finals of the Coca-Cola Cup. Every fan stood up and stayed on their feet as the final seconds ticked away — final seconds in which the Stockport keeper somehow got his outstretched fingertips to a wicked Le Tissier free-kick that looked to be soaring into the top corner.

Again, eyes were fixed to watches... 89 minutes, 89-and-a-half, 90 — blow the whistle! And then, the sweetest sound of them all breaks the tension and County have done it — against all the odds.

"It was unbelievable, here was Stockport County in the semi-finals of a major competition. For a Second Division side to get there was amazing," said Jones. "After the game, Graeme Souness gave us full credit. He said we deserved it, that it wasn't a lucky win or anything like that. And the press were frightening — I mean it was a big story for them, fairytale stuff, wasn't it? It was that night we started to get called 'Shockport'. And, again, we were doing it the right way; we weren't clogging our way through matches, we were playing the game properly."

Back on the pitch, the players and travelling fans were lapping up every moment. "I thought Tom Bennett was magnificent that night, he ran the show with Mazza. The defence was superb — and we attacked and counter attacked; it was great to watch," says Jones proudly.

****

The silence in David Jones' office is broken by the 'ring ring' of the telephone. Jones picks it up, and there's an agent on the end of the line. The agent wants to know if Jones is planning to quit his job; because, if so, there's a First Division club ready to make him their manager.

And that's how close Jones came to walking out of Edgeley Park. Suddenly he was a hot property, and news spread like wildfire that he hadn't got a contract to keep him at Stockport. The press seized on the story, and every other phone call seemed to be a reporter, or an agent, demanding to know whether Jones was going to quit.

It should have been the greatest moment of his managerial career; he

David Jones...Seventies sex symbol?

had just guided County to the semi-finals of one of the nation's most important cup competitions. County had beaten not one, not two, but three Premier League sides and they could almost see the Twin Towers looming on the horizon. It should have been a time for champagne and laughter; but, instead, the seeds of doubt started to grow in Jones' mind. The constant barrage of questions: "Why haven't you got a contract?" — "Why are you only on £50,000?" — "Don't you realise other clubs want you?" — all began to prey on the mind of the besieged County boss.

Basically, the press were jumping on the fact that Jones had taken the County job on a handshake — that was the extent of his contract with chairman Brendan Elwood. And, up until now, that had been fine. Jones knew when he accepted the job he was being given an exceptional opportunity to break into management, and in return he realised he could hardly expect a glittering deal.

But 18 months down the road, he was now proving he could handle the job. And the sudden barrage of interest from agents, hungry to get Jones to another club, and the press, hungry to manufacture a 'Jones To Quit' shock/horror story, began to make Jones uncomfortable.

"I was depressed because things were going well and the press were really bombarding me," admitted Jones. "Every time I did an interview, the final question would be: "Have you got a contract?" I was getting a little bit fed up. In all honesty, they were putting the thought in my head — and then you start thinking about security for your family.

"It started to concern a lot of people that I wasn't on a contract — because the team was doing so well, they were pointing a finger at the chairman, saying: 'Why isn't he giving David Jones a contract?' But I'd never asked for one. I thought if you do the business, then you'll earn it. I'd shook hands with the chairman and I was building a relationship with him where our word was our contract. I trusted him completely. He'd given me a handshake, and that was as good a contract to me as a written one."

But word was out — and Oldham Athletic and West Bromwich Albion were just two of the clubs suddenly linked with Jones.

"I was getting phone calls from middle-men, yeah; asking me whether I would like this job, or that job," revealed Jones. "They were clubs where jobs were available — Oldham and West Brom were mentioned — but there were others as well, including another First Division side and a couple of Second Division clubs. But it would be unfair to mention names.

"The middle-men were asking me if I was unhappy. I always said no, but if they wanted they could go through the proper channels. They knew I didn't have a contract, so they were quite entitled to approach the club in the proper way.

"In one respect, it was very flattering because all of a sudden I was being appreciated. I must have been doing something right to get people to notice me."

Not surprisingly, Elwood heard the rumours, read the stories, and offered Jones a new deal. But it wasn't the one Jones was hoping to see, and for one critical moment his Stockport County future hung in the balance. "I wasn't happy with the initial contract he offered me — basically he just offered to improve my bonus incentives," said Jones.

****

QUESTION: "Would David Jones have walked out on Stockport County at this stage?"

ANSWER: "There would have been a possibility."

****

"I think if the chairman's honest, he was a bit frightened of giving contracts out because of what had happened with Danny Bergara. When he came up with what he was offering me, I went away and sat down with Ann and had a good, long think about it. And we decided the best thing was to have a proper chat with the chairman."

And so it was over lunch with Brendan Elwood that David Jones' future at Stockport County was decided: "I think he was depressed about it all as well. We spoke about team things and then he said: 'Right, let's get down to the nitty-gritty'. I told him I thought I was worth a little bit more. He asked me how much I wanted, I told him, and he replied: 'OK, fine'. It was as simple as that."

But Jones admits his days as manager of Stockport County would have been numbered had Elwood failed to deliver over that critical lunch meeting.

"If the chairman hadn't improved on his original offer I wouldn't have signed it," he confirmed. "I would probably have gone along with what I was already on, done my job to the best of my ability, and if any offers had come in, considered them. And if a good offer came in — even at that stage of the season — I would have gone for another long chat with the chairman."

It didn't come to it, thank God. Had Jones carried on, disenchanted, unwilling to accept the contract he was initially offered, who knows what impact that may have had on the team. "Obviously the players were aware of what was going on, and they were asking me whether I'd signed or not. It was unsettling a lot of people," he admits. "But I honestly felt the chairman would look after me. I just felt at the time the relationship I had with him was getting stronger and stronger."

In the aftermath, once the Jones signature was on the Elwood contract, the County boss asked his chairman what he'd really thought of the demand he'd made at their lunch meeting: "I asked him whether I could have got any more and his words to me were: 'I think you were spot on. If you'd asked for any less, I'd have been surprised, if you'd asked for any more I would have had to go away and think about it....'"

****

Stockport County 0, Middlesbrough 2
Middlesbrough 0, Stockport County 1

One of the world's highest-paid footballers, Fabrizio Ravanelli, tangles with one of the world's lowest paid — County skipper Mike Flynn — on the halfway line. Flynnie is sent sprawling to the muddy ground, blatantly shoved by a player renowned for the way he barges players out of his way.

Edgeley Park waits for the free-kick to be awarded. The whistle is raised agonisingly towards the referee's mouth. David Jones is waiting for the inevitable sound that will halt play, but it never comes. The hand that carries the whistle stays suspended in mid-air, frozen, the whistle mute, the play continuing. Middlesbrough break clear and bungle the ball in the net to take an unassailable 2-0 lead.

Bloody referee.

Bloody David Elleray.

****

David Jones is ADAMANT he never once thought about leading County out of the players' tunnel at Wembley; adamant he never imagined the famous terraces bedecked in blue and white; adamant he never heard the delirious fans chanting: 'David Jones' Blue and White Army.'

County were one step from heaven — in the semi-finals of the Coca-

Cola Cup — and two steps from Europe, and the prospect of facing Barcelona, or Inter Milan.

Bloody Elleray.

The other Coca-Cola Cup semi-finalists were Middlesbrough, Leicester City and Wimbledon — and the way County were playing, it really didn't matter who they drew. Confidence was sky-high, and absolutely everyone had forgotten Stockport were only a Second Division team.

Except for Jones.

"Honest to God — and this is the truth — I was still totally focused on the league," he insists. "If someone had said to me; 'You can't play this game, but you're going to go up', I'd have said forget the game — we'll go up instead. I honestly looked on all these games as bonuses.

"Going to Wembley would have been goodbye to the league, because of all the hype that goes with it. You're getting measured for suits; you're on this TV show; you're needed for such-and-such an interview. But all I wanted was the league.

"One or two of the players may have been dreaming of Wembley, but I wouldn't have it. Yes, we're in the semi, and sure we're only two games from Wembley in a major competition; but I can honestly say we never mentioned the word Wembley. I didn't want it."

Reaching the semi-finals of a major competition had taken just about everyone by surprise. Bonus deals suddenly had to be re-arranged to included the possibility of actually winning the darned thing, and sponsors had to take another look at their contracts with the club.

"The contracts for major competitions would only go so far — maybe up to round four or five," explained Jones. "We had a contract with Adidas and there was nothing written in about extra money for playing in the semi-finals of the FA Cup or the Coca-Cola. Obviously, no-one dreamt we would get there."

But there they were, and the name out of the hat was Middlesbrough — easily the most glamorous of the remaining teams in the competition.

Bryan Robson's side had hit the headlines when they suddenly signed big foreign superstars for incredible sums of money: the Brazilians Emerson, £4 million from Porto; Juninho, £4.75m from Sao Paulo; plus the biggest star of them all — the Italian Ravanelli, £7m from Juventus. By contrast, County's record signing was Brett Angell, £100,000 from Sunderland.

Ravanelli was being paid a phenomenal £42,000 A WEEK by Middlesbrough chairman Steve Gibson — more than Stockport's entire wage bill for the same period. His distinctive, closely-cropped silvery hair made him one of the most recognisable players in the country — and, when he scored, everybody knew he would run round the pitch with his red shirt stretched back over his face, revealing his muscular torso to anyone who cared to look. Love him, or loathe him, you knew who Fabrizio Ravanelli was.

And this was who Stockport were now up against. It was an awesome prospect. Again, County's opponents were locked in a relegation fight — which they would ultimately lose — but by the time the semi-final came around Middlesbrough were suddenly hitting a streak of form.

Nobody really gave County much of a chance. Except for David Jones.

"The draw didn't really matter: the semi-final was our final — and we said that against West Ham, against Southampton and now we were saying it again against Middlesbrough," said Jones. "People were saying we were there just to make the numbers up, but we weren't too sure about that. We felt we could make a good game of it. And that's what we did."

Jones stuck to exactly the same pre-match regime that had served County so well in their previous cup encounters: "We didn't make any special allowance for Ravanelli and the like. We hadn't done it with any other players in the other cup games, and we didn't feel the occasion warranted it now. Players get used to set ways and if you start changing things that late in the season, they'll become confused. So we stuck to our guns."

As with the Southampton game, the first fixture had to be cancelled, this time because of torrential rain, and even the re-scheduled game looked in doubt when the heavens opened yet again.

But that was the least of Jones' problems. There was something far more worrying concerning the Stockport boss — the man selected to referee the first leg, David Elleray.

Elleray is considered one of the country's top referees, but he's also one of the most controversial, often clashing with Premier League stars — usually Arsenal's Ian Wright!

And he had left an indelible mark on Jones during County's heartbreaking play-off final against Peterborough at Wembley. It was Elleray who decided that Ken Charlery's shot had crashed off the crossbar and rebounded over the line for a Posh goal: even though he was a good 18 yards away and the linesman level with play hadn't raised his flag. And it was Elleray who then disallowed Kevin Francis' header, when everyone else at Wembley was convinced a perfectly-good goal had been scored.

Bloody Elleray.

The County manager could neither forgive nor forget, and is still willing today to face an FA disrepute charge to let his feelings towards Elleray be known.

"Of all the referees, he was the one we did not want to get," says Jones. "We'd experienced him at Wembley before and — I might get in trouble for this, but I don't care — although everyone else thinks he's a good referee, I certainly don't. We'd come across him in the past and we definitely didn't want him. The fans didn't want him either, and given the choice, I wouldn't have had him for sure."

Elleray was reluctant to give the re-arranged fixture the go-ahead after more torrential rain had turned the sodden Edgeley park pitch into a mudbath. But he relented when both Jones, and 'Boro boss Bryan Robson, pleaded for the game to go-ahead.

"It was lashing down," recalled Jones. "But Bryan and I wanted to play it, and so did the players. After West Ham and Southampton, we thought the likes of Ravanelli would walk down our dingy tunnel out on to a pitch that was awful, with the rain chucking down, and not be too keen. But all credit to them, they proved to be good professionals."

So the game went ahead, and the first half was tense and tight; neither side stamping their authority, although County created a couple of half chances early on. 0-0 at half-time was about right.

"I was happy with our first-half performance," recalled Jones. "It was a case at half-time of: 'Keep it going, don't lose concentration, keep it tight'. They posed a danger all over the pitch — but so long as we kept our concentration, I felt we'd be all right."

Inevitably, it was a suicidal lapse of concentration that cost County the opening goal. Just when the game seemed destined to remain goal-less, the ball was threaded through Stockport's static defence and Danish international Mikkel Beck found himself with space and time to fire 'Boro into the lead.

Admits Jones: "We lost concentration, it's as simple as that. At first, I thought it was offside but the replays proved that Kizza had kept them onside, which annoyed me even more. Instead of one our full-backs keeping them on, it was one of my wide fellas."

Until then, there had been so little between the two sides, that Jones still believed another incredible County comeback was on the cards: "At 1-0, I'm thinking don't let them score the second; it was important that didn't happen. But because of what we'd done against West Ham and Southampton, I thought we were still capable of pulling it back."

Enter David Elleray, and the questionable decision that would ultimately dump Stockport out of the Coca-Cola Cup. The decision was a mirror image of the one 47 years earlier, when 27,000 Stockport fans had waited for the referee to blow his whistle against Liverpool — and the whistle never came.

"The lad Ravanelli jumped in front of Flynnie and Elleray, who was right by it, put his whistle to his mouth to blow up — but didn't," recalls Jones, smarting at the bitter memory. "The ball dropped, Flynnie tried to clear it, but completely mis-kicked — and it went straight to their lad; and they broke away and scored.

"I was fuming, totally incensed, because we should have got a free kick on the half-way line. Don't try to tell me Elleray's a good referee! Now it's 2-0, and I'm thinking please don't score a third; let us get one back — but it just wasn't to be."

When Elleray did finally blow the whistle, it was to signal the end; and the disappointment that swept across Edgeley Park was as torrential as the relentless rain — saturating spirits, hopes and dreams.

Recalls Jones: "It was very quiet in the dressing room afterwards, but we'd had a great run. And I told the players: 'Everyone thinks we're out of it — but why should we be? Let's go there and show them what we've got — we've still got a sting in our tail.'"

Jones then had to suffer the indignity of a live television interview afterwards, alongside jubilant Boro boss Bryan Robson. Now the nation would see just how furious he was with Elleray.

"I didn't want to do that interview with Robbo, because I was still livid," he admitted. "Bryan was happy with the result — obviously, he wasn't going to say it was a foul. They'd come and done a good professional job as far as he was concerned. But I didn't want to go on TV and be interviewed and say: 'Well done'. There definitely wasn't two goals in it on the night, and I felt we deserved a lot better than a 2-0 defeat."

County were written off now. Nobody expected them to go to a packed Riverside Stadium and claw back a two-goal deficit. Middlesbrough had already started to celebrate reaching Wembley; their marketing men were so confident, they splashed out over £200,000 on new Cup final shirts, suits and merchandise.

However, Jones had other ideas. "We turned our attention back to the league the next day," he said. "Everyone thought we were out, so we just decided to approach the return game as and when it came up."

So when that time came, County went about their usual pre-match routine. The only concession this time was their decision to stay overnight AFTER the game, rather than face the wearying journey home from Middlesbrough late at night. "We decided to let the lads have a couple of beers and then get off to bed," explained Jones.

"We hadn't given up hope — we never do. We felt if we could score early on we would have a chance. Everybody thought it was all over, but we felt the one thing Middlesbrough didn't really have was a good defence. We thought we might be able to exploit that."

Jones' final words, as his players walked out into the Teesside night air, were still ringing through their minds: 'Get at them, get at them.'

The Boro fans were in a party mood; swathes of red and white rocking and swaying to the famous anthem: 'Wem-ber-lee'. But the blue and white was out in force as well; packed behind the goal, giving everything they had to lift Jones' team. At least the fans hadn't given up hope....

The astonishing start County gave them was a fitting reward for their unwavering loyalty; the Second Division no-hopers tore into Middlesbrough and when Sean Connolly thundered home his first goal for the club, the ferocity of the shot mirrored the ferocity of County's commitment.

They weren't dead yet.

"It was a brilliant goal," said Jones. "When it went in I thought we could do it — I really thought then we were capable of getting a second one."

Juninho had missed the first leg, but was back playing now — and doing his utmost to terrorise County's defence. But Stockport held on, and it was Bryan Robson who went in at half-time a worried man. Going to Wembley didn't seem such a forgone conclusion now, and the marketing men were thinking of the £200,000 already spent on new suits....

"We knew chances were going to be scarce, very scarce, and we had to take them when we got them," said Jones.

The chance that mattered came midway through the second-half; when Luis Cavaco burst into the box, with only Middlesbrough's giant keeper, Shwarzer, to beat.

It was as simple as that: one-on-one. There was nothing between Cavaco and the keeper. Cavaco, the little Portuguese winger who had so brilliantly saved County at Upton Park against West Ham; Shwarzer, the £1 million buy from Bradford, who had made his debut for Boro against County in the first leg.

All Luis had to do was blast it past Shwarzer and run to the delirious County fans, now barely able to watch in the stand directly behind the goal. That was all! It was a clear chance; an instant to think about it, and — in that moment — Cavaco decided to place the ball, rather than blast it. He made his choice, hit the ball firmly, and Shwarzer swooped brilliantly down to save. 1-0 Stockport — still.

"The best bit of business I thought Bryan Robson did was to buy that goalkeeper," said Jones. "If they'd had anyone else in goal, we would have got a better result at Edgeley — and at theirs. That was the difference between the two sides — their goalkeeper doing the job on the night."

There was still more drama to come: Tony Dinning was about to be cruelly sent off after clashing with — that man again — Ravanelli.

"Again, the decision to send the lad off was totally unjustified; but once he was sent off, I knew that was it, we weren't going to get the second goal," said Jones. "If Tony had stayed on, we still had a chance of the equaliser.

"It was a diabolical decision, it really was. Unbelievable. I wouldn't have minded if Ravanelli had held the leg that was supposed to have been kicked! All it warranted was a booking. Ravanelli's renowned for these situations, and Tony got suckered — but he's a young lad and he'll learn from it. I was more disappointed in the linesman, because he got it totally wrong — and the referee acted on the linesman's decision. The officials got it wrong that night."

And so it was over; but, in defeat, there was immense pride. County had gone out the way Jones would have wanted: by giving it a go. "It was all over and we'd won the game — but lost the tie. I felt really sorry for the players because they'd given it everything," he said. "The players swapped shirts and I told them they had been absolutely brilliant."

And for once Jones, the party pooper, the man who usually says: 'Right, it's back to the league now', broke all his own rules. County were booked into a hotel for the night, and now was the time to enjoy the celebration their astonishing cup adventure had merited.

Eat football, sleep football — drink Coca-Cola. Only it wasn't cans of Coke the players drank that night.

"The plan was to go to bed early — but it didn't quite work out like that," he smiles. "In fact we didn't get to bed until five in the morning. I thought: 'Blow it, they deserve it, let's have a party and enjoy the success' — and it was success.

"We hadn't got to the final, but there was success in getting to the semis — and, once again, we'd beaten another Premiership side on their ground. So we had a right good piss-up! It wasn't part of the plan, but they deserved it — they'd earned it.

"The chairman was quietly disappointed, but he realised what the players had achieved for the club was phenomenal. He was proud to be chairman of Stockport that night, and I was proud to be manager.

"The players deserved their piss-up. They should have been in bed by 1 o'clock, but I thought: 'Sod it, let them drink the night away' — and they did! And they still went to Peterborough the following Saturday and won!

"The players knew they'd played well and couldn't have given any more. We had a great night, with a great bunch of lads, and it was a privilege to be involved with all of them."

Taking it all in was a job in itself. What County had achieved was monumental. They'd become the talk of football across the land; for once Stockport County wasn't the punchline to a cheap joke. Stockport County meant something at last.

Looking back on it all now, Jones reflects: "I thought we matched all these big teams in every department; and I mean every department. The players were brilliant, they played to their potential and proved to me that each and everyone of them wouldn't look out of place in a Premiership side.

"I think the directors enjoyed it — not for the money, but because they were going to these big grounds and really living it up, rubbing shoulders with big and famous people. The club was growing and the directors were starting to get big ideas, talking to all these big people.

"And we needed the cup run to get us out of this division. Regardless of all the games we played, the cup kept everything going, and the players got a belief they could win every game.

"It was a great experience for the players, because I think it gave them something they wanted more of. They were successful and they wanted more. They tasted it — and that stood us in good stead for the league. If we had lost everything because of the cup run I would have felt gutted. Our own success would have been our downfall — and I'd have felt shattered because the lads had given everything they had."

And the abiding memory? The moment that will linger more than any other during the epic battles and heroic deeds?

"The greatest moment was going to Middlesbrough and doing what we did; winning the game there," replies Jones. "We proved that we were a team that could defy the odds. Everyone had written us off and we gave Middlesbrough the biggest fright of their lives. I looked at Bryan's face at the end of the game and there was a lot of relief there. And the 'Boro fans around the ground were getting really panicky. We came so close that night.

"But probably the biggest memory was of us growing as a football team. I felt every game we played we were growing and getting confidence and really believing in ourselves. I could see the players maturing and becoming winners and not being frightened of certain things."

Eat football, sleep football, drink Coca-Cola. It had been the greatest Cup adventure of them all.

Until the next one....

****

The Vanquished

The following managers all have one thing in common: they all tasted Coca-Cola Cup defeat at the hands of Stockport County and David Jones.

From John Duncan in the first round, all the way through to Bryan Robson in the semi-final second leg, here's what they thought of the tournament's biggest giantkiller:

JOHN DUNCAN (Chesterfield manager): "Taking over from Danny Bergara wasn't an easy act to follow and it's a credit to David Jones that he's done it so quickly and successfully.

"He put his stamp on the team straight away. For a young man to pick up the trade of management so instantly and impose his own style is a tremendous achievement.

"A lot is made of Stockport's footballing style, but I'm not fooled by that argument. They can mix it up as well, you know. In British football,

Picture by Martin Rickett, News Team Manchester

It's good to talk. Ravanelli head to head with Lee Todd

you can't just play a passing game, or a long-ball game, you have to discover the right blend, and David Jones has done that for Stockport.

"They used that mixture to knock us out of the cup, and they were always the best team in the league over the full season. They got a wee bit distracted by their success in the cup, but came good in the end through the quality of their football.

"They kept stuffing us every time we played them; but that didn't stop me giving David Jones my vote for Second Division manager of the year! I'm sure he's going to go a long way and enjoy even greater success."

HOWARD KENDALL (Sheffield United manager): "Stockport dominated the first leg and we were very lucky to get away with only a 2-1 defeat. But with the second leg at Bramall Lane, and us scoring an away goal, I still felt confident.

"But Stockport absolutely battered us — and they did it through playing good football. They looked a good, well-balanced side; they beat us comfortably and they deserved to win by the margin they did.

"That's the biggest compliment I can pay them. I told David Jones immediately after the second leg that they deserved their success and the feeling within our camp was that we fancied them to go to Blackburn and win there, too.

"They are well organised, Dave has got the balance of his side right, and they play the type of football I admire. I'm delighted that Dave has had so much success this season."

RAY HARFORD (former Blackburn manager): "I have every reason to remember David Jones and Stockport County. Their victory over us in the Coca-Cola Cup signalled the end of my spell as manager of Blackburn.

"I'd seen them play a couple of weeks earlier and, to be honest, I didn't think they could threaten us. But when it came to the game, they surprised us with the quality of their football. They passed the ball around in a way you don't normally expect from a Second Division team.

"It was one of those nights which is tailor-made for a cup upset. They scored a rather flukey goal when our goalkeeper, Tim Flowers, attempted to punch the ball away — and it hit Tim Sherwood on the head and went into the net.

"But there is no denying that Stockport deserved their win. We defended awfully and they just got better and better. I remember their two midfield players, Tom Bennett and Chris Marsden, controlling the match with their composure and experience.

"I was also impressed with the way David Jones handled himself afterwards. Often managers of giantkilling teams are a bit full of themselves and get carried away with the occasion. But he didn't gloat and certainly wasn't cocky about the victory.

"I've also been impressed by the way Stockport played their way out of the Second Division. It's always argued that you have to have power and strength to bulldoze your way to promotion from the lower divisions; but Stockport have proved you can do it the proper way."

HARRY REDKNAPP (West Ham United manager): "David Jones has done an incredible job at Stockport and his lads did exceptionally well against us.

"They came to Upton Park and, to be fair, they did excellently and went away with a draw. We were looking comfortable; but they came back and scored, and really got into the game. They thoroughly deserved their result at the end of it; they played some tremendous football, and I knew they were a very good side.

"We started the replay at Edgeley Park really well — going a goal up. Then Iain Dowie scored the most bizarre own goal I think I've ever seen. That goal put Stockport back into the game and within a minute we were 2-1 down.

"They kept hitting us on the break, and creating chances of their own, and I've got absolutely no qualms about the result. They did ever so well and I was very impressed with them as a team.

"David Jones and John Sainty have done a brilliant job there. They're a good club, I've met their chairman a couple of times and he's a good man. I'm sure if they continue to play as well as they did last season, they'll have no problems in Division One. They proved they can beat anyone on their day — and I'm sure not many teams will relish going to face Stockport next season."

GRAEME SOUNESS (former Southampton manager): "When you talk about David Jones, you can only talk about one year — but it's been one hell of a year!

"To be perfectly honest I did not know an awful lot about him — but he's suddenly arrived as far as I'm concerned. From my meetings with him, I found him a very warm, pleasant personality, a real nice guy. And what's even more important, it was obvious his players liked him as well.

"He's done a terrific job for Stockport; but his problem now is to be able to sustain what has been an incredible season. But if he can do it in the lower leagues, then there's absolutely no reason why he can't do it at the very top.

"People like David Jones have to work tremendously hard. They have to operate on desperately small budgets, and to come to Premier League sides like Southampton, and to win, is a mark of the man's expertise.

"The Joneses of this world are the real heroes; they give the communities they operate in a real sense of pride in their team. They provide these communities with a link to the big time, and when they beat a big side — like they did against Southampton — I'm sure the victory seems even more precious, even more important."

BRYAN ROBSON (Middlesbrough manager): "Jonesy and I got to know one another when we were in the England Under 21 squad. Right from the start he was the kind of bloke you know you can get on with.

"He's straightforward, honest and can't stand being messed around. He also has a very quiet sense of humour. But never let the fact he is so quiet fool you. For a start, he has a deep knowledge of the game.

"And, as he showed against us, he wants his players to play cultured, organised football. A lot of people were surprised by the way Stockport played against us and other Premiership teams, but I already knew he had his team playing in the right way.

"Make no mistakes, they gave us a fright. Even in the second leg of the Coca-Cola Cup semi-final, when people thought our job was done, they gave us a lot of anxious moments — because Stockport don't hump the ball forward, they think their way forward.

"It is for that reason that I think Dave will survive quite comfortably in the First Division. He has instilled quality right through the team — and if he can hang on to people like his centre half and his strikers, then Stockport will be a lot of fun to watch.

"Certainly Dave deserved his new contract. He has given Stockport a whole new profile and he's worth every penny they are paying him.

"Indeed, Stockport's biggest problem might be holding on to him. He has raised his own profile no end, and shown everybody in his efficient, quiet way, that he's one of the game's top young managers."

****

Coke Is Not The Only Cup

Stockport County waited 108 years to go to Wembley; three years later no-one would have bothered if they ever saw the place again.

The first time was magical, and County fans were like children following the Yellow Brick Road, as Danny Bergara led his Blue and White Army down the M1.

County were facing Stoke City in the final of the Autoglass Trophy; the tournament that gives Division Two and Three minnows a realistic crack at actually walking out on the hallowed turf. It's not exactly the Coca Cola Cup or the FA Cup, but try telling that to a fan who has spent a lifetime dreaming of seeing his side walk out a Wembley. In that moment, the Autoglass Trophy becomes the greatest tournament in the land.

County lost that hot, sunny day; and they lost once again in the same tournament against Port Vale. No fan should have to suffer the hurt of two Wembley defeats; but there was worse to follow as County suffered two defeats in the play-off finals as well.

But time heals all wounds, and in season 1996-7, David Jones brought the Twin Towers sharply back into focus again. Few really expected County to make it to the Coca-Cola Cup final, although their heroic bid surpassed all expectations, but the Autoglass — now subtly renamed the Auto Windscreen Shield — became a strong possibility once again.

Only this time, the Stockport County manager wasn't as keen to go there as might be expected.

County's first tie was against Third Division Doncaster; who looked like pulling off a shock win when they went into a deserved 1-0 lead. "It was a terrible game, the players were looking jaded, we weren't doing it," recalled Jones. "And that was the first time I introduced Kiko, and the kid went on and turned everyone inside out."

Like Luis Cavaco, Kiko Charana had arrived from Portugal, and had been held back in the reserve team until Jones felt he was ready for the rigorous demands of first-team football. "He came on with half an hour to go and turned the game," recounts Jones. "He ran at people; he was up to his little tricks, and twists and turns, and he did really well."

It was Kiko who levelled the scores, and then his fellow countryman, Cavaco, made it a Portuguese one-two with the winner. But it didn't prove to be the breakthrough Kiko hoped for: "It was probably the worst thing that could have happened to the kid — because he thought he'd done it then. But he still needed to learn the game and how to adjust to it," explains Jones.

Bitter local rivals Burnley were waiting in the next round. The game was repeatedly called off, to allow County's Coca-Cola Cup fixtures take preference; and when a free date did become available, the weather made the Turf Moor pitch unplayable.

The Burnley fixture finally took place on 4th February — and, by then, County were facing an appalling fixture backlog. League games were piling up and Jones was anxious that his weary players were wilting under the strain of so many games in such a short space of time.

Suddenly, the Autoglass Windscreen Shield seemed a luxury County could do without. In 1991, such thoughts would have been sacrilege. County had never been to Wembley then, and the magnetic pull of the Twin Towers was overpowering. Now, with County dreaming of Coca-Cola Cup glory, and mounting an increasingly convincing promotion challenge, nobody really cared about the little old Autoglass.

And so David Jones put out almost a reserve side against Burnley — and got the biggest shock of the season.

"The first-team players were absolutely shattered so we decided to play the reserves. In all honesty I would say yes, I expected them to lose; especially as Burnley had already beaten us 5-2 earlier in the season," confessed Jones.

Jim Gannon, Lee Todd and Kieron Durkan were the only regular first-teamers that night. "I told the players I wanted them to win it and it was an opportunity for them to show me what they could do," added Jones. And they certainly did. They tore Burnley apart.

"I'm standing there looking at Saint and saying: 'What the hell's going on?' because the team Burnley put out was almost full strength. I realised then that the squad we had was half-decent!"

The Gods were smiling down on County — Martin Nash scored the only goal of the game, Neil Edwards saved his first penalty in professional football, and Damon Searle was sent off.

"We needed to win it, but I was thinking at the time: 'Bloody hell, we don't need this'. I didn't want to lose games. But the number of games we were playing was too much. It seemed to be big game after big game....."

County then faced another tough fixture, this time against Bury, and the problems mounted for Jones. The game dragged on into extra-time, and both sides were suddenly faced with a new innovation — the golden goal, whereby the first team to score would immediately win the game.

"The last thing we wanted was another long, drawn-out match," said Jones. "But then Brett scored just after we kicked off, which was a blessing in disguise because it saved us from another thirty minutes. I thought the golden goal thing was a good idea, although I wouldn't have been so happy with it if we had lost!"

Again fate seemed to be contriving to keep County in the competition. Angell's goal came after a neat one-two with Ade Mike — and he shouldn't have even been on the pitch!

"Alun Armstrong was meant to be playing, but he pulled his hamstring half an hour before kick-off, while he was warming up," explained Jones. "Ade was having a pint and some nuts in the stand and we had to bring him out and put him in the subs' bench. Then he comes on and sets up the goal."

Crewe were next, and suddenly those old Twin Towers were flaunting their irresistible charms. "Having beaten Burnley and Bury, we're now thinking: 'If we beat Crewe, we're only a couple of games away from Wembley'," admitted Jones.

And again, the thrilling and totally exhausting match went into extra time; only this time nobody scored the golden goal that would break the deadlock.

"It was end to end, either side could have won the game during the golden goal period — we were having balls cleared off the line, they were having balls cleared off the line," recalled Jones. "Even I was getting a little bit excited, because it was so end to end."

The game went into a penalty decider, something Jones hadn't foreseen and County were totally unprepared for. "We hadn't even decided who would take them beforehand — it was just a case of who fancied it," said Jones.

And to the complete astonishment of everyone at Gresty Road that night — including Jones himself — it was County's giant goalkeeper, Paul Jones, who fancied it the most.

County were leading 4-3 — after Crewe had blasted one penalty wide. Jones recalled: "Sean was due to take the fifth when, suddenly, up steps the big fella, and takes the ball off him."

The County keeper was a man on a mission. There was no stopping him.

"The whole place went quiet," recalled Jones. "The Crewe fans were laughing and chuckling away to themselves, our supporters had a look of horror on their faces. I didn't expect him to do it, but I wasn't going to argue with a big 6ft 3 inches tall honey monster like Jonah!

"He'd never practised any before in training, but up he stepped and smashed the ball in the back of the net to win the game."

And so Stockport County, despite their worst efforts, were now in the regional final — merely a two legs from the famous stadium.

"Now we were thinking of Wembley," confessed Jones, "but what kept gnawing away at me was a real fear that if we went there, we would kiss the league goodbye.

"I was always in two minds as to what I wanted; although I kept those thoughts to myself — behind closed doors. I told the players to go for it."

Third Division pace-setters Carlisle were the opposition. On paper County were favourites. "We went up there for the first leg, and totally controlled the game," said Jones. "They scored a good goal against the run of play, but I never felt in any danger whatsoever. I'd have been very happy to come back to Edgeley Park just 1-0 down."

But then came one of those moments of sheer insanity that could have cost County far more than a chance to play in the Auto Windscreen Shield final.

Chris Marsden, one of County's key players, was sent off for brawling. As he left the pitch, head hung in shame, Jones could see County's hopes of winning promotion — never mind the Auto Windscreen — disappearing down the players' tunnel with the disgraced midfielder.

"I felt like throttling him," admitted Jones. "I thought he'd outgrown that; and I knew when he got sent off he'd be banned for at least four games.

"In fact, it turned out to be five because he'd been sent off earlier in the season against Wrexham. I just couldn't believe it, I was fuming.

"I felt he'd let himself down and the players down and I completely flipped my lid. He couldn't say anything in reply and, in all fairness, he took it on the chin."

Marsden was fined a week's wages; and Jones immediately brought in the immensely experienced Gordon Cowans, who was languishing in Bradford City's reserves, as emergency cover.

Although County went into the home leg trailing 2-0, Jones was confident his side could turn the score round. But he wasn't all that sure whether he really wanted them to.

County's Coca-Cola Cup semi-final was looming, and league matches were coming thick and fast. And the league was ALL that mattered.

"We felt we could win if we got an early goal," he said. "But there was an eerie feeling within the club. When I talked to the fans they didn't seem all that bothered."

Jones was proven to be right: County could only draw 0-0, losing 2-0 on aggregate; and blowing their best chance of getting to Wembley. "Normally if you get beaten there are moans and groans, but this time there weren't any," said Jones.

"I can honestly say I was disappointed that we didn't get to Wembley, but I was also a little bit glad as well. I knew the programme we had ahead

Picture courtesy Manchester Evening News

Angell rises....and West Ham falls

of us was horrendous and I just felt Wembley would have completely taken over the club.

"It would have diverted us away from our main objective — winning promotion. I have no doubt at all that if we had beaten Carlisle that night, we would have never made it out of Division Two."

CHAPTER 6
Flynnie's Secret Torment

THIS chapter is dedicated to Mike Flynn — Flynnie — the man David Jones chose to be Stockport captain; and the man who has been the bedrock of County's defence all season. The man who miraculously hurled himself through the air, in the dying seconds against Southampton, to head clear a Matthew Le Tissier chip that was arrowing towards the empty Stockport goal. In that one heroic moment, he guaranteed County would stay in the Coca-Cola Cup quarter final — and go on to greater glory. However, the man who pulled on that blue number six shirt each week — and who had the strength and courage every manager would want in a captain — was, unknown to the fans and many of his team-mates, bravely struggling with a dark secret which was haunting his family.....

David Jones is sitting alone in his tiny office buried beneath the main stand at Edgeley Park. There's nobody around — the players haven't arrived for training yet; there are no autograph hunters; no hangers on and no sponsors. He's just alone with his thoughts — and right now Jones can barely believe what he's thinking about. Stockport County's boss is thinking about a killing — about a woman stabbing her husband in a wild, frenzied attack. A mental picture of screaming and hysteria is flashing through his mind.

He regains his senses and thinks about all the times he would have happily killed that fat slob of a supporter, who's always giving him earache behind the dug-out. That thought makes Jones smile; it relieves the tension. Because, and he's pinching himself to believe it, this is the real thing. There is a terrible event to worry about at Stockport County — and Jones is wondering how the hell, out of the 92 clubs in the Football League, he's landed a job that comes with this.

****

The unthinkable is happening: Stockport are losing 1-0 at home to Third Division minnows Doncaster Rovers in the first round of the FA Cup. The side that had produced the biggest Cup shocks of the year in the Coca-Cola Cup are suddenly finding out what it's like to be on the receiving end themselves— and the newspapers are ready to run the headline: "Rover and out for Jones."

Short on inspiration and ideas — frankly looking down and out — County unexpectedly win a free kick, which Chris Marsden optimistically swings into the box. In a flash, a blue shirt is towering high over the Doncaster defence to power home a header that swings the game in one breathtaking moment. The blue shirt belongs to Mike Flynn; and that's why David Jones made him captain....

Jones got the first inclinations something was horrifically wrong with Flynnie when, ironically, he was trying to cope with his own family nightmare. It was the period when Jones's youngest daughter, Georgina, was undergoing distressing tests for meningitis. The County manager was by her bedside at Southport Infirmary when his mobile phone started to ring. Unable to answer, Jones waited until he had left the hospital to see if the caller had left a message.

He recalled: "It was Flynnie, and he was asking for permission to miss training; but, to be honest, it was difficult to understand why at this stage. The message was very garbled, there was loads of interference — perhaps because I was in hospital and their electrical equipment may have been affecting the signal to the mobile phone, I don't really know. To be honest, I shouldn't really have had the phone on in the hospital in the first place.

"There was something about his father-in-law being involved in an accident, and that he was in hospital. But I had no idea whether it was a car accident, or what on earth it was."

Somewhat puzzled by the call, Jones headed home and tried several times to call Flynn back that afternoon, without success. Something was gnawing away at Jones — it was unlike Flynnie to ask permission to miss training — and the County manager gave it another try later that evening. Jones picked up the phone, rang the number he almost knew off-by-heart,

Picture courtesy Manchester Evening News

It feels this good! County's Paul Jones celebrates the win over Blackburn Rovers

and patiently waited. The shrill tone sounded all too familiar to Jones — it was even beginning to sound like it was coming from an empty house — when suddenly the monotonous: 'Ring, ring, ring, ring' was broken and there was a voice at the other end of the line. It was Flynn. Had Jones got the slightest inclination of the appalling trauma that had turned Flynn's life upside down, he may have felt some embarrassment or awkwardness talking to the County captain. But Jones was blissfully unaware: he greeted his skipper in the way he always would — bright, chatty, the broad Scouse drawl in full flow as he asked: "Everything all right, Flynnie?"

There are times in life when we are asked to deal with the unexpected, when our ability to withstand extreme shock — and, in a flash, to know all the right things to say and do — is stretched to the limit. It is in these moments that we can truly judge ourselves; it is here that our true natures are exposed. That moment was about to come for Jones. Deep down, he expected Flynn to say something like: "My father-in-law's been involved in a car crash; yes, he's in hospital; yes, the family are distressed but, no, it isn't too serious. So is it OK if I miss training tomorrow, boss?" And, of course, Jones was going to say: "Sure you can Flynnie," — and probably crack some joke.

Instead he listened, speechless, as the captain of Stockport County tried to explain the real reason why he needed to miss training the next day. Recalled Jones: "He started off by saying there had been some 'trouble' between his mother-in-law and father-in-law. I remember he used the word 'trouble', and when I asked what sort of trouble, he explained there had been a disagreement and that she had stabbed him. I instinctively asked whether the father-in-law was going to be all right, and Flynnie said no, they didn't expect him to see the night through."

****

It's the last home game of the season, against Wycombe, and Stockport HAVE to win. Edgeley Park is packed: the 9,000 fans are so desperate for County to go up they'll sing and chant until they're hoarse, in the hope the noise urges their heroes on. Anything less than victory would be a disaster — almost certainly condemning County to the play-offs. And everyone knows County are too tired for the play-offs. Jones wants an early goal, so do the fans. Four minutes have gone when Mike Flynn picks up the ball, toys with it between his huge hands, and hurls one of his trademark long throws into the Wycombe box. Like a guided missile it finds Kieron Durkan, who back-heads the ball into Alun Armstrong's path; and the blond striker rifles home his first goal for 19 matches. 1-0 Stockport and the ground erupts: 'Super, Super Al....' But it's too early to score, and County need a second to be safe. Enter Flynn again — 31 minutes have gone by, when he sends over another of those explosive long throws. This one causes widespread panic and, like a bouncing bomb, it shoots out of control off the head of Wycombe defender, Michael Forsyth — and straight into the net for an own goal. 2-0 Stockport; and the ground erupts again: 'We're Going Up, We're Going Up...' And that's why David Jones made Mike Flynn captain...

****

Stabbed. Flynn said stabbed — there wasn't time for the full horror of what had happened to sink in; Flynnie was on the end of the phone, waiting for a reply. Everybody thinks they know how to handle a crisis. With the benefit of hindsight, we're all experts at knowing what we would have done in the same circumstances. It was in this moment, in this instant, that Jones would reveal his true self. Would he handle this crisis as the manager of Stockport County — dealing with a problem confronting the captain of Stockport County — or would he react as a human being, shedding all the responsibilities that come with the job, and try to help a colleague, a friend, through an unspeakable tragedy. Judge for yourselves....

"There's lots of little things that crop up in life, in management, and all you can do is deal with them naturally, in the best way you can," said Jones. "My first and foremost concern was for Flynnie and his wife. I was worried that if the press got hold of this they might start pestering the family. So I told Flynnie that if they wanted to get away, the club would sort it out. As far as I was concerned, we had to get them to a hotel, or somewhere, and give them some peace and quiet to sort things out.

"At that moment I thought that was the best way I could help Flynnie. I knew that if he was fine, then he would make certain his wife was properly looked after. And after everything Flynnie had done for our club, the way he's looked after us out on the pitch, it was time for us to look after him — no matter what the cost. If he needed to get away, I would have gone to war with the chairman to send him wherever he wanted. I would have done that for any of my players, to be honest, because they are family. If I don't look after them then they're not going to help me and the club."

****

County are making the weary journey back from Vicarage Road, after losing 1-0 to Watford. They'd been stuffed; everyone knew it and Mike Flynn was angry. "Oh yes, he's not afraid to speak his mind," says Jones. "If he thinks someone is crap, he'll tell them they're crap to their face. On the coach back, he's not frightened to say what he thinks — and that's not a bad thing. Flynnie will speak his mind; if we've lost, or he thinks someone hasn't done it, he'll say so. If a forward has missed some good chances, he'll have a go. He's not a bully, or domineering, or anything like that. If it's bubbling up at half-time, he might stand up and shout: 'Why don't you do this, or you do that', but really he leads by example — by the way he plays." That's why David Jones made Mike Flynn captain....

It was another two days before Jones met Flynn face-to-face for the first time since that phone conversation. That was two days to guess what had happened, to imagine all sorts of horrific images — and to wonder whether or not Flynn's father-in-law had died as a result of his wounds. Jones had spent that time carrying out all the usual tasks that come with the job: overseeing training; chatting with players; answering letters; taking phone calls; talking to sponsors; talking to directors; talking to office girls; talking to the man who cleans the stands; and the lady who makes the tea. These are the nuts and bolts of the job; this was the daily routine he was used to at Edgeley Park. But now it was different. Now he had something unthinkable, unspeakable, to deal with. There was never a moment when he wasn't anxious for Flynn, and his family — never a moment when he wasn't wondering what he could do to help. But to the outside world, life was going on as normal.

He shared the gruesome secret with his wife, Ann, and they naturally drew on their own traumatic experiences when they discussed how best to handle the situation. Twice they'd suffered extreme anxiety in their family life: Ann, seized with terror as she watched their daughter Chloe horrifically flung from a fairground ride; David, desperately trying to hold down two-and-a-half year old Georgina, as she underwent tests for suspected meningitis. "Yes, that all came flooding back for us," confessed Jones. "We reacted to those problems in the best way we could at the time, we tried to stay calm, do the right things, and I guess that's how I tried to handle this."

Jones also shared the secret with his chairman at Edgeley Park, Brendan Elwood, and his most-trusted colleague and righthand man, Sainty. But there were no grand announcements to the players, nobody got on the tannoy and broadcasted it round the ground. This was something private, too private to even talk about, and the only person Jones was willing to discuss it with, in detail, was the man at the centre of this tragedy; Flynn. Jones knew Flynn was coming to Edgeley Park on this particular day — for the record, it was Thursday — and he felt his usual calm, self-assured self as he drove to the ground. This is the Jones trademark; when everyone is busy flapping and panicking, Jones stays cool, in charge, clear-headed. He doesn't go in for histrionics; he doesn't throw his head into his hands in grand, theatrical gestures. "I wasn't embarrassed, or even nervous about seeing Flynnie," he insisted. "I just wanted to know that he was OK."

Jones headed for his office beneath the main stand at Edgeley Park. Jones calls it the pit — a man could go mad in there. There are no windows, the stark whitewashed walls remind you of a hospital waiting room, and the sloping ceiling hangs so low you wonder whether you should stoop to enter, or just get down on your hands and knees and crawl in. Jones was opening some letters when there was a polite knock on the door, and in came Flynn. His imposing 6ft frame instantly filled what little room there was in Jones' office; and for the first time in two days, the manager of Stockport County was eye to eye with the man he'd made captain. To this day, Jones has never forgotten the look on Flynn's face.

"He looked white; he looked like he'd never slept," recalled Jones. "I asked him whether his father-in-law had died, and he replied: 'Yeah, he died in the night'." So that was it: he'd been killed. Before coming into soccer management, in the bleak period when Jones had to quit playing the game because of injury, he had trained to become a social worker. Were those influences at work now — was he instinctively putting into practise all the theory he had learnt at college? "I don't honestly know," he replies. "Maybe, subconsciously, something like that was going on. I don't think Flynnie found it difficult to come to me — he had to tell somebody."

Again the instinct to help, to want to ease the pain, dominated the conversation: "I asked him if there was anything we could do, anything at all.

He needed to find a solicitor, so I put him in touch with my mate, but his main concern was for his wife. He was really worried about her. He'd had everything to cope with: the funeral, the police, the family, looking after their baby — and looking after his wife.

"It was hardly surprising he wasn't his usual self. I don't think he understood why it had happened; I don't think his wife, or even his mother-in-law, knew why it had happened. It was just a huge shock to the whole family. It must have been a nightmare for them. It must have been absolutely horrendous."

It seemed crass, an insignificance, but there was another problem that had to be dealt with — County had a match two days later, and Jones needed to know whether his skipper wanted to play. The answer would be portentous; it would tell Jones whether Flynn was being crushed under the unbearable burden he was now shouldering, or whether he had the incredible strength to let life go on. "We didn't know whether to play him, we weren't sure whether he would be up for it," said Jones. "But he wanted to play, and I think that was the way he decided to deal with it. Everyone deals with situations differently themselves. It's no good me saying I would have done this, or done that, because it's not happened to me. Until it does, you can never know what you'd do. But I can't praise him highly enough. Despite all the things that were going on in his life — all the things that were happening to his family — he just came in and wanted to get on with it. He was being paid to be a footballer, and so he got on with his job.

"If he had said: 'Look, I don't want to play', we would have quite understood. But the only game he missed from then on was against Burnley — and it was us who pulled him out of that.

"Eventually the whole thing went to court, and Flynnie had to go along and be there. But he always kept us in line with what was going on, and whether he would be unavailable for training because he had to be in court. But he still never missed a game."

****

Mike Flynn has arrived from Preston — Danny Bergara is still in charge at County — and all Flynn's capable of doing is hoofing the ball like it's something disgusting, something to get rid of as quickly as possible. "Danny bought him because he's got this incredible long throw and he wanted someone who could chuck the ball towards Kevin Francis," remembers Jones. "Everyone still talks about the long throw when they talk about Flynnie, but really they've got to talk about him as a player as well — because he's got a lot better. When he came, he just came as a destroyer and, incredibly, Danny threw him into midfield. But in midfield you have to be a bit more creative than that, so Sainty and I started chipping away at him, coaching, talking to him in training, teaching him how to be confident on the ball. He's worked really hard at his game, and it's fair to say he's doing things now that he didn't think he was capable of doing.

"Under his old boss at Preston, John Beck, he was told he had to kick the ball as far forward as he could — but we got him passing the ball 40 yards with the outside of his foot, getting the ball down and playing; not just hoofing it.

"Flynnie wears his heart on his sleeve. That's him all the time, that's how he plays. He loves a big battle and the more players he comes up against where he's really got to fight and scrap, then the happier and better he is. He just leads by example, that is him as a captain. He's actually very quiet out on the field, funnily enough. I told him when he took over, he needed to learn how to be a captain — some players are born into the role, but he's had to learn how to be one. He just gets better and better at it. He's popular with the players — he even runs a savings account for them. The lads put money away each week, some are saving for holidays, or whatever, and he keeps that account for them.

"Sometimes me and Sainty might call him in and ask him to have a quiet word with a player who's not performing; or one who we think has a personal problem. Sometimes, something like that is better coming from him — it's less daunting for a player to talk to Flynnie than to talk to the boss." That's why David Jones made Mike Flynn captain....

The way the players reacted to the nightmare confronting Flynn proved to Jones that there was an incredible loyalty at the club. Naturally, word got around; but it was a subject nobody spoke about openly, and it was one that never leaked outside the club. As Jones explains: "Gradually, the players got to know about it — although not for some time. I suppose once one player got to know, he told another and so on; but the one thing they are good at is keeping things in-house.

"It was never a subject you could go up to Flynnie and approach him with. It would have been easy for the players to go around talking about it, so again that shows what sort of spirit there is in the camp. Very rarely does anything get out — and this proved it. Nobody spoke about it, and it's remained that way right up to today. The way Flynnie handled what he went through is a credit to him — but also to the lads. They never put him under any pressure to talk about it; the bond within the club is very strong — and this proved it."

This episode in Jones' managerial career is over now. This is the first time he has ever spoken about it publicly, the first time he has shared the secret with strangers — and, naturally, he asked Flynn's permission first. If Flynn had said no, then the subject would have remained closed. But Flynn consented and, who knows, perhaps this, for him, is part of his healing process. Certain details have been deliberately omitted from this book: dates, addresses and most of all names. Because it was Flynn's in-laws, his name was never associated with the tragedy, and the press never made the connection. When the case came to court, Flynn's mother-in-law pleaded guilty to manslaughter and she received a prison sentence.

"Everybody suffers deaths in their family, and it's a terrible time, but at end of the day life must go on," said Jones. "Mick probably dealt with his crisis in the best way, although none of us really knows for sure how he dealt with it at home. I've seen his wife at a game, now and then, and always asked whether she was OK — although to be honest, we were always checking with Flynnie how she was coping. I think I know Flynnie very well — I have a good relationship with him, I can speak my mind to him, and he does the same with me. If something is bothering him he just gets out there and gets on with playing football — and that's the best way he knows how.

"To do what he did; well, I will always have so much admiration for him. To go through all that took remarkable strength and courage, and that's what Flynnie has in abundance. I can only draw on my own experiences, when my daughters were in hospital, and I needed to work as well to stop me worrying. Of course, I'd still be worried deep down, but you need to occupy your mind with something else, and that's what Mick did.

"We watched him very closely to be honest — what he was like around the training ground, how it was affecting him on the pitch, whether he was making bad decisions, things like that. We were keeping an eye on him from a distance but he never once showed any signs of being affected. In my short time in management — and even in my experiences outside the game — for him to do what he did, and to handle it in the way he did, leaves me full of admiration. It proves to me a great deal of character."

****

It's the third round of the Coca-Cola Cup and Stockport have been handed an away draw at Premier League giants Blackburn Rovers — after beating Chesterfield and Sheffield United in the earlier rounds. There's a large contingent of County fans making the trip; they're feeling optimistic after the Sheffield result and when County step out of the players' tunnel onto the Ewood Park pitch, it's the 'Barmy Stockport Army' making the most noise. It will prove to be one of the greatest night's in the club history — not so much for the result, but for the manner in which County stun their big-time neighbours.

Stockport look in control right from the start; dictating the pace, imposing their will on a Premier League team managed by Ray Harford — the silent partner when Kenny Dalglish led Blackburn to the richest jewel of them all, the league title. There's no doubt County deserve a lead — but where's the goal coming from? Who will be the man to produce one moment of inspiration, and give the Second Division minnows their just reward?

County win a throw-in and Mike Flynn picks up the ball, almost level with Blackburn's 18-yard box. Jones knows what's coming, the players know — and every County fan knows. He inches himself back as far as he can towards the perimeter wall, twists the ball around in the palm of his hands — until he's happy with the grip — and then hurls himself forward; firing the ball high towards the Blackburn goal like a human rocket launcher. All eyes shoot to the night sky and wait in eager anticipation to see where the ball is going to land. Panic breaks out in the Blackburn goalmouth and their goalkeeper — England No.3, Tim Flowers — rushes to the near-post. Flowers' upraised arm flails about above the mass of heads — he desperately tries to punch the ball clear, only to see it ricochet off the head of Blackburn skipper, Tim Sherwood, and rebound back into the empty net. County are 1-0 up and that's the way it will stay. That's why David Jones made Mike Flynn captain......

CHAPTER **7**

On The Edge

Crewe Alexandra 1, Stockport County 0 *(Saturday, August 17)*
Stockport County 0, Notts County 0 *(Saturday, August 24)*
Stockport County 0, Bournemouth 1 *(Tuesday, August 27)*
Bristol Rovers 1, Stockport County 1 *(Saturday, August 31)*
Watford 1, Stockport County 0 *(Saturday, September 7)*
Stockport County 0, Wrexham 2 *(Tuesday, September 10)*

THE crazed eyes are filled with hate; the ugly, bloated face contorted with vicious anger. A torrent of vitriolic abuse pours out of the snarling mouth, like a sewer over-flowing, and it's all directed at one man: Stockport County manager, David Jones. The season is only four weeks old and this deranged fan, so consumed with ferocious anger, wants Jones sacked. And he's not the only one; the poisonous words: 'Jones out' are echoing around Edgeley Park.

And that's how the greatest season in Stockport County's history started for the greatest manager the club has ever known. Reviled, despised, Jones faced the biggest crisis of his short managerial career.

Like every Stockport fan, like the chairman, like the directors, Jones

Picture courtesy Manchester Evening News

Promotion a-spire-ations. D-day at Saltergate

approached the new season back in August full of confidence, full of hope. However, within a few desperate weeks, he was receiving hate mail and the humiliating chants of: 'Jones out', 'Board out', were spreading from the unforgiving terraces.

The first match of the 1996-1997 campaign was away at Crewe; and Jones had been busy during the preceding summer months, strengthening his squad — discovering the magical skills of Luis Cavaco in Portugal, and bringing in the Wolves keeper Paul Jones.

The arrival of the latter raised a few eyebrows: County already had a supremely talented keeper in the diminutive Neil Edwards. But, as far as the County boss was concerned, size mattered, and Edwards was too short. Big was beautiful.

Persuading the giant Wolves keeper to drop a division — and accept a hefty cut in wages — was a problem however and, for a while, Jones feared he wouldn't get his man. "I'd seen Jonah play, but I'd never met him in person," recalled the County boss. "I was in America at the time and spoke to him on the phone, inviting him to come down to the ground and have a look round. Andy Mutch met him — they'd been team-mates at Molineux — and Saint gave him the guided tour; trying to sell him the club, before our secretary gave him a run-down on what we could afford.

"But Jonah phoned me later on in America and said the deal's off, he'd be losing too much money. That was three or four days before I was due back. As soon as I returned, I phoned the chairman and asked him if the deal was dead — and the chairman just said let me have a chat with him.

"And that's what happened. Jonah walked into the place, and the chairman — who's a big bloke himself — took one look at him, saw how huge he was, and said: 'If you want him, you can have him!'"

County paid Wolves £60,000, and made their new keeper one of the club's highest-paid players. "The chairman backed me all the way," said Jones. Again, it would prove to be a wise investment.

Jones' other big find was little Luis Cavaco, a precious gem he discovered on a scouting tour to Portugal. Jones and his chairman Brendan Elwood, were keen to see if County could exploit the new Bosman ruling; which allowed European players out of contract to move to any club they chose — with no bloated transfer fee involved.

"The chairman phoned me up and asked where would be the best place to go looking for players," said Jones. "I knew Spain had already been looked at — and Holland was getting drained — but I felt Portugal might be a good, untapped source."

Before setting off, Jones contacted the former England boss, Bobby Robson; who was out there managing Porto. "I asked Bobby if he could recommend an agent to me, someone who knew the players, and he gave me the name of a contact called Jorge Gama," recalled Jones.

So the County party took off to sunny Portugal — and took in an Estoril game. It was there they got their first look at Cavaco. "We were actually looking at two other players who'd been recommended, but I didn't fancy either of them," said Jones. "But Luis caught my eye, we made some enquiries; but the boy seemed to be tied up with Estoril, and that was that."

Jones arranged for County to return to Portugal for a pre-season tour, where they played three matches — including one against Benfica's feeder club. "The next thing, Cavaco turns up completely out of the blue," continued Jones, "and wants to know whether we're interested in him! I thought he was one for the future, and we signed him for nothing!

"A lot of people thought it was Bobby Robson who introduced me to Cavaco, but it wasn't. Bobby just introduced me to the agent. We also took another lad, Kiko; and a young 18-year-old called Nelson has signed now, so our contacts are quite strong over there.

"Believe it or not, we're headline news in Portugal now. They saw our Cup runs on Sky TV, and really picked up on the fact that Cavaco was playing so well for us.

"It was a brilliant education for me to go abroad and have a look at their players. I went to Benfica as well, and had a look at their training facilities; and we'll be going back to Portugal for another pre-season tour. I'm like a big sponge, I gather in as much information as I can, and I learnt a lot out there."

County came back from their Portuguese break feeling buoyant, fresh and raring to go. They played two tough friendlies against Birmingham and Tranmere; and won both so convincingly that Jones felt supremely confident.

"I remember Trevor Francis having a moan about the grass being too long, but it hadn't stopped us; we played some really good stuff against Birmingham. Then we beat Tranmere away — which was no mean feat. Everything seemed to be taking off," said Jones.

"I felt this was the strongest squad of players the club had ever had, and everything was starting to fall into place for promotion."

In fact, the County boss was so confident he even threw down a remarkable challenge to his team before their first league game at Crewe.

"It was a scorching hot day, and we all felt this was going to be the start of something big for the club," said Jones. "We just didn't feel we could lose because of the pre-season we'd had.

"I actually asked the lads before the game whether they thought it was possible for us to go through the campaign and not lose a league game. I remembered Leeds United nearly did it; and I felt so confident, that was my team talk. I wasn't being blasé, or anything like that. I just asked them: 'Can it be done? Let's see if it's possible'.

Forty-five minutes later, the optimism was starting to wane. It was 0-0, and County weren't looking a good bet for promotion.

"I absolutely blasted them at half-time, because all they were doing was passing the ball — nobody was prepared to shoot. I could never see Crewe scoring, but I could never see us scoring, either."

Jones got it wrong — Crewe did score, in the last minute; and his dream of going through the season unbeaten was abruptly shattered.

"We were all bitterly disappointed," he recalled. "We'd really felt we were going to steamroller everybody who came in front of us — but it hadn't happened.

"I was very annoyed afterwards: you can't go through a game of football and just pass, pass, pass. Too many players were taking the easy way out. But then you start making excuses, and start thinking: 'OK, it's the first game of the season; it was a really hot day, the pace of the game was slow, it's a minor blip.'"

Jones responded to the early setback by persuading Sunderland to release former County striker Brett Angell on loan — seven years after he'd left Edgeley Park. It was a significant move; County went on to pay a club record £100,000 to sign Angell permanently. He would be worth every penny.

But before that, there was worse to come. County struggled their way through a 0-0 draw at home to Notts County, and then slumped to 21st in the division — after a humiliating 1-0 home defeat against Bournemouth, in front of 3,000 disenchanted fans. "We lost to a fabulous goal, an overhead kick, and all of a sudden you're thinking to yourself: 'Hang on, what's going on here?'" said Jones. "It was as if someone had stuck a syringe in our players, and drained out all their confidence."

County then faced an exhausting journey to Bristol Rovers. Where there'd been exuberance, there was now despondency; players were starting to get on each other's nerves, niggling rows were breaking out on and off the pitch. The mood was in stark contrast to the coach trip to Crewe just three weeks earlier, when players were lapping up the sunshine in T-shirts and shorts, ready to conquer the world.

Rovers were in party mood — this was the inaugural game in their brand new home, the Memorial Ground. But dispirited County were in no frame of mind to join in the celebrations, and Jones still remembers a conversation he shared with Chris Marsden shortly before kick off.

"I was standing outside the changing room and Mazza, who was injured, came up to me and said: 'Are you all right gaffer?' I told him I was fine but wanted to know why he'd asked, and he replied: 'Because you look a little bit down in the dumps. You must get your head up, we'll turn this around'.

"Now that meant a lot to me. It was a nice thing to have in the camp, because it proved that the players also cared about what was going on."

It only took Rovers 12 minutes to take the lead; but John Jeffers brought temporary relief with a crashing 25-yard equaliser that soared into the roof of the net. Final score 1-1, and County faced another long trek — this time to Watford — wondering if they'd turned the corner.

But they hadn't. "We lost to a dubious penalty and all of a sudden you can feel heads are starting to drop," recalled Jones. "I was baffled. I couldn't figure out why we'd been scoring so freely in pre-season but now we couldn't hit the back of the net."

The Coca-Cola Cup seemed to offer the only respite; County had beaten Chesterfield over two legs. But they were still 22nd in the table, and now faced Wrexham at home in the league.

It was to be the lowest point of Jones' managerial career. County lost 2-0, Chris Marsden was sent off, and the 4,000 crowd were baying for blood. David Jones' blood. "Wrexham at home was probably the poorest I'd ever seen us play since I'd been in charge," he confessed.

Jones had to walk a gauntlet of hate that night, inside and outside Edgeley Park. For the first time in his managerial career, the words ringing in his ears were foul, abusive, menacing.

The loudmouths in the crowd seized their chance to stick the knife in, and took it with spiteful vengeance: 'Get out Jones' — 'You're shit' — 'You don't know what the f*** you're doing'. It had all come down to this. A season that had started off with so much hope, had disintegrated into two measly points from six games — and the contorted faces of angry fans feverishly blaming Jones.

"All of a sudden the knives were out," said Jones. "People were being abusive as I was walking off the pitch, shouting: 'Get out' and 'Sack the board' — stuff like that.

"There was one supporter who slaughtered me. I know who he is — a big, fat fella, I have a good memory — and he absolutely slaughtered me. But I had to be prepared to take the flak. To be honest, it made me more determined — I wanted to rub a few faces in the mud after that; especially his. Whenever things were going wrong, it was always him yelling: 'Get him on' — 'Take him off.' Everyone has an opinion, and everyone's opinion is right, it's just I have the final say. But people like that will always find something wrong.

"I'd never experienced that in my life before; as a player, coach or manager. All of a sudden, I'm experiencing the other side of the coin — and it wasn't nice."

Jones made straight for the sanctuary of his cramped office — squashed beneath the iron girders of the main stand — and waited for the chairman to arrive as he usually did after a home game.

Outside, he could still hear the angry, accusing voices, and when Elwood walked into the room, closing the door behind him, it was difficult to look the chairman straight in the eye.

"I felt a bit embarrassed, because here's this man who'd given me the opportunity, who'd placed his faith in me, and things weren't working out for him," recalls Jones.

"Everybody thought he'd come down to give me a right bollocking, but he hadn't. He'd come down to reassure me, to tell me he was 100 per cent behind me. It was never, ever, a vote of confidence, because he didn't go to the press and say anything. This was between me and the chairman.

"He knew himself we were on the verge of something big, but all of a sudden the wheels had fallen off somewhere. I was even asking him questions like: 'What the bloody hell's gone wrong?!'"

"He reminded me I was a young manager coming in, and I needed time to settle in. We'd changed the style of play, we'd got rid of the long-ball, and he didn't expect things to happen overnight."

But the baying mob hadn't finished with Jones yet; there was more back-stabbing to come, this time from the press. "One paper — The Sun — told me I had 24 hours to put things right, which I found virtually impossible, because we didn't play again until the following Saturday. I found that quite amusing, really. Then I was standing next to the chairman when one reporter asked: "Is your job on the line?"

The key question. Six short words on which a man's future could hang. Jones is shoulder to shoulder with his boss — the man who pulls the strings — and suddenly a hush descends on the crowded room. Was Jones going to get the bullet?

"The chairman said: 'Don't be stupid, we're only six games into the season. If we're like this after 15 games, then maybe I'll have to look at it'.

"I thought that was fair enough," remembers Jones. "At least he was giving me 15 games and not one, as one reporter had suggested."

But Jones' head was spinning, he couldn't define what was going wrong: "It wasn't that the players weren't trying, it was just everything they tried wasn't coming off. And that's when people start to hide. I remember sitting in the manager's room afterwards, talking to Wrexham's Kevin Reeves and Joey Jones and they were telling me they'd been down the same road in the past themselves.

"But I just couldn't believe it — I was looking at our players and they weren't the players we'd done such a good a pre-season with. It was as if somebody had cloned them and put out a different set of players. I couldn't work out what had gone wrong.

"I never really doubted myself, but I questioned myself once or twice. I looked at myself hard and asked whether what I was doing was the right way of playing. And I decided: 'Yes, that's my philosophy, these are my principles.'"

But when the knives are out, their sharpened blades can be long and piercing. The vitriol didn't end with one heated press conference.

That same night, the seething fans vented their anger on the local radio stations, and over the following days the Edgeley Park postbags were suddenly filled with hate mail — all directed at Jones.

"I was getting some pretty poisonous letters sent to the club, telling me to get out; people were phoning up radio stations saying they'd chosen the wrong man; I didn't know what I was doing; they should have picked a more experienced manager.

"After the Wrexham game I went on the radio myself. I knew I was putting my head on the chopping block; but I wanted to tell people that I still honestly felt this was the best team Stockport had ever had — and we'd be working flat out to put the problems right. I always felt it would only be a matter of time because the players we had were too good."

Jones left Edgeley Park that night dispirited, disillusioned; a million-and-one voices pounding through his brain: 'Why don't you do this?' 'Why don't you try that?' 'Why don't you quit?'

He faced a bleak 50-mile car journey home to Southport, and set off into the night anxious to leave the Wrexham debacle — and the voices of hate that still echoed in his mind — far behind him.

And it was then, during that drive home, that a truth began to dawn — and Jones made the first, monumental, step towards solving the Stockport County crisis.

"I was driving home, thinking to myself: 'What the hell's gone wrong?'

— and I just couldn't put my finger on it," revealed Jones. "And then I suddenly realised I was listening to too many people, rather than doing my own thing and making my own decisions. And that's not normally like me.

"I phoned Saint there and then on the car phone, and told him we should hold a meeting of all the senior players — not the entire team, just the senior pros — in my office and hammer the thing out. And, if it was close to the bone, then so be it."

By the time Jones got home, his wife Ann was fast asleep in bed. Jones knew she would have been listening to the radio phone-ins, and would have shared the pain — as each irate fan delivered their damning verdicts on her husband.

"Ann was very quiet the next day; of course she was worried," said Jones. "She heard it all, and it must have been hard to take. I tried to reassure her not to be worried, but of course she was. All of a sudden she's thinking no contract, no security, what happens if I get the sack. I knew these things were on her mind.

"She gets uptight — she listens to the games, she's a winner as well and she wants us to win.

"The darkest moment for all of us were those first six games. I'm not a worrier; Ann and the family worry enough, without me doing it, I tend to bottle things up a little bit and keep it all to myself. But it was a hell of a pressure for Ann — she told me later on that she'd been really anxious.

"She'd ask me things, and I'd tell her not to worry and just let me get on with it. She'd even try to pick the team for me, and find out what I was going to say to the players.

"I just tried to convince her that if they sacked me after only six games, it wasn't worth being in the job anyway. That's the way I looked at it."

But Jones wasn't throwing in the towel. He'd rediscovered his self belief, he knew his football principles were sound, and he knew he had the right players to make them work. He now needed to impose his strength, his will, on the team — and not be distracted by other people's opinions.

"No player means to go out on the pitch and play badly; but we were going out and just waiting for things to automatically happen," he said.

"Everybody was working hard; but they weren't working hard as a team. I felt one or two things needed to be pointed out — we weren't all pulling together, it was a case of getting our heads out of the sand and rediscovering some self-belief."

And so, two days after the Wrexham debacle, Jones sat in his office waiting for his most senior players to walk through the door.

It would be the mother of all meetings....

****

Stockport County 3, Plymouth Argyle 1 *(Saturday, September 14)*

David Jones is sat in his office — 'the pit' — waiting for his senior pro's to enter. It's appropriate they are going to meet in 'the pit' because, quite frankly, that's exactly where Stockport County are right now — and deep in it.

One by one they come in and Jones watches each in turn: skipper Mike Flynn; Jim Gannon; Brett Angell; Andy Mutch; Chris Marsden; Tom Bennett and Paul Jones.

There's no room here for Alun Armstrong, Luis Cavaco, Lee Todd, Sean Connolly, Kieron Durkan, John Jeffers. They are excluded — right now Jones wants to have it out with the men he relies on more than any others out on the pitch.

The players sit side by side, squeezed together in the confined space of the tiny room. There's no hiding place in here; and everyone is at the mercy of each other.

And this will be no place for faint hearts; Jones kicks off the meeting by giving the players the chance to duck out straight away. He knows some home-truths are going to be flying around, and he needs men with broad enough shoulders to let the flak bounce right off.

"I told them it wasn't a slagging match; but if people didn't want to hear what was being said then they could leave the room there and then. Deep down, I felt these were the players who would be big enough, and strong enough, to accept the things that would be thrown at them," he said.

Jones was desperate to hear the players' grievances; and desperate to repair the shattered morale that had seen his talented squad score just one goal in six league games. This meeting was designed to let the players have their say, in the hope they could talk out their problems and rediscover the form that had been so electrifying during pre-season.

The County boss had become increasingly alarmed at the back biting and squabbling that had broken out on the pitch. His frustrated players were starting to row among themselves; to blame each other but never themselves, and Jones knew he had to fix that immediately. But first he had to coax them into speaking their minds.

As he explained: "I'm a big believer in not letting things fester; you bring them to the fore. I said if they had anything on their chest, this was the time to say it.

"Against Wrexham, Saint and I had noticed the players snarling at one another, backbiting, arguing on the pitch — and we'd never really had that before. It worried us because we knew if we couldn't get a grip on that, then we would lose the whole lot. We needed to start working together and helping one another. You don't need to tell someone he's given a bad ball, what you need to do is get his head up and encourage him. If he's not doing what he should be doing, then you hand out a bollocking; but if the lad's trying his best and it isn't coming off, you try to lift him up.

"I didn't feel we were doing that — as soon as someone gave a bad ball, he was getting a bollocking on the pitch and that needed to be stamped out."

Jones invited his assembled players to spill their hearts — and they seized the opportunity. Predictably though, they all pointed the finger at one another.

"That was normal; we'd expected that to happen," recalls Jones. "The safety valve for any player is to blame someone else. That happens in all walks of life and we knew that was coming; and, sure enough, certain players thought that others weren't pulling their weight."

The fingers pointed at big Jim Gannon, the man who had served Stockport longer than any of the others squashed into one tiny room.

Just about all Gannon's playing career had been spent at Edgeley Park; he still carried the wounds of County's bloody play-off battles at Wembley. Now he was being knifed again.

Revealed Jones: "Jim got the worst flak. Someone accused him of always having a moan out on the pitch. If he made a mistake he was blaming someone else — it wasn't that he'd given a bad ball, it was that the other player wasn't there to receive it.

"One by one the other players started to jump on the bandwagon and said they felt the same. It was pretty heated — the atmosphere built up, then it calmed down. But it was what we wanted. We'd told them not to be frightened to say what they felt — but we'd also promised we wouldn't let it turn into a slagging match."

Picture courtesy Manchester Evening News

End of the road at the Riverside

Gannon wasn't the only one who came under fire: Chris Marsden and Paul Jones also had to contend with their share of criticism: "The players felt that Mazza was running all over the show," says Jones. "He was trying too hard, and he wasn't sticking to the one specific thing he was meant to do — help Tom and be creative in midfield. He was charging down the right wing, down the left wing, he was running all over the show and there was no pattern to our play.

"And big Jonah. We'd brought him in to dominate his back four, but it wasn't happening. It was all things like that."

Slowly but surely, the players were letting the painful truths come out; giving Jones the chance to identify their anxieties, and then, hopefully, do something about them. The language may have been industrial — and it wasn't exactly half an hour on the psychiatrist's couch — but it was the remedy Stockport County badly needed.

"Yes, it was heated at times but they weren't at each other's throats, they weren't fighting. They didn't know themselves why it was going wrong on the pitch — they were bemused, and it was a case of reassuring them that they were good players, and that they had the ability to turn it round. We had to convince them that you don't just become bad players over night."

Even Jones couldn't escape the glaring spotlight he had switched on during that meeting. He'd sat and watched the players tear each other apart — now it was their turn to watch him squirm. The County manager had encouraged them to speak their minds, and these men were strong enough to tell their gaffer what they thought he was doing wrong.

"Some of the players felt Saint and I hadn't worked enough on set-pieces in training," recalls Jones. "I didn't mind, it was a fair comment. I mean, if I open up a meeting I've got to be prepared to take the flak myself — and I told them that.

"The set-pieces thing was probably my fault. I assumed the players I'd brought into the club would do everything for themselves; they were good players and they would sort out all the problems. But that doesn't always happen, and I should have been aware of that."

The meeting that would bring about the resurrection of Stockport County lasted a mere 30 minutes. Two lessons were learned: the need to encourage one another out on the pitch; and the need for greater discipline. Players had to stick to the tasks they were required to do, and not run all over the place as if they were one-man teams.

"I felt a lot better afterwards, because they'd got things off their chests and we'd got some off ours," admitted Jones. "When the meeting finished there was a feeling of: 'Right, let's start afresh'. It was like a new beginning for us."

Jones ordered his players straight back on to the training ground after the meeting, to play five-a-sides and keep ball. "The players who hadn't been in the meeting were dying to know what had gone on," smiles Jones. "Saint and I knew the players would tell them — that's why we'd chosen the senior ones in the first place. It was a collective thing, and we expected them to spread the word."

The boss held another training session the following day, Friday, and he recalled: "That went really well — you could feel the confidence returning in them. They were laughing and joking again — a bit bubbly — and they worked on a few set-pieces, free-kicks, which went down well."

County were playing Plymouth at home on the Saturday, and Jones arrived at Edgeley Park with a feeling he had not known for some weeks: overwhelming confidence.

"I just felt whoever we were going to play at home that day was going to get a hiding — be it Plymouth, Liverpool or Manchester United. Everything seemed to be falling back into place," he said.

Only two minutes into the game and Jones had every reason to feel that way: Tom Bennett floated a dangerous free-kick towards the far post and big Jim Gannon rose to power home a ferocious header.

The same Tom Bennett who'd had the guts in THAT meeting to accuse his boss of not spending enough time practising free-kicks; the same Jim Gannon who'd stood accused by his own team-mates of blaming everyone except himself, of moaning and groaning at them all.

Now they were all working together, in harmony, and it had taken just two minutes.

Recalled Jones: "It made them feel better because they'd asked us to work on free-kicks; so we worked on a few things, and then two minutes into the next game they go and score from one!"

County won 3-1, with Gannon bagging another and Alun Armstrong netting his first goal for the club. "It was a huge relief," confessed Jones. "When Jim scored that first, I was thinking: 'Hell, we CAN score goals'; then we get a second, then a third — and next thing I'm thinking is that there's going to be an avalanche of goals.

"When we got to 3-1, the lads really started to knock the ball about and the crowd were loving it. They could now see what they'd seen in pre-season and the back-end of last year. I think they'd been in shock as well; but now they were seeing that we could play and that was a big relief."

Jones identifies that game as the most significant in the astonishing season that still lay ahead. "I know it was the turning point," he says, adamantly. How much of it was down to that no-holds-barred meeting is one for the psychiatrists to debate. Perhaps British Telecom know best — after all, they're the ones who insist: 'It's good to talk'.

****

York City 1, Stockport County 2 *(Saturday, September 21)*
Stockport County 2, Gillingham 1 *(Saturday, September 28)*
Millwall 3, Stockport County 4 *(Wednesday, October 2)*
Burnley 5, Stockport County 2 *(Saturday, October 5)*
Stockport County 1, Preston North End 0 *(Saturday, October 12)*
Stockport County 1, Luton Town 1 *(Tuesday, October 15)*
Wycombe Wanderers 0, Stockport County 2 *(Saturday, October 19)*
Walsall 1, Stockport County 1 *(Saturday, October 26)*

Stockport County 1, Chesterfield 0 *(Tuesday, October 29)*
Stockport County 1, Bristol City 1 *(Saturday, November 2)*
Brentford 2, Stockport County 2 *(Saturday, November 9)*
Stockport County 2, Doncaster R 1 *(FA Cup1: Saturday, November 16)*
Stockport County 1, Blackpool 0 *(Tuesday, November 19)*
Shrewsbury Town 3, Stockport County 2 *(Saturday, November 23)*
Stockport County 2, Walsall 0 *(Saturday, November 30)*
Rotherham United 0, Stockport County 1 *(Tuesday, December 3)*

****

It's 9.45 in the evening, and David Jones is standing in the manager's room. On the walls hang photographs — some black and white, others colour — of County's great moments. There they are winning promotion from Division Three — the jubilation, the ecstasy etched on all the faces. There's the lads at Wembley, proudly coming out of the most famous players' tunnel in Britain, to lap up the warm sunshine and the unforgettable atmosphere.

Jones knows these pictures intimately — he was there when they were taken; he recognises the players in an instant, and one quick glance is enough to bring the memories tumbling back.

But tonight there's a big difference — because David Jones isn't standing in his office, and this isn't Edgeley Park.

This is Rotherham; and Jones is standing in their new manager's office. Their new manager is Danny Bergara; hanging on the walls are the pictures that Jones helped a distraught Bergara remove on that heart-rending day when he was kicked out of Edgeley Park.

These are pictures Bergara still cherishes, nearly two years later, because there they are, hanging on the walls of his office — even though he's now manager of Rotherham.

The dethroned Stockport boss is standing opposite Jones. They were master and pupil when all those photographs were taken; now they're equals, facing each other for the first time since Bergara's traumatic exit.

The words wouldn't flow easily between Jones and Bergara that night. Too much had happened in their lives in between.....

****

Jones had been elated by County's performance against Plymouth. It had given him hope and confidence — whereas, before, doubt and concern had beaten their poisonous paths to his door. Jones is essentially an optimistic man; he approaches problems with an inherent belief that they can be overcome. He doesn't surrender easily; but like all County fans, he needed that victory over Plymouth to feel the faith flowing through his veins again.

Jones was convinced that the squad of players he had assembled at the beginning of the season was good enough to play the fluid, passing game he believed would get the club out of Division Two. Perhaps it needs an optimistic person to believe in the beautiful game; and maybe that person also has to have an obstinate belief in his principles.

Because no matter how disheartening County's pitiful start to the season had been — and at this stage they were a colossal 18 points adrift of the top — Jones was never once tempted to revert to the long-ball game he finds so abhorrent. The man was not for turning. And, over the next few games, that unwavering resolve would be rewarded.

After Plymouth came victory in the league at York City, Brett Angell grabbing both goals in a 2-1 triumph. After the game, Jones and Angell were alone in the dressing room with the York YTS trainees — who were busy cleaning the boots of players they hoped one day to emulate.

"They didn't know who we were," recalled Jones, "but I remember them asking us how come we were in such a bad position in the table; because we had absolutely battered York. We'd played some brilliant football, and these kids couldn't believe we were nearly bottom of the league. I think Brett turned to them and said: 'Well, watch us climb the table, youngster.'"

The 5-2 mauling of Sheffield United in the Coca-Cola Cup followed; a 2-1 home win over Gillingham came next and then there was the game that really proved to Jones what his side could accomplish.

Up to this point, Jones had abandoned all the thoughts of promotion that had filled him with such hope at the beginning of the season. That seemed too distant a goal — the immediate objective was to steer County steadily up the table.

But Millwall, away, was to be the turning point; the moment when Jones sensed this was to be the year. "Over the entire season it was probably our best game," he confirmed. "I don't think anyone in the league could have touched us that night."

County had raced into a 3-1 lead with goals from Kieron Durkan, Alun

Armstrong and Jim Gannon — after Millwall had gone ahead through Anton Rogan.

Stockport were exhilarating that night — and deserved their emphatic lead against a Millwall side that had been setting the pace at the top of the table. "I remember Saint saying at half-time that it was frightening," says Jones. "Never in his wildest dreams did Saint think the lads could play as well as that. You couldn't single out one player; they were all spot on. Everything you do in training; everything you say, and everything you coach — it was just all coming together."

But the night wasn't quite over — there were a few twists and turns to survive before Jones and Saint would come away dreaming once again of promotion. Explained Jones: "The referee made one almighty cock-up. Toddy gave a back pass — with his knee — but the ref blew, thinking it was an offence.

"I remember running down the touchline, and steaming on to the pitch — with all the players — and having a right go at him. He suddenly realised he'd made a mistake, and decided to drop the ball; which Millwall booted out for a throw-in, right by the corner flag.

"We took the throw-in, lost the ball, they crossed it and scored. That's how they got back into it. If the referee hadn't made that mistake we'd have probably won by five or six."

But, suddenly, Millwall could see light, and roared on by the partisan New Den support, they grabbed a dramatic equaliser through substitute Paul Hartley — bringing the score to 3-3.

"I remember turning round to Saint and saying: 'How the bloody hell has this happened?' We'd totally dominated the game and now it's 3-3."

But County weren't dead. The minutes were ticking away, and Jones was trying to convince himself a draw was still a good result, when — in his words: "Tom Bennett did a bit of magic on the edge of the box, slipped the ball across to Alun Armstrong, who finished it off." Final score: 4-3. Justice was done and Stockport County, tenth in the division, were heading for promotion.

"The players couldn't believe it afterwards," said Jones. "They absolutely slaughtered Millwall — I mean really slaughtered them —and some of the football they'd played had been incredible. I'd always thought they had the ability, and that night I felt very proud. And that was the first time that we really started to think, hang on, we can win this league — we were on a roll, and the belief in the camp was starting to grow. It was only four league games since the Wrexham defeat at home — so four games after our worst performance, I'd suddenly seen the best of us. Now we were starting to play like a team."

It was John Lennon who wrote: 'Life's what happens to you when you're busy making other plans.' And Jones and Saint were busy making plans for promotion, when they went to Burnley three days later. They were euphoric; they'd turned the tide, and now they expected to carry over all the good work from the New Den to Turf Moor.

Every truly passionate fan has an irrational, but deep-seated, need to loathe one opposing team more than any other —it's an essential part of football nature. Arsenal despise Tottenham and vice-versa; and the depth of their bigotry makes the north London derby one of the most compelling fixtures in football.

And so it is with Stockport and Burnley. The chances of seeing both sets of fans enjoying a convivial day out at the seaside together are about as remote as Vinny Jones winning a fair-play award.

Losing to Burnley is far harder to take than losing to anyone else; when they beat County 2-1 in the play-off final at Wembley the hurt was just about as bad as it gets. And now, three days after County's greatest win of the season, it was Burnley, of all people, who were to deliver the worst league pasting of the season: 5-2, with Paul Barnes grabbing ALL five goals.

Jones chuckles now at the memory, although he didn't know whether to laugh or cry on the day: "I was walking across the pitch with Saint afterwards and said to him: 'Were we really that bad?' — because the game could have ended up ten-all. As an attacking team we were brilliant, as a defensive team we were bloody awful."

Jones had little doubt as to where the blame lay, and he wasted little time letting that player know. The man who took all the flak during that make-or-break players' meeting was about to get it again.

According to Jones: "We just weren't marking, we weren't doing the things you should be doing. Their lad scored all five goals, so whoever was meant to be picking him up obviously wasn't doing his job — and that was Jim Gannon.

"I blamed him squarely, I asked him: 'Where's the bloody marking?' Jim was saying things like: 'I thought he was going to do this, I thought he was going to do that'. In other words, he was trying to think the other lad's game, instead of concentrating on his own.

"As an attacking display we played some great stuff. Every time we attacked we looked like we were going to score; every time they attacked they did score!

"Everyone of the defence was bloody awful. Toddy and Jim even ran into one another at one point — and that let them in for one of their goals. It was a total disaster.

"The fans were on a roller coaster — one minute up, the next down, and of course the one team they don't want to lose to is Burnley."

Stoical to the last, Jones made a virtue of defeat, convincing his crestfallen players that it was a short, sharp shock they could learn from: "After Millwall, they'd started to feel like they had at the beginning of the season: all they had to do was put a shirt on, go out and it would all automatically happen. They'd forgotten you've also got to work your socks off."

Once again, Jones the Optimist proved correct: County beat Preston 1-0 at home, with a Brett Angell goal after 70 seconds, and then faced another one of the Second Division pacesetters — Luton at Edgeley Park.

"They were one of the favourites to go up, and in the first half they absolutely battered us. They really did, they looked the strongest team and the best team I'd seen all season," recalled Jones.

Steve Davis headed Luton ahead after 27 minutes — but Brett Angell notched his seventh goal in seven games after the break to level the scores. "The second half was a complete turnaround and we absolutely pulverised them," explains Jones. "I'd kept my half-time talk calm; I told them to keep playing, to be patient and it would come. And it did — Brett was on a hot streak by then. And if their keeper hadn't been six foot six, he'd never have pulled off a brilliant save at the end."

'Angell's Delight' started to become a recurring headline in the newspapers: the County striker grabbed two more in County's next game — a 2-0 win at Wycombe. "They must have had 20 corners in the second half," remembers Jones. "But it became easy for us because they kept lobbing the same ball into the same area — and in the end Flynnie found it all a bit mundane, a bit straightforward."

County's majestic win at Blackburn in the Coca-Cola Cup followed and suddenly confidence was flowing through the side. But Jones was worried about After the Lord Mayor's Show syndrome — having scaled the sublime peaks at Ewood Park, would County come plummeting down to ridiculous depths at Walsall, three days later?

"That was my biggest concern," he confessed. "In the past, when we played a big team, we'd always lose the next game afterwards. We went to Walsall, which was never going to be easy for us, and we drew 1-1; Kizza scoring in the last minute. But what pleased me more than anything was that we kept playing, even when we went 1-0 down. We didn't just lump the ball into the box, we kept playing and playing."

Although County were winning — they beat Chesterfield next, 1-0, in a bruising battle at Edgeley Park — their league position remained frustrating. The poor start to the season was still taking its toll, and as hard as they tried, County seemed unable to get any higher than tenth in the table.

Next they faced Bristol City at home, also title contenders at this stage, and Jones was happy to come away with a 1-1 draw — Tom Bennett cancelling out Clayton Blackmore's opener — leaving County with just one defeat in 14 League and Cup games.

"That was a hard game — two good sides, I thought, hammering one another. A great game to watch," said Jones. "I didn't mind the draw; I'd always insisted that four points every two games would keep me happy, and we'd won the previous game."

County's promotion year is punctuated with key games where something — an incident, an event, a twist of fate, a slice of luck — played a significant part in shaping the club's success. Jones identifies Millwall away as one of those games — that was the night he really knew, deep down, his players were good enough.

Brentford, away, was another one of those games, and the key moment came when Jones played his wild card: the Portuguese winger, Luis Cavaco.

County were trailing 2-0 to the side everyone was tipping for promotion. They were top of the table and County's streak of form appeared to be on the brink of an abrupt halt. So far, he'd only used Cavaco as substitute in a handful of games. Jones knew this man could play, he knew he had the exhilarating touches of a predatory winger; but he wasn't sure he had the temperament, or experience yet for the English game. However, it was to be the day Cavaco came of age.

"We were two down when I brought on Luis," explains Jones. "He'd played a couple of games, always coming on as a substitute — but mentally and physically he hadn't been ready, although I knew he could play. We just felt it was a case of bringing him on at the right time."

It's a common misconception that Jones plays a 4-2-4 formation, although County certainly won promotion using a flat back four. The players who shoulder the biggest responsibility in a David Jones line-up are his wide men, but they have to do an awful lot more than stick on the wings and charge up and down the channels.

"The way I play, the most important people in my team are the wide fellas," explained Jones. "They are up and down, inside and out — they have to be everywhere. They have to be defenders, they have to be attackers, they have to be midfielders.

"If you look back over the season, the four players I've rotated the most have been the wide men: John Jeffers; Kieron Durkan; 'Coops' and Luis Cavaco. The rest of the team has been virtually settled."

Jones deliberately held Cavaco back until he could handle the different demands of that system: "His problem, at first, was that he wouldn't get into the game enough. We'd play him in the reserves; and he thought one run in 15 minutes was enough.

"I saw him as right-sided midfielder-cum-attacker, but we needed him to fit into our system; to learn that he had to cover and get tucked in where we wanted him. He'd never played like that before."

Cavaco was plunged in at the deep end at Brentford — just as County were sinking. They'd fallen two behind, with only 16 minutes left, although Angell threw a lifeline when he pulled a goal back.

And then Cavaco seized his chance. With the faintest jink of his shoulders, he swerved in from the right — cutting through the Brentford defence. This was the moment when Jones needed a player to be out of the ordinary — to think for himself, and not stick to some robotic plan drilled home during brain-numbing sessions on a practise ground. The coaching manuals were out of the window now; Jones was about to discover whether he'd discovered a real footballer, or just another Second Division journeyman. This was when Cavaco had to show flair, individuality — the strength of character to go it alone.

The little Portuguese winger charged forward, carving open enough space to unleash a shot — which curled round the keeper, and into the Brentford net for a breathtaking equaliser. 2-2 — and Stockport County had discovered Luis Cavaco.

"It was a great goal and I was pleased for him, because when he scored that goal he established himself at the football club," said Jones. "I think that's when the players realised this little bugger could play."

County then moved on to the first-round of the FA Cup — and a home tie against Third Division Doncaster. Jones' team by now were the talk of the nation after their giantkilling exploits in the Coca-Cola Cup; now it was nearly their turn to be on the receiving end.

The Yorkshire 'minnows' went into a deserved lead; and only quick-fire strikes from skipper Mike Flynn and Andy Mutch woke County from their lethargic display.

Back to the league, and another bruising encounter; this time at home to Blackpool. The Seasiders had two goals disallowed for offside, and their frustration boiled over when Micky Mellon was sent off for arguing with the referee. "It was a very, very physical game and they lost it due to their own lack of discipline," says Jones. "Some of their players seemed hell-bent on kicking us rather than playing, even though they're a good side. On the night they should have got something out of the game, but Tom Bennett scored what I consider to be our goal of the season. He got to the edge of the box, flicked the ball over the top of their centre half, and then buried it with his left foot on the volley. It was a great goal; especially after such a hard game."

Jones met up with the Blackpool boss, his old pal Gary Megson, after the game — and recognised a man going through the same trauma he'd experienced earlier in the season.

"Just like us, they were a good side, but they couldn't win games. I chatted to him, and told him to keep working away at it, but he was blaming Billy Bingham. Billy was their director of football, or something like that, and Gary felt he was poking his nose into too many things."

Jones can recall the highs of season 1996-97 with amazing clarity — seemingly minor details come flooding back with ease as he relives the magic moments that guaranteed Stockport promotion.

But there were also moments of intense disappointment last season when the cause looked lost, the dream shattered. They too have lodged themselves permanently in his memory. Saturday, November 23rd, is one of those.

"That day will stick in my mind for a long, long time. In fact it took nearly two months to get it out of my system," he revealed.

It takes something extraordinary to make Jones really lose his temper. The ice-cool facade rarely cracks; he reacts to pressure by staying calm. Tantrums, rages, foul-mouthed tirades are not Jones' trademarks — Channel Four could follow Jones for a season, Graham-Taylor style, and not have to worry about the number of F-words.

Or at least that was the case until the day County travelled to Shrewsbury — and lost 3-2 after totally dominating the game. Angell — who else? — had put County ahead; and even though Ian Stevens and Steve Anthrobus turned it round to 2-1, Chris Marsden grabbed an equaliser seven minutes from time.

But it wasn't over, and after looking comfortably the better side throughout, County threw it away in the last minute — when Paul Evans scored a spectacular winner.

"Our attacking had been good; but defensively, it was a case of déjà vu the Burnley game,'" said Jones. "I wasn't happy one bit. I threw my dummy out! It was probably the first time I'd had a tantrum in the changing room."

David Jones, a tantrum? "I told them they were absolute arseholes; they were useless to throw a game like that away — after dominating it so much. I was incensed that we'd thrown away at least a point — especially since we should have got all three.

It's Hammer time. County strike back

"I'm not normally that way inclined; I'm not a swearer, to be honest. In fact, I think the players know I'm angry when I'm quiet. But this time I was really seething. I think one of the press-men said it was the angriest he'd ever seen me.

"Again, I blamed Jim Gannon. Jim thought I was picking on him — but it just so happened that it was his fault! I still kept playing him afterwards because I believed in him; even though he might not have thought so sometimes.

"But that result really got to me. Even when I gave my team talk on the morning of the West Ham game in the Coca-Cola Cup, I brought the Shrewsbury match up again.

"It was a classic example of falling into bad habits; we'd done it against Wrexham; we'd done it against Burnley; and there we were doing it again, against Shrewsbury."

But what really rankled with Jones was the knowledge that County had blown a great chance to jump up the table: "We could have shot up about four places, and that would have been a huge psychological boost for us, because we were getting sick at always being stuck in either tenth or eleventh place."

Was it a coincidence that County's next game was against West Ham? Was it conceivable those players were mentally half-way down the motorway to Upton Park when that last-minute winner went in? "No, it was just a crap performance!" says Jones bluntly, still wincing at the memory.

County redeemed themselves in heroic fashion at West Ham, but then had to get back to the real world at home to Walsall three days later. Would they be able to get back to basics, after the glitter of Premier League opposition?

"We played our hearts out at West Ham and, obviously, I was worried it would be followed by another bad performance," admitted Jones.

"But we absolutely slaughtered Walsall 2-0 — Brett got both — and I felt we were starting to learn a lesson. But we were still tenth, we weren't moving anywhere! The Walsall game was on November 30th — and we'd been stuck in tenth place since the 2nd of October. In two months, we hadn't moved — and yet we'd won all those games!"

By now, County were having to cancel league games, because of their cup run, and Jones knew a backlog of matches was starting to build up. "I still felt we were steadily climbing the ladder, and we just had to keep at it.

But we were a long way off the top teams — the likes of Brentford, Luton, and Millwall."

And then came another one of those dates that will stick in Jones' memory for a long time to come: Tuesday, December 3rd. His first encounter with the man whose legacy had haunted Jones ever since he became Stockport manager — Danny Bergara, now manager of Rotherham.

The press billed it as the ultimate clash — the master against the pupil. The man who had taken County to the dizzy heights of Wembley, against the young pretender who thought he could go one better. It was the ultimate clash of ideologies; the passing game versus the long-ball game — the Beautiful Game against the Ugly Game.

The two men hadn't come face to face; hadn't spoken to each other since that awful day nearly two years ago, when Bergara was sacked, and Jones was handed his job ten minutes later.

Their final moments together then had been a mixture of deep sadness and deep embarrassment. It had been Jones who told Bergara he was succeeding him as County manager. And it was Jones who helped the distraught Uruguayan pack up his belongings — including the treasured photographs that hung on his office wall — and leave Edgeley Park for the last time.

Now they were to come face to face again, no longer colleagues united by a football club, but adversaries hell-bent on putting the other down.

To this day, Jones is adamant he didn't approach this clash with an ulterior motive. As much as the newspapers wanted to believe otherwise, Jones saw it solely as an opportunity to pick up three points — irrespective of the manager of the opposition. "The press had been making a big thing about my first encounter with Danny. I wasn't really bothered — honest to God. I'd be lying if I said otherwise.

"I never said anything to the players about him, even in the team talk. I just wanted to win and I didn't give two monkeys about Danny. Three-quarters of my team didn't know who he was, so it didn't warrant mentioning his name."

The pair did not meet before the game, and it wasn't until the two teams were walking down the players' tunnel, out on to the pitch, that Jones caught his first glimpse of the man who had plucked him from non-league obscurity and brought him to Stockport: "Danny was walking down the tunnel before me and I heard the fans chanting his name, they gave him a good reception," he recalled. "We didn't talk to each other going out of the tunnel. I just winked at him as I walked past his dug-out and shook his hand. I asked him how he was, he said: 'All right', and then it was on with the game."

The game was dominated by the abominable weather that night — incessant rain lashed across the pitch, and the howling wind made the torrential downpour all the more ferocious.

Only Kieron Durkan weathered the storm: his powerful free-kick flying through the sodden night air high into the net for the only goal of the game. The result consigned Rotherham to bottom of the table... Danny Bergara 0, David Jones 1.

"They couldn't live with us; they didn't know what they were doing, they were all at sixes and sevens — they didn't have a clue," said Jones. "They were just putting balls into corners. They had the Danny Bergara trademark all over them — endless balls into corners and chasing down to try and put you under pressure.

"I had no feelings whatsoever afterwards; all I wanted was those three points. It wouldn't have mattered whether it was against Danny or any other manager. I did hear their fans having a right go at him: telling him to get out, he was useless, crap — all that. I felt sorry for him then; but after the game he didn't shake hands with me, he just went storming off up the tunnel. He was probably annoyed with his team."

But Jones went looking for Bergara once the players had changed — and found him in his new office, surrounded by all those old pictures of County days-gone-by. And it was then that the clash of ideologies, the fundamental difference between the two men, came to the fore.

"I'll never forget it," said Jones. "I met him in his room, shook his hand and he said to me: 'You'll never play your way out of this division, Jonesy'. I just looked at him and said: 'Well, I'm going to give it one hell of a go, Dan.'

"I think he was still annoyed at his own players, he knew he had a big job on his hands— which he said — and he knew we had been too good for them on the night."

The victory put County into seventh spot — away from the despised tenth spot where they'd seemed permanently marooned. But Jones was in no mood to gloat — as he stood in Bergara's room, he started to recognise all the pictures hanging on the walls. "It was like déjà vu," he recalls. "He'd taken all his pictures from his old office at Edgeley Park and put them all up in his new office. It was like going into a time-warp."

The pair spent 30 minutes together; Bergara clutching a glass of whisky — "he always had a glass of whisky after a game," remarks Jones. Occasionally they referred to old times, but in the main they stuck to the two jobs in hand. Conversation didn't come easily; particularly for Bergara.

It wasn't that long ago that the Uruguayan had been the main man; revered by Jones, idolised by the County fans — an icon who could do no wrong. Now the tables had turned — it was Jones earning the plaudits for County's exhilarating style of football and Cup heroics; and it was Bergara — the man who lifted County from the Third Division doldrums — who was rock bottom.

Recalls Jones: "He asked me how it was going — he'd seen we'd done well in the cup — but I think it was hard for him, very, very hard for him to speak. It was just a feeling I got, I dunno, I think he found it difficult. It wasn't so much embarrassment; I think he just maybe reflected on what might have been. That's the feeling I got — but I might be totally wrong.

"Things weren't right at Rotherham, the players were ordinary and, knowing Danny like I did, he would have known they weren't up to it."

****

Mansfield Town 0, Stockport County 3 (FA Cup 2: Saturday, December 7)
Stockport County 0, Peterborough United 0 (Saturday, December 14)
Bury 0, Stockport County 0 (Saturday, December 21)
Wrexham 2, Stockport County 3 (Thursday, December 26)

David Jones can still hear the yob voices spitting their venomous hatred at him the night County's season hit the depth of despair: the 2-0 home defeat against Wrexham. The menacing chants of: 'Jones Out' have lodged in his memory; perhaps as a brutal reminder of what management's like at both ends of the spectrum. Jones may be in the penthouse now, but after that harrowing night against Wrexham, he knows how rapidly a manager can plummet to the basement.

Wrexham at home was County's nadir; Wrexham away the moment for sweet revenge. But it was also another moment of intense intimidation for Jones. As had been the case on that fraught night at Edgeley Park, the

County manager once again left the pitch confronted by the twisted behaviour of 'yob culture' — only this time it was far more menacing, far more threatening....

****

County were in seventh place now, and following their win at Rotherham, faced a second round FA Cup tie away to Mansfield. "It was an important game, because once again we were looking for a big team in the third round," said Jones. County won, 3-0, with Kieron Durkan grabbing two goals — including one spectacular free kick bent Brazilian-style around the wall. "The weather was really bad — in fact I thought the game would be called off," added Jones. "It was so foggy I didn't even see one of our goals going in!"

Back in the league, County struggled to a disappointing goal-less draw at home to Peterborough although, ironically. it was still enough to lift them a place in the table. "I found that very amusing," recalled Jones, "because we'd gone two months without moving and then we draw, and go from seventh to sixth."

County then scaled the Coca-Cola Cup heights again with their magnificent victory over West Ham. By now they were getting used to rubbing shoulders with world-class players — the big time had landed at Edgeley Park, and Jones' squad were lapping it up.

"It was funny to see all these foreigners prancing and posing around Edgeley Park: I swear every time you saw one, they had a mobile phone stuck to their ears," he chuckled. "It gave us a great feeling of being in the big time, and our players rose to the occasion. And they took it in their stride; no-one was getting big-headed, which was nice, and everyone kept their feet on the ground."

But the harsh truth was that the Coca-Cola Cup was a fantasy; and Bury, at Gigg Lane three days later, was the reality. Beating the Premier League boys counted for nothing if, at the end of the season, County were still in Division Two.

"Bury were flying then," reflects Jones, "but we played well against them and came away with a 0-0 draw. It was a good performance. We'd played all the big teams at the top by then, and I felt that Luton were the best we'd played. But I didn't think we had anything to fear."

And then came Wrexham: The Return! It was Boxing Day, and proved to be the best present Jones would receive that Christmas.

County had fallen 2-0 behind, both goals coming from corners. Jones tore into his team at half time: "I had a moan and a groan; I didn't care it was Christmas. We weren't getting in behind them, and our forwards were coming short all the time."

Armstrong and Gannon responded, pulling County level after the break, and then Tony Dinning dramatically converted a penalty, after Scott Williams had clumsily dragged down Luis Cavaco in the box.

Jones could barely contain himself. Victory would put County into fifth place, and the fact they were beating Wrexham made it extra satisfying. But, throughout the game, he had been the target for some abusive taunts and insults from one deranged fan in the stand immediately behind the County dug-out.

Jones usually enjoys a good-natured banter with rival fans. Stockport supporters are used to seeing their manager standing next to the dug-out during a game; as a former player it brings him closer to the action, he feels part of the play, he wants to be out there, making the passes, making the runs....

But the sight of a visiting manager standing by the touchline sometimes infuriates the home supporters — and Jones is used to the cries of: 'Sit down' from the terraces. And he's not averse to answering back.

But this was different, more sinister, more threatening.

"This one fella was giving me some right stick — the things he was saying were unprintable," recalled Jones. "Then, when we got to 2-2, I turned round and said: 'You've gone a bit quiet, mate.'"

What happened next took Jones totally by surprise. Incandescent with rage, the fan rushed towards the County manager, lanched himself across the perimeter wall and, with his ugly face screwed up in sheer fury, spat straight at Jones — sending an ugly dollop of saliva splattering over his jacket.

For once, Jones lost his cool, and anger got the better of him. With the benefit of hindsight, Jones should have remained his usual, calm self. But he didn't, and to this day is ashamed to admit he responded crudely. "I had an all-wool coat on, and I just looked at him and said: 'You've probably shagged this in the past, mate,'" he confesses. "That's the only time I've ever been offensive back."

County won the game — but there was still trouble to come for Jones. When a game finishes at Wrexham, the Racecourse Ground stewards close two wire-meshed gates to create a players' tunnel — allowing the teams to walk back into the main stand without having to fight their way through the crowd.

"I was walking round the pitch," says Jones, "and they'd just closed the gates so the players could get down the tunnel — when the same fella ran at the gate like a man possessed. If he could have got at me I swear he would have killed me. He had pure hatred in his face, it was unbelievable. If he could have got over the gate, I'm sure he would have gone for me."

The ugly confrontation took the gloss off a crucial victory for County. The three points lifted them into fifth place; the last time they played Wrexham, just three months earlier, they had slumped to 23rd. "It was a big win for us," confirms Jones, who that December picked up his first — but not his last — manager of the month award.

****

**Stoke City 0, Stockport County 2 *(FA Cup 3: Wednesday, January 15)*
Stockport County 5, Millwall 1 *(Saturday, January 18)*
Birmingham City 3, Stockport County 1 *(FA Cup 4: Saturday, January 25)*
Stockport County 1, Brentford 2 *(Saturday, February 1)*
Bristol City 1, Stockport County 1 *(Friday, February 7)***

Joe Jordan used to be a big brute of a footballer, in the traditional mould of centre forwards who frightened the living daylights out of defenders. A tough, rugged Scot, who made it to the top with Manchester United — ruling by fear and scoring goals by the bucketful. County had come across him before: he gave United the lead on that memorable night in 1978, when Stockport came so close to stunning the Reds at Old Trafford; and it was Jordan who won the diabolical penalty, that finally killed off Mike Summerbee's brave battlers.

David Jones knew Jordan well from his own playing days. He knew the only way to handle Jordan was to meet strength with strength, tackle with tackle, and to remain — at all times — defiant.

Now, many years later, that experience would prove invaluable — as he was about to encounter the Jordan temper once again....

****

County's promotion push was put on ice over the Christmas period — literally. After their superb victory at Wrexham on December 26, 1996, they didn't play another competitive match until January 15, 1997, as frozen grounds ruled out game after game.

"We were getting concerned," admitted Jones. "We were grateful for a rest, because we'd been playing two games a week but we didn't want 21 days off."

The big freeze also ruled out use of County's training ground; and Jones needed to find somewhere else to keep his squad in shape. During Euro 96, the luxurious facilities at Mottram Hall had been used by the tournament's eventual winners, so Jones decided: "If it's good enough for Germany, it's probably good enough for us!"

But, as the frozen days ticked by, and County tried to survive on five-a-sides and keep ball, Jones became increasingly concerned at their lack of match practice. It was then he turned to another former Manchester United star, Sammy McIlroy — manager of eventual Vauxhall Conference champions Macclesfield — for help.

"I phoned up Sammy and asked him if they would play a match against us at Mottram," explains Jones. "They were due to play a Conference game themselves, but weren't having a pitch inspection until 9 o'clock on the morning of their match. I told him the Mottram pitch was softish; we'd be there anyway — and if his game was cancelled, then come up and play us."

Macclesfield's game was postponed, and McIlroy took up the offer. "It was probably the best thing that happened to us," said Jones. "I realised when we played Sammy's team that we were half a yard off the pace because we'd gone so long without a game. "We beat them 3-2 and it was a good, strong game. We got a great workout and I'll always be grateful to Sammy for bringing his team over. We needed it."

That was on the Saturday; four days later County were facing a tough third round FA Cup tie away at First Division Stoke. Jones was concerned on two fronts: would the game go ahead; and, if so, was his side fit enough?

"We were sitting in the Stoke PostHouse hotel, when one of the match policemen phoned me up on my mobile and said: 'The referee's inspecting the pitch, he's going to call it off because of fog,'" recalls Jones. "Saint and I got a lift to the ground, walked out onto the pitch and could see quite clearly from goal-to-goal. We couldn't understand what all the fuss was about. I asked where the referee was, and one of the Stoke groundsmen pointed over my shoulder and said: 'He's up there, in the back row of the far stand!'"

Laughing at the absurdity of the situation, Jones continues: "I couldn't believe it! It wasn't a case of whether the ref could see post to post, it was whether the fans in the back row of the stand could get a decent view. "I shouted up to him: 'You're not referring from up there, you're meant to be down on the pitch!' And I told him it wouldn't be a full house, so he could always move the fans forward 20 rows. The point was, I really didn't want another game called off."

The referee left his decision until the last minute, eventually giving the game the all-clear. And it was rampant County who left their opponents fog-bound that night. Goals from Kieron Durkan and Alun Armstrong sealed a stunning 2-0 triumph over a Stoke side that had been on fire themselves in Division One. "We were brilliant but I was especially happy because all my fears of how we looked in the Macclesfield game had now gone," said Jones.

"I couldn't believe how well we played, especially as we'd not had a proper match for 21 days. We'd been playing some of our best stuff before the big freeze, and it was a relief to see we could still do it."

Once again an inspirational cup match provided the springboard for

Tom Bennett

Picture courtesy Manchester Evening News

greater success in the league. The victory over Stoke was yet another phenomenal piece of giantkilling by Stockport, one that never quite got the recognition it deserved. But in a way, that was understandable: County were used to beating Premier League opposition by now — they were becoming so good at it, everybody expected them to dispose of mere Division One sides with consummate ease!

However, there was always a fear lurking in the background that County would ultimately pay for their cup exploits, that it would all catch up with them, and battle-weary limbs would eventually be over-run in league games.

That wasn't to be. Each time County excelled in the cup, they carried that inspirational form over into the league. Stoke was no different. Three days after that thrilling performance, his side produced what Jones considers to be their second best display of the season — at home to Millwall; on whose ground County had put on their finest show back in October.

The legendary Ray 'Butch' Wilkins had just signed for Millwall. Wilkins and Jones had become mates during their days together in the England Under 21s; and although the distinctive Wilkins hairline may have receded more and more over the years, his ability to slice open a defence with one breathtaking 30-yard pass hadn't. Jones knew his old pal would provide stiff opposition. "I thought Butch would be a good challenge for Mazza and Tom, because they would be coming up against a world-class midfield player," he recalls, still glowing at the memory of what happened that afternoon.

County were electrifying. Their sweeping moves and intricate one-twos were carving through the Millwall defence with ease; their accuracy and skill would have been a credit to Wilkins in his prime.

Goals from Flynn, Mutch, Armstrong and Cavaco (two) were the icing on a stunning 5-1 victory, that left Jones purring: "We absolutely battered them. After the game, Ray admitted we'd played really well; I think he was a bit shellshocked.

"We'd closed him down really well, and we looked awesome going forward. I put that performance almost on a par with Millwall away — they were just unfortunate and unlucky to meet us twice when we were at our best."

It's mid-January now, and Brentford are looking uncatchable at the top of the Division. Second place is up for grabs though; but, once again, the league is pushed aside as County plough on with their cup exploits, first drawing 2-2 at home to Southampton — and then facing another difficult clash, this time at First Division Birmingham in the FA Cup fourth round.

County lost this 3-1 and some fans may have secretly breathed a sigh of relief. It meant one less distraction from the thing that really mattered.

But Jones does not include himself in that category; he came away from St Andrews fuming at the way County had been robbed of yet another piece of giantkilling. And, not for the first time, he pointed the finger of blame straight at the "abysmal" referee; who, he believes, was over-awed by Birmingham's famous new signing: the former Manchester United skipper Steve Bruce. "We should have won it," insists Jones. "I was really disappointed with the referee, I thought he was absolutely crap.

"It was the Steve Bruce show. If we tackled Steve Bruce; or if Steve Bruce asked for anything, he got it. And Steve Bruce used all his experience, his expertise, to milk that — and he did an absolutely brilliant job on us. He was magnificent, he conned the referee left, right and centre. And the referee — a fella called Paul Jones, from Loughborough — fell for it. He was absolutely useless. I was very disappointed to lose that game. The way we lost really did rile me. I just felt for an experienced referee to be conned, in the way he was, was an absolute joke."

To add insult to injury, the man who had been the spearhead of County's side during the Bergara years — Kevin Francis — stuck the knife in his old team-mates, scoring one of Birmingham's goals.

County picked themselves up from that setback to beat Southampton 2-1 in their epic Coca-Cola Cup quarter-final clash. Now they faced their biggest challenge of the league campaign so far: a home clash against the Division Two run-away leaders, Brentford. This was a real six pointer, the chance to peg the leaders back, the chance to prove County had the pedigree to get out of Division Two.

And they blew it.

Edgeley Park was still glowing from the stunning Southampton clash, when Brett Angell rocketed County into the lead. The Coca-Cola Cup, promotion, the Auto Windscreen Shield — hell, County were going to win the lot!

But Brentford hit back, equalising from a free kick — and then taking the lead and hanging on to a morale-busting 2-1 victory. "It was a big setback," conceded Jones. "Everyone was on a high after the Southampton game, and this was a really great chance to pull back on the top side.

"I was very, very unhappy at the way we lost it — and especially their equaliser, which was from a set-piece. We'd worked and worked in training on how to defend those; and then when they go and score from one it made it even more frustrating." County paid a heavy price for that blunder: dropping from fourth to eighth in the time it takes one piece of sloppy defending to lead to a goal.

The Auto Windscreen was becoming a distraction by now, and Jones deliberately rested his first-team players for the second-round tie at Burnley.

Fixtures were piling up thick and fast, and training just about went out of the window: "We couldn't get the team that had played on a Saturday to train together, because they were carrying knocks, or they were tired. We were virtually just ticking over."

And then came the confrontation with Bristol City boss, Joe Jordan.

Just like their manager in his playing days, Bristol were a ruthless, bruising side, and the tackles were as crude as they were effective.

"Me and Joe Jordan were having a right go at one another on the touchline," said Jones. "I was getting upset at some of the tackles and the decisions, and he was shouting back: 'You haven't won anything yet Dave'. I must admit that annoyed me. I got the feeling he thought we were getting a bit too big for our boots after all our cup games. I was thinking 'What's he saying that for?' Yes, I was shouting, but that was at the tackles, but then he started shouting back, and then me and him ended up arguing with one another."

It was a classic touchline confrontation. The shouts and insults grew in ferocity and, to the delight of the impassioned fans, the two over-heated managers squared up to one another in front of their dug-outs, toe-to-toe, eye-to eye.

It takes either a lot of courage, a lot of indignation, or a total loss of control to square up to Joe Jordan. He could take a man out with one ferocious stare, but an enraged Jones was beyond the point of no return. "We were face to face, pointing and yelling at one another — I think the fans were loving it," he recalled. "I was telling him to shut up; to keep his mouth shut. I'd played against him many times, I wasn't intimidated by him then and I wasn't intimidated by him now."

The warring managers were finally separated, and County went on to keep their composure and earn a 1-1 draw — thanks to an Alun Armstrong goal. Both managers walked off together, shaking hands. It had been handbags at dawn, and both Jones and Jordan were wise enough, and experienced enough, to shrug it off. "We had a beer afterwards and it was all forgotten, which it's got to be," said Jones. "It's all part of the hurly-burly of the game.

"I think Mazza was a bit in awe of Joe Jordan — because of his reputation and everything — and he turned to me after the game and said: 'Bloody hell, gaffer, you shouldn't be going up against the likes of him.' But it didn't bother me, I'd played against him lots of times. It was just typical Joe, he stands up and he intimidates people — and that's all part and parcel of his game."

****

Stockport County 3, Shrewsbury Town 1 *(Saturday, February 15)*
Blackpool 2, Stockport County 1 *(Saturday, February 22)*
Stockport County 0, Rotherham United 0 *(Saturday, March 1)*
Stockport County 2, Bury 1 *(Saturday, March 8)*
Peterborough United 0, Stockport County 2 *(Saturday, March 15)*
Notts County 1, Stockport County 2 *(Saturday, March 22)*

David Jones is sitting by the telephone in his office, scrolling down the names on the piece of paper in front of him. This is his hitlist; each name that of a footballer he desperately wants to bring to Edgeley Park.

And time is running out: County's exhilarating but totally unexpected success in the Coca-Cola Cup, the Auto Windscreen Shield and — to a lesser extent — the FA Cup, is taking its toll. They are facing a daunting backlog of games; matches that were postponed to let them continue their cup adventures. Injuries are piling up and two senior players are facing long suspensions after being sent off in suicidal fashion.

Jones can hear the alarm bells ringing; everything he's worked towards is on a knife-edge. The cup run, the injuries, the postponed games, the suspensions are sour ingredients for the most indigestible truth of them all — they're perilously close to blowing their chance of promotion.

Reinforcements are needed, fresh players to rejuvenate a tiring squad, to provide cover for injuries and suspensions. But the transfer deadline, after which clubs are no longer permitted to buy or sell players for the remainder of the season, is only days away.

Jones looks at the list he has drawn up after lengthy talks with his trusted right-hand man Sainty. He decides to go straight to the man at the top; he picks up the phone, and rings Birmingham City manager Trevor Francis.

The man Jones wants to bring to Stockport County right now is the former Blackburn striker, Mike Newell; the man who partnered England skipper Alan Shearer when Rovers won the Premiership title under Kenny Dalglish. An undisputed goalscorer, a player with the quality and experience to make a mockery of Second Division defences.

It was no secret in soccer circles that Newell had fallen out big-time with the Birmingham boss; and the club's owner, soft porn king David Sullivan, was ready to unload the troubled striker. As ever, Jones was optimistic.

"I knew Brett Angell was struggling with a knee injury," he confessed. "So I went for Mike Newell on loan — but we couldn't afford his money. He was on something like £6,000 a week, and there was no way we were going to be able to do that."

But this was a crisis. If Jones couldn't have Newell, there were other players on the hitlist he was determined to land.....

****

After the showdown with Jordan, County's next home league game was against Shrewsbury, the kind of opposition that has to be beaten if promotion is a realistic proposition. After 60 minutes, Edgeley Park was stunned into silence as Peter Whiston gave the lowly visitors the lead — but once again, towering Brett Angell came to the rescue, scoring two in a minute, before Alun Armstrong wrapped up the three precious points.

But this was to be a topsy-turvey period for County: each time they took a step forward, they were suddenly forced into a step back. They travelled to the seaside; and just like those famous big-dipper rides, plummeted with alarming speed to crash 2-1 against Blackpool. Goals from Northern Ireland international, Jimmy Quinn, and Tony Ellis, killed off County, although Andy Mutch grabbed a last-minute consolation. Were they going off the rails?

"After beating Shrewsbury I started to look at how many games we had left," said Jones. "We'd reached the points we wanted by now — we always said 52 points in February would be a good springboard for promotion.

"So we looked like we were on target — and then we go and lose to

Blackpool, which was a major disappointment. We didn't play well and I thought everyone looked tired — not so much physically, more mentally drained, after all the Coca-Cola Cup hype and everything."

"Blackpool deserved their points," conceded Jones. "We played Middlesbrough at home next in the Coca-Cola, and even though it was terribly disappointing to lose that match 2-0, Blackpool was a far worse setback.

"I was really thinking of automatic promotion now because I could see we had loads of games in hand. But Blackpool brought us right back down to earth."

The frustration and doubts continued, and with them the growing realisation that Jones would have to bring in new players to bolster his tiring squad. And that was underlined again in County's next match. No sooner had Ravanelli and Co. left Edgeley Park, than another 'legend' walked in: Danny Bergara.

This was Bergara's first return to Edgeley since his traumatic sacking two years earlier. He would have had his own private reasons for not wanting to come away empty-handed. Once again, Jones and Bergara found no opportunity to chat before the game, but this time it was the Uruguayan who got the upper-hand.

The match ended goal-less, although it was Bergara's team who had threatened to steal all the points. "Danny just came, packed his defence and stopped us from playing," said Jones. "And they should have won the game — they had a couple of good chances near the end. We were going flat out for three points after losing at Blackpool — we really needed all three — but at the end I was grateful for the point. It was a terrible game.

"We didn't play well, and I was getting concerned because I knew we had all these cup games — and all these re-arranged league matches — to fit in. This was the first time this all really worried me. I thought the players were starting to look a little bit jaded. Now it was a case of picking them up again and giving it a right good bash."

By now, Jones and Sainty had begun to draw up the hitlist of players they would like to bring to Edgeley Park. The transfer deadline wasn't far away, and the pair spent hours locked in talks together, carefully identifying the sort of players who could slot quickly, easily, and comfortably into the County system — without causing disruption and panic among the existing squad.

But the most immediate problem was the next league game: a real crunch home tie against Bury, who were now second in the division.

"This was another big one; it was so important. And we pulverised them," smiles Jones, almost gloating at the memory. Andy Mutch gave County a dream start, shooting them ahead after just two minutes, and John Jeffers added a second. "We were playing some cracking stuff but then they scored from a long throw, and it was all hands to the pumps then. That's the first time I think the supporters started to get edgy, because they knew we were starting to get close to things."

But County hung on, to claim their first league win for three matches. "I thought Bury were a big, strong side," said Jones. "I was a little bit surprised they were doing so well, but I knew their manager, Stan Ternent, had got them well organised."

County's valiant, but ultimately fruitless, victory at the Riverside Stadium over Middlesbrough followed. Crashing out of the Coca-Cola Cup semi-final in such an heroic manner was bitterly disappointing; but at least it made the future objective more defined, more focused.

Explained Jones: "Now we knew what we had to concentrate on, it was one less distraction. If we had beaten Middlesbrough, I honestly don't think we would have gone up; what with all the hype of getting to Wembley, of getting 'suited up' and everything.

"And I would have rather got promoted. After such a long, hard, slog of a season, gaining promotion was the ultimate goal. If we'd have got to Wembley, we would have kissed that goodbye.

"We came away from Middlesbrough with a lot of credit, it had been nail-biting right until the end, and to go there and win was a great boost for our confidence. It did our league campaign a lot of good — and that was the main thing."

Three days later, County were at struggling Peterborough; and goals from Marsden and Cavaco clinched another crucial 2-0 win. "It was an awful game, on an awful pitch, but it was a must we got those three points. We couldn't afford the luxury now of losing to teams at the bottom," said Jones.

But teams at the bottom can be formidable opposition — espescially when they too are fighting for points, and County faced another tricky away game at Notts County next. Luck was on their side though; while Brett Angell was accredited with Stockport's first goal in the 2-1 triumph —

even though it smacked of an own goal — there was absolutely no doubt about the fortuitous winner.

"It was a flukey goal, right at the end," confessed Jones. "The ball was played into the box, their keeper shouted and their centre-half — the former Manchester United player Graeme Hogg — tried to flick it back to him. Instead he just flicked it straight over his head. We'd deserved a draw — but probably not all three points."

It was a precious win but the danger signs were there. Jones' exhausted players were facing a monumental backlog of fixtures, and transfer deadline day was getting closer and closer. "I knew with the number of games coming up — we still had Watford and Plymouth and Gillingham to squeeze into the last month — that we had to do something," confessed Jones.

Bringing in new players at the start of the season is a gamble, bringing them in when an entire season's hopes and dreams are hanging in the balance has the potential to be devastating.

Most of Jones' and Sainty's spare time is spent scouring the country looking for players. It's not a glamorous occupation, this is the bread and butter of management; traipsing hundreds of miles to dire reserve games, in the hope that a player lives up to his reputation.

"If you spoke to my wife, she would say if there was a game of football going on, I'd be there," admitted Jones. "Sometimes I go out of the house at eight in the morning and I won't see Ann until the following morning, because by the time I get back, she's long been in bed. This season alone, I've flown to Portugal and Ireland looking for players; I've been up to Scotland, I've been down to Plymouth, I've been all over the place, clocking up an awful lot of miles. And most of the time, it comes to nothing.

"I'll try to watch a player a couple of times, and every one of my staff will try to watch them at least once as well. But I can go to a game and the player can be absolutely crap. I've looked at players and thought they weren't good enough, then another manager has gone along and seen them play absolutely brilliantly and got them.

"You just have to be in the right place at the right time and back your judgement. You've got to put your neck on the line. You can't 'um and ah' about a player; if you feel he's worth it, then go and do it."

Jones wanted a reserve keeper — second choice Neil Edwards needed a knee operation; a wide player — John Jeffers was struggling with a groin injury; a strong front man to cover for Brett Angell, who faced cartilage problems; and an experienced midfielder who could replace Chris Marsden, while he served a suspension.

It was the familiar cry of most managers at the beginning of the season: 'I just need four more players!' But this wasn't the beginning, it was much more important than that: it was the crunch. "Yes, I was tampering with the side," agrees Jones, "but Saint and I had long chats about it. I told the chairman it was a must. It wasn't an easy thing, but the chairman knew it had to be done."

****

QUESTION: Was it a panic measure?

ANSWER: "No, it was a calculated move. Every time you make a transfer it's a gamble but everything was done with a lot of thought behind it. It wasn't just a case of going out and grabbing a player at the last minute. We had a hitlist and we touched lucky, in that we got the ones we wanted."

****

Picture courtesy Manchester Evening News

Allun Armstrong

The first to arrive was a young keeper from Newcastle, Steve Harper. And it was while he was conducting that piece of business that Jones was encouraged to look at his next signing: Kevin Cooper, at Derby County. I'd been talking on the phone to Kenny Dalglish about Harper," explains Jones, "when I got transferred through to Arthur Cox — who used to be manager at Derby. I asked him if he'd seen any players worth looking at and he said there was a good lad at the Baseball Ground he remembered from when he'd been there.

So Saint and I went to look at him in about four reserve games. He was quick, had good feet, and seemed an intelligent player. I always think the more intelligent a player is, the better chance you've got."

Jones contacted Derby boss, Jim Smith, who at first seemed reluctant to part with Cooper: "But he phoned me back, and agreed to a loan deal."

It proved to be a significant phone call. Cooper was to score vital goals as County surged towards promotion. "It wasn't hard to convince him to come because he wanted first-team football, he'd seen us on television in our cup games and he was happy to move," added Jones.

Next came the evergreen Gordon 'Sid' Cowans; the man who had picked up more silverware in a sparkling career than County had lifted in their 114-year history. "I knew I was losing Chris Marsden through suspension for four or five games — we didn't know exactly how many then — so I needed an experienced player who had seen it, done it, and knew what it was all about. Those players are normally in the first team: the only one I could find was Sid."

Once again, Jones had spotted his man in a reserve-team game: "I'd gone to see Bradford reserves and he stuck in my mind. So I phoned up my mate, Chris Kamara, who was Bradford's manager, asked him whether Sid was available —and he said if I took over his contract, we could have him."

The transfer raised a few eyebrows. Surely Cowans, who in his heyday was an England international and the nucleus of Aston Villa's midfield, was past it? Jones disagrees: "Sid's 37. He's fit, he can still read the game, he's a good passer," answers Jones. "I knew he wouldn't have the legs to play three games in one week — which was starting to happen to us — but I felt it was vital we got someone with that experience. If I'd have brought in another youngster I think the players in the dressing room would have wondered what was going on. But to bring in an experienced player, and a famous one at that, gives people a lift.

"That's why I went and got Sid. Now we've got a player who's been in much bigger situations — such as European Cup games. We were always aware that the only people who had been in really big games at our club were the staff. But, sometimes, it's hard to transmit the calmness you need in those situations from the bench out to the field. Now Sid could do it for us."

The final target was Ken Charlery, a striker who had been a sharp thorn in County's side — particularly after his two goals at Wembley clinched promotion for Peterborough in the play-off final at Stockport's expense. But first Jones had to get past Posh's flamboyant manager, Barry Fry.

"It was the longest bit of transfer negotiating I'd ever done — because of Barry Fry," he laughs. "Barry's Barry — he kept moving the goalposts. One minute he wanted more money, then he didn't, then he did, and eventually we went back to the original offer we'd made — £60,000. Barry wanted £150,000 at first, but settled for sixty grand when I pointed out Charlery was 32 now and was going nowhere.

"But we had to agree to cough up another £10,000 if we got promotion — which we thought was a fair price to pay for going up."

****

Stockport County 1, Crewe Alexandra 0 *(Saturday, March 29)*
Bournemouth 0, Stockport County 0 *(Tuesday, April 1)*
Stockport County 1, Bristol Rovers 0 *(Saturday, April 5)*
Plymouth Argyle 0, Stockport County 0 *(Tuesday, April 8)*
Stockport County 1, Burnley 0 *(Saturday, April 12)*
Stockport County 1, Watford 0 *(Monday, April 14)*
Gillingham 1, Stockport County 0 *(Wednesday, April 16)*
Preston North End 1, Stockport County 0 *(Saturday, April 19)*
Stockport County 2, York City 1 *(Tuesday, April 22)*
Stockport County 2, Wycombe Wanderers 1 *(Saturday, April 26)*
Chesterfield 0, Stockport County 1 *(Tuesday, April 29)*
Luton Town 1, Stockport County 1 *(Saturday, May 3)*

There are 9,000 Stockport fans packed into Edgeley Park and the sound of their silence is shattering. The eerie noise reverberates through David Jones' head like a great, loud pneumatic drill pounding through the earth. Jones wants to cover his ears, to ward off the incredible sound: the sound of 9,000 fans mute with fear and panic.....

****

Having survived the threat from the bottom of the table, County were catapulted back to the top with two tough games — against Crewe and Burnley.

The new recruits were plunged into the deep end, and the Jones gamble paid dividends straight away, when Kevin Cooper scored a classy goal to clinch a 1-0 triumph at home to Crewe. "It was a great goal," recalled Jones. "Tom Bennett slid a lovely ball between their centre back and full back, Coops ran on to it and slotted the ball beyond their keeper."

Not only did that goal help erase the bitter memories of that desperately disappointing opening day defeat at Crewe, it also saw County leapfrog them in the table. The win lifted Jones' boys into fourth spot.

"It was great for Coops, it took the pressure off him," recalls Jones. "You don't know how a new player is going to react, but he settled in quickly, whereas Ken didn't settle in as well as we expected; perhaps because he had a big point to prove."

County were facing their 57th match of a season that was still far from over — this time away to Bournemouth. Although they came away with a goal-less draw, Jones was smarting with his young striker, Alun Armstrong, who had been sent off for foul-mouthing the referee. Armstrong had been petulant when he should have stayed cool; that was down to inexperience, but Jones knew County would pay dearly. Armstrong would now be suspended; it was April the 1st and Jones had no doubt who the April Fool was.

According to Jones: "Alun told the referee he was crap — which, of course, we all agreed with; but he just voiced his opinions. I had a right go at him, because we were now getting players sent off — like Mazza and Tom Bennett in the Auto Windscreen — at the wrong time of the season. We were starting to lose our discipline.

"I was annoyed because you can't mouth off to the referees. The ref may have deserved it, but in the end there's only going to be one winner."

Armstrong was fined 25 per cent of his week's wages for a first sending off, and Jones turned his attentions to Bristol Rovers at home. Once again, new arrival Cooper was the hero; calmly slotting home a penalty four minutes from time, after Rovers' substitute, Jamie Clapham, had hand-balled in the area. It was a far from easy win — "They got everyone behind the ball and made it very difficult for us," recalled Jones.

An exhausting coach trip to Plymouth followed — but County returned with a vital point after another 0-0 draw; although Armstrong came desperately close to making amends for his stupidity at Bournemouth, when his powerful header crashed against the bar.

April is renowned for its showers; and for Stockport it was the month when the matches came raining down on them in one almighty downpour. If you blinked you'd miss a game, if it wasn't in your diary, you'd be stranded. If Monday was Watford, then Wednesday must be Gillingham, which means Saturday has to be Preston. It was as crazy as that.

This was the month when Manchester United boss Alex Ferguson complained his pampered stars were playing too many games, and he pleaded with the Premier League to re-arrange games to ease United's congested fixture programme. That brought a wry smile from Jones; by the end of the season his side would play a staggering 67 matches, more than any other club in the entire Football League.

He knew there would be no favours for his weary players; it was a case of shut up and get on with it. And the harsh reality was that, if County were to go up, they would somehow have to contend with four games in eight days; stretching to six in 14 days, which became eight in 21, finally ending with ten games in 29 body-aching, limb-wearying days of April football. And, if all went to plan, at the end of that exhausting trail would be the Holy Grail: promotion. It was a tall order for a club which doesn't have a fraction of the resources of a Manchester United; but at least it was still within their sights.

After Plymouth, County faced their bitter local rivals, Burnley, at home. The game seemed gridlocked at 0-0, frustration was seeping through the terraces and one County supporter started having a go at Jones.

For once, it was the best bit of heckling Jones endured all season. Still chuckling at the memory, Jones recalls: "I'd got Andy Mutch running up and down the touchline warming up, and this fella in the crowd is giving me so much abuse — stuff like: 'You don't know what you're doing Jones', 'Get Mutchy on', 'We want Mutchy'.

"It was really getting to me, so I made a point that I wasn't going to put Andy on. It was actually a case of: 'I'll show that supporter who's boss round here!'

"Then Alun Armstrong got injured — so I had no choice but to put Andy on. And lo-and-behold, he goes and scores the winner! I don't mind admitting it, I wasn't going to put him on out of principle. I really wanted to teach that fat bastard in the stand a lesson!"

County were now seven games from their Holy Grail, and Watford at home was the next hurdle. John Jeffers got the only goal of the game — but nobody felt like celebrating; County paid a terrible price for their victory.

After just 12 minutes of the game, little Luis Cavaco slumped to the ground after an innocuous looking challenge. Jones leapt from his dug-out in a flash; he recognised the tell-tale sign — Cavaco wasn't moving.

"I knew it was bad as soon as it happened," he recalled. "When a player's down and they're motionless you know something's gone. It's when they're wriggling around you know it's not that serious."

The Portuguese winger, who had won the hearts of every County fan with his breathtaking runs, lay prone for five long minutes; the pain of an horrendous double break to his right leg racking his body.

Jones stood, helpless; remembering the chilling night when a reckless tackle in a reserve team game against Derby erased his own playing career. He can still feel the pain of that night; the crunch of boot against limb, and now, looking at Cavaco's motionless body, his heart went out to the brave winger. He knew from bitter experience that Cavaco would face a long, agonising haul back.

"It's part and parcel of the game but it wasn't a bad tackle; it was nothing, no-one was to blame," said Jones. "Luis was on fire then, he was flying past people at that stage in his career and the one thing that frightens defenders is pace. Although we won 1-0, it was a big disappointment to lose the kid. I really felt for him and his wife."

Cavaco was stretchered off, dazed, unable to take in the consequences of what had happened to him in one cruel second of a football match. He had come a long way from the obscurity of Portuguese football, but his goal against West Ham United at Upton Park had thrilled the nation — and the ovation he received as he was carried off spoke volumes. County fans knew how invaluable his magical twists and turns had been.

The victory over Watford just about ended their manager Graham

Taylor's promotion hopes, and put County into the prized second automatic promotion spot for the first time. "All of a sudden we've picked up nine points from three games and we're really looking set up," said Jones.

And then disaster struck; County came crashing from their lofty perch with a 1-0 defeat at Gillingham. It was their first reverse in ten games; but the timing stank, and all of a sudden the players were looking shattered after 62 exhausting games.

Said Jones: "Out of the three games — Burnley, Watford and Gillingham — everyone thought Gillingham was going to be the easy one. But I always felt it would be the hardest, because it was coming off the back of two tough matches. On top of that, we'd been travelling the length and breadth of the country to play games: Bournemouth, Plymouth, they're all long coach journeys and they tire you out. All of a sudden we're not doing half-hour journeys, we're doing five or six hour ones.

"I remember going down to Gillingham, and the lads were huddled up in corners of the coach, fast asleep. They were absolutely shattered — and this is the day before the match! They didn't look like a team that was going to win promotion."

Tired or not, Jones still didn't think his side would actually lose at Gillingham. "Yes, during the first half we were still on the coach; but after the break we came alive. There was no way we could have been tired and play like that. But the ball wouldn't go in the net for us."

It was an unwelcome — and unexpected — defeat, but Jones wasn't panicking because County still had games in hand. But the frustration continued at Preston, where they completely dominated the match — and came away 1-0 losers yet again. "That was the biggest massacre 1-0 defeat you will ever see," smiles Jones. "They had one shot, scored — that's not a bad average: one shot, one goal."

Twice Armstrong came agonisingly close: first, his fierce free-kick crashed against a post; and then he fluffed a glorious opportunity when he somehow blasted the ball hopelessly wide with only the keeper to beat. "It just wouldn't go in for us," shrugs Jones.

But Preston's Ian Bryson showed the way, when his long-range shot from 25 yards flew into the net, just eleven minutes from time —leaving Jones facing an exasperating drive back to Southport.

"I remember listening to a phone-in on the car radio, I don't know why I had it on — because normally I listen to music — when a Stockport supporter phoned up and started slaughtering the team — saying we weren't good enough to go up or anything. He'd forgotten all about the Burnleys and the Watfords. Just because we'd lost against Preston and Gillingham he thought the world had caved in."

However, even Jones found it hard to lift his own spirits that night. The sight of his players slumped in the back of the team coach, fast asleep on the way to Gillingham, had been a shock. This dizzy season — when these shattered players had given everything they had to slay the giants from the Premier League — was catching up on them. Now County were running out of time and matches.

Automatic promotion was everything now — the thought of going into the play-offs was simply too horrendous to contemplate. "We were starting to look very jaded," admitted Jones. "Deep down I knew we would have lost in the play-offs, because the likes of Crewe and Bristol and Brentford were all starting to come good again. We were starting off our games now like a house on fire but then dying near the end. It was all getting too much."

At least County's next two games were at home; but both were against teams desperate to avoid relegation, York and Wycombe. Nothing was going to be easy.

And, to make matters worse, after 20 minutes against York disaster struck; striker Neil Tolson pouncing on a rare Tom Bennett mistake to fire York into a shock lead. "I couldn't believe it," said Jones. "Flynnie and Jim, and the back four, could have had a Barbeque the amount of time we spent in their half. But they had one chance, broke away and scored."

The hallmark of County's season had been the ability to stay calm in crisis; to keep their shape and belief, and play their way back into games that looked to be slipping away.

That spirit was exemplified at Upton Park in the Coca-Cola Cup; West Ham scored, but County regrouped and carried on playing the football their manager so passionately believed in.

But the stakes were even higher now; the consequences of County losing to York were unthinkable. The temptation to hoof the ball and hope was almost irresistible, but Jones was having none of it. That system of securing promotion had been tried — and failed — under Danny Bergara; and Jones was determined to stick to his beliefs: "I told them at half time to keep playing, to keep passing, to keep their shape — to go back out and be Stockport County. They did, and we won 2-1."

Bennett made amends for his error when he headed home Marsden's free kick to level the scores. Relief exploded from the terraces — and the stage was set for the return of big Brett Angell.

Just 18 days earlier, Angell had been under a surgeon's knife for a cartilage operation. Now he was being thrown back into the firing line as a second-half substitute, and just 14 minutes later, he nodded home his 19th goal of the season after Bennett's ferocious drive was deflected back into his path by York skipper Tony Barras.

That heroic goal clinched a 2-1 win, and everyone at Stockport now knew the truth — two wins out of the last three games of the season would send them up.

Their last home game — the 65th match in a phenomenal year that had surpassed the wildest expectations of the even most-frenzied Stockport fan — would see the visit of struggling Wycombe Wanderers.

County were assured of a play-off place at least; but nobody was talking about that. In the past, clinching a place in the play-offs had been received with euphoria; now, nobody wanted to know. It was an unmentionable last resort. But the fact was that anything less than a win against Wycombe would surely have consigned County to the play-off lottery. Bury looked certain champions; Stockport and Luton were slugging it out for second place.

Once again, fate stepped in and conjured up a final sting in the tail: County's last game was to be at Kenilworth Road — and nobody relished the prospect of travelling there, if County needed a win to go up.

No, they HAD to win at home to Wycombe, and then they HAD to win away at Chesterfield — in the penultimate game of the season — so everyone could get on with the mother of all parties.

David Jones knew how critical the Wanderers' game was: "We had to win against Wycombe, then regardless of how the other results went, we knew we had the Chesterfield game to come — that was now our game in hand."

Mathematically, County could do it just by beating Wycombe alone — providing a string of other results went their way. Jones thought that scenario was as likely as him winning the lottery. But the danger was that Wycombe were still not safe from relegation themselves. While County were fighting for promotion, Wycombe were fighting for their lives.

And that's when teams are at their most dangerous. In that desperate situation, players aren't just playing for the pride of their fans or their club; they're playing for their own futures. They know contracts will be screwed up if they get relegated; mortgages could go unpaid; they're out on the scrapheap. Who wants a relegated player?

Ironically, both teams had their eyes on one other key fixture that day: Luton versus Peterborough. If Luton won, then Wycombe were safe — and County would go to Chesterfield knowing that only victory would guarantee promotion.

The Wycombe game attracted County's biggest league gate of the season, and at least 9,000 of the fans packed into Edgeley Park were signed up members of the David Jones Blue and White Army.

This was why football is truly 'the Beautiful Game': mums and dads; kids; teenagers; self-employed; the unemployed; the old; the young; all united, all craving the same thing that had been denied Stockport for 60 long years. It was getting close... it was coming home.

And for the first time that season, the unflappable, the ice-cool, the nerves-of-steel Mr David Jones actually felt the unbearable tension that could tear the County fans apart; David Jones cracked. He was human after all.

County got off to a dream start, when Armstrong scored after just four minutes; Kieron Durkan back-heading one of Flynn's monstrous long throws straight into the blond striker's path. It was Armstrong first goal for 19 barren matches, and he drove it confidently into the net. Relief swept across the terraces, and then, after 31 minutes, came euphoria.

Flynn sent another explosive throw into the Wycombe defence, the ball looped back off the head of Wycombe's central defender Michael Forsyth, and into the net for a cruel — but, for Stockport fans, beautiful — own goal.

County went in at the break 2-0 up, looking assured and well on course. Jones didn't need to say much, there was no great inspirational team-talk from the manager, just a: 'Keep it going, lads'.

Good advice — but in the 71st minute Lee Todd handled in the area, and Wycombe's Dave Carroll blasted home the penalty to throw the Division Two strugglers a lifeline. That signalled the worst 19 minutes of relentless tension suffered that season. If Jones felt it, then it had to be bad.

"The crowd was about 9,500 that day, and 9,000 of them were our fans" he recalls. "And with 15 minutes to go, 9,000 of them were absolutely crapping themselves! They really were — the atmosphere in the ground was unbearable.

"I never realised so many people could make so little noise. Everyone was stunned into silence, and then I'd hear a single voice screaming out from somewhere: 'Get your subs on'. But I didn't have any left!

"I'm not an emotional person — all my emotions are kept inside me — but I was getting closer and closer to the touchline to try to help our players. But, of course, there was nothing I could do. You can shout and bawl in a situation like that; but the players aren't going to hear you, and they'd only lose their concentration if they did.

"All you can do is pray you've got enough experience out there to steady things down."

Wave upon wave of Wycombe attacks descended on County's weary players; and the anxiety on the terraces intensified as the defending got more and more desperate.

"They were throwing players forward willy nilly," he remembers with a shudder. "We couldn't get out. They were hurling everything at us and every time they swept forward I could see them scoring. It was as if they were throwing bricks and stones at us; having a right go at it, and we were looking tired, scrappy — totally shellshocked.

"But I knew our players wanted it because they were dying for it. Toddy was flinging himself in front of the ball; Jonesy was pulling off saves, but we just couldn't get out of our own half.

"The fans were so silent — that was the first time in 65 games I felt: 'Bloody hell, blow the whistle ref, please don't let them score'."

If Jones could have darted on the pitch at that moment, rolled back the years and got stuck in, he wouldn't have hesitated. This was purgatory; as a player, he could influence the outcome of a game, now, as a manager he had to stand and suffer — just like a fan.

Nearly 200 miles away, Luton were beating Peterborough 2-0, but the Wycombe players were unaware of the score; unaware they were now free from the claws of relegation. "Their manager, John Gregory, was standing up screaming: 'Come on, come on, just one more,'" recalled Jones.

The pressure was relentless for all the players — but one, Chris Marsden, had extra reason to be wilting under the strain. Just 12 hours earlier he'd been holding his girlfriend's hand as she gave birth to their son, Matthew, in the middle of the night. Now he was struggling to stay on his feet.

According to Jones: "Mazza came up to me before the game and said: 'Gaffer, I've been up all night and if I get tired during the match, I'll give you the nod'. Mazza gave me the nod with 15 minutes to go and I just nodded back at him! He kept looking at me — and when I brought our sub on, he started walking towards the bench. But I just screamed: 'No, bugger off, get back on!'

"He told me afterwards he was completely knackered and I said: 'I know, I was knackered watching you!'"

The minutes trickled away, and as they agonisingly crept into seconds, pleading eyes turned towards for relief from the referee's whistle: 'Blow it, for God's sake, blow it'.

And then it came — the most welcome sound of all.

"Normally a few fans start to leave the ground before the end, but not this time," said Jones. "It was like they were all to scared to move from their seats. And when the whistle went it was unbelievable — there was a great roar as if all the tension was lifted off."

Jones and Sainty stood by the tunnel entrance and watched their shattered players drag their aching limbs round Edgeley Park for a lap of hon-

Picture courtesy Manchester Evening News

Mike Flynn

our, a farewell to the fans who were just as exhausted from the tension as the players themselves. "I was slapping them on their shoulders as they came back in, and their shirts were absolutely drenched," recalled Jones. "Everybody on that day gave everything they had. They'd run themselves into the ground, none of them had any more to give."

In the changing room the mood was subdued, quiet. The players sat, drained, sapped of energy, unable to find the strength to celebrate their victory. News spread that Luton had won at Peterborough; and with it came the realisation that Wycombe were safe — their incredible onslaught had been for nothing — and that County needed to win at Chesterfield to guarantee promotion.

"I spoke to their manager after the game and said: 'You wouldn't bloody lie down would you!'" said Jones. "He said: 'Well, we didn't know we were safe'. And I thought, damn, if I'd have had a radio I could have shouted to him during the game: 'Hey, John, you're safe — now pack it in will you!'"

By this time, everybody's focusing on Chesterfield; and wondering whether County have any strength left to go there and win. Sainty reminds Jones that County have already beaten them three times so far — and then adds: 'But no side's ever beaten a team four times in a season.'

Smiles Jones: "Saint comes up with these little quips every now and then — and I'm thinking 'Cheers, pal!' He's a master at it!"

The boss made his way up to the lounge after the Wycombe match, to chat to the sponsors and directors. He walked in to a barrage of questions; it was clear only one thing was on everyone's mind: "It was as if everyone was in a daze — can we be this close, are we still going to miss out? People were asking: 'Can we do it, can we do it?' They wanted to know what I was going to say to the players; things like that.

"Then, when I walked out to my car it was more of the same. Complete strangers, fans, were coming up saying: 'Do you think we'll do it?' — 'Is everybody fit?' — 'What are you going to say?' — 'What are you going to do?' Everybody in the town knew we really were close."

The Chesterfield game was just three days later; and Jones knew it would be futile to put his players through a vigorous training session.

"We trained on the Monday — or rather we had a walk around! We hadn't trained for two months now, we'd just played games. We had a little five-a-side, and I remember Jonah pulling out. He was still shattered and he went to sit alongside Saint for a chat. People were just going through the motions; it was walking pace. Almost slow motion.

"We just kept them ticking over. There was no use hammering them in any way because there was nothing left to give. They were giving everything they had and that was the most important thing.

"In the last two-and-a-half months of the season, we didn't work on anything. We could never train the day before a game with the team we wanted to put out, because players were either carrying knocks, or just resting. It was uncanny.

"You couldn't go out and practise things with players, because they were having treatment. You could only talk about things, and go over the stuff we'd drilled into them during the early part of the season."

Jones felt confident on the morning of the Chesterfield game. Yes, his players were tired, but so too were Chesterfield's. They also had thrilled the country with their valiant FA Cup run, and they too had a backlog of games to plough through.

John Duncan's team also had an outside chance of reaching the play-offs, but Jones felt that was to County's advantage. He reasoned that Chesterfield would have no option but to go for it — and that would leave them vulnerable at the back.

Victory was paramount. Jones did not want to go to Luton knowing he had to win there to clinch automatic promotion. This was a far more realistic prospect.

And so County dragged their weary limbs to Chesterfield for one more Herculean effort. As his players assembled in the dressing room, all Jones could do now was pass on his confidence, his optimism, as his side waited for their date with destiny.

He has long realised that the attention span of an average footballer is no more than a couple of minutes. He doesn't go in for long, rambling speeches before a game — he keeps his message simple, concise and straight to the point.

And so it was at Chesterfield.

He recalls: "I made a rallying call, something like: 'We've worked our bollocks off for 65 games to get to this position. We've always wanted to keep our fate in our own hands, and not be dependant on other results — well, it's in our hands now. I'd rather you go out now and lose the game than draw, so go out all guns blazing. Let's show the people what we're about.'"

And that was it, those were the words with which Jones equipped his players as they faced the most monumental match of the season. Yes, Blackburn, West Ham, Southampton, Middlesbrough had been big games — but they were for fun. This was for real.

It was County's tenth game in just 29 days, and they somehow found the strength to overcome their aching tiredness to produce a display that would propel Stockport into the big time after 60 years in the wilderness.

The record books will record that Stockport County sealed promotion with a 1-0 win at Chesterfield on Tuesday, April 29.

But the record books don't reveal the drama, the tension, the triumph of sheer mental willpower over sheer physical exhaustion. It was an heroic performance, and it had given every County fan the glory they had been craving during the club's many bleak, barren years.

The County manager was as elated as anyone when the referee finally blew his whistle after six agonising minutes of injury time. He had proved his managerial pedigree in only his second full season in the job, and proved that a passing game could get a club like Stockport out of the Second Division.

But it still wasn't enough for Jones. He craved something extra — he wanted his players to pull one last heroic deed out of the bag. He wanted the title.....

Jones is ruthlessly ambitious, and he doesn't settle for second best. He knew that if County won at Luton four days later, and Millwall could hold Bury to a draw at Gigg Lane, then County would finish the season as champions. And that sounded good....

"It was great to finish second but I wanted to be top," he admitted. "It was a tall order — because I knew Millwall had nothing to play for but pride at Bury — but I really wanted us to go for it."

County travelled down to Luton the day before their game, and spent a relaxing night in a local hotel. There were no wild booze ups, no sing-songs. That could all wait; there was still a job to be done.

And once again, Jones's men rose to the occasion, and for a while the cherished tag of champions was within their grasp. County took the lead when Luton keeper Ian Feuer upended Alun Armstrong in the box, and Kevin Cooper slotted home the penalty. "We played some great stuff; but their keeper should have been sent off," said Jones. "How can you bring down a lad in the penalty area and not even get booked?"

It looked good — but a rare Mike Flynn error let Andy Fotiadis in for a Luton equaliser; and, as news that Bury were beating Millwall, 2-0, swept around the ground, the game petered out into a 1-1 draw.

"There were no real celebrations after the game — we'd done all that at Chesterfield," said Jones. "We cracked open a bottle of champagne, had a few sips and that was it."

But if the players weren't ready to party, the chairman and the fans certainly were. The longest season in the club's history was at last over, and Stockport had got what they so richly deserved — and if that wasn't a good cause to celebrate, what was? The following night, chairman Brendan Elwood arranged a cabaret night at Cottons, in Knutsford, for the players, wives and girlfriends. "The cabaret lasted 20 minutes — the lads absolutely slaughtered him," chuckles Jones at the memory. "The chairman had booked an impressionist — he came on as Al Jolson and as soon as the players saw him, Brett Angell shouted: 'Yeah, he died as well!' But it was a great night, it got everyone together."

And then it was the fans' turn to party, to show their heroes just how much promotion meant to them. For 60 years, Stockport fans had been forced to survive on odd scraps of glory — a cup run here, a cup run there, promotion from the lowest division. But the occasional highs were always overshadowed by the almost constant lows; most of County's time was spent flirting with relegation — and even re-election. And, all the time, the two bullies from Manchester — United and City — were lapping up the silverware, the money, the fans, the headlines.

But now, in one beautiful season, those dismal days were swept away. The older generation could savour a moment they'd been patiently waiting years and years for; the younger generation could look to the future, to mouthwatering league games next year against the likes of Nottingham Forest and Manchester City. At last, Stockport County fans had something meaningful to celebrate.

An open-topped bus tour from Edgeley Park to Stockport Town Hall had been arranged for the next day, and all the players duly arrived the following morning; bringing their wives, children — and their hangovers from the night before — with them. "I remember getting up in the morning and it was absolutely chucking it down and I was thinking: 'Who the hell's going to turn up?'" says Jones.

"But when we got to the ground there were thousands of fans already there. All the lads parked their cars — had a bucks-fizz reception at the club shop — and then everyone got on the bus and set off for the Town Hall.

"There were thousands of people lining the streets, waving their flags, singing and chanting — it was brilliant. And they all followed the bus as we moved along; it took us half an hour just to get off when we reached the Town Hall. I knew these supporters were fanatical; so it was nice that our wives and children could see just how much it meant as well."

The County heroes were then ushered inside Stockport Town Hall, re-emerging minutes later on a balcony that overlooked the thousands of jubilant fans gathered down below. "They'd allowed the press and some of the supporters on the balcony as well," said Jones. "It was pretty congested up there and we had to stand on a ledge — which was only six inches wide — so we could wave and shout to the crowd down below. I'm up there on this ledge, when a fella suddenly slaps me on the back and says: 'Well done Jonesy' and it's nearly sent me flying over the top! The lads were loving it and the banter was really good: Brett Angell's got bad eyesight and all the lads were saying: 'The crowd's over there, Brett!'

"There was no microphone, and I was trying to shout to the fans. I'm sure they couldn't hear, but it didn't matter because they were loving it. Then the players got up in turn and the fans cheered them all, one by one.

"Even the chairman got up and the crowd started singing: 'There's only one Brendan Elwood.' I looked over to him and he had this great big cheesy grin on his face! I was made up for him, I really was. He'd put the money in, he'd done it and I thought it was brilliant that he was standing there getting the applause — he deserved it, he'd earned it."

They all had — every last one of them. It had been a long, hard season, but this explosion of joy had made each muscle-sapping moment of it so memorably worthwhile.

****

How often does it happen? After triumph comes disaster; it's a sad but almost inevitable fact of life. The good times take on greater meaning because of the bad times. Just when we've climbed to the top, something unforeseen comes along to steal our moment of glory.

Everyone at Edgeley Park was still celebrating County's greatest moment when the club was suddenly sent reeling by its greatest loss — the tragic death of Mr Stockport, Trevor Porteous.

Porteous was a servant in the true sense of the word; his sweat, toil and devotion to the club was ingrained in every corner of the ground. He was a friend to everyone — and anyone — who had blue blood running through their veins; he ate, slept and drank Stockport County.

Inevitably, Porteous befriended David Jones the moment the fresh-faced Scouser walked through the doors of Edgeley Park to take over County's youth policy. As Jones climbed the ladder — eventually succeeding Danny Bergara — their friendship grew stronger and stronger.

Porteous was a man Jones could turn to through the good times and — more imprtantly — the bad times; he'd been there, seen it, done it, and his immense experience and wisdom was a guiding light for County's new boss.

"I'd speak to Trevor virtually every day," remembers Jones, fondly. "He'd come in for an hour or so, sit around the place, do a little bit of mail for me, answer the phone — he was just there. Trevor was always there and he was the nicest person you could ever hope to meet. He was a good counsellor for me, I suppose. He'd listen to me, and I'd bounce ideas off him. I had long chats with him when I was coach and, certainly, when I was manager; I played golf with him and I miss him already.

"I just relaxed with Trevor. He always told me to keep my head up, to keep doing it my way; some days I would go in and I must have looked down in the dumps — but he was always there to pick me up."

Jones was on holiday in Marbella with County chairman Brendan Elwood, and some of the club directors, when they heard the tragic news. They returned in time to attend the funeral, where Jones made a speech in front of a packed congregation.

"I just said he was Mr Stockport County. He'd been at the club for over 40 years as player; manager; youth coach; assistant manager; physio; kitman. It was in his blood. He wasn't employed by the club any more, but he'd come in, do a little bit of scouting, help out. He knew Stockport County inside out. If we were bringing young kids into the club, Trevor was the one to meet them; the one to make them feel welcome. Nobody had a bad word to say about him. It's a big loss for the club. We've lost a friend as well as a colleague."

Thankfully, Porteous lived to see his beloved Stockport County clinch promotion to Division One; something he craved for 40 long years with the club.

Promotion was for Porteous, for everyone: for Jones; Elwood; the directors; sponsors; office staff; fans; everyone who has shared the dream that one day little Stockport County would stand shoulder-to-shoulder with the elite.

In life, Trevor Porteous honoured Stockport with his devotion, loyalty and service. In death Stockport County honoured him by fulfilling the dream he worked so hard to make come true....

CHAPTER **8**
The Saints Came Marching In

THE blazing sun beats down on yet another beautiful blue day in Majorca; so blue that the sky and sea have fused into one — elbowing the horizon out of the way — and turning the world into a huge dome of sparkling sapphire.

The sounds of people on holiday fill the crystal-clear air — children laughing and splashing in a great blue swimming pool, parents, teenagers, lovers, engrossed in idle chit-chat over ice-cool drinks. It's paradise here.

David Jones can bear the heat no longer; he slips into the alluring pool and, as the cool water laps refreshingly around him, he lifts baby Georgia to his shoulder so he can dip her tiny feet in and out of the delicious coolness.

The Stockport manager hasn't a care in the world. His year's work is done; County are promoted, and all the pressures and tensions of a long, taut season are floating away with every lap of water that splashes against his body. His wife, Ann, is stretched out on a sunbed; daughter Chloe close by her side. On days like this, reaching out for a tube of suncream seems like hard work.

Picture courtesy Manchester Evening News

Luis Cavaco

The noises of the swimming pool engulf Jones; not surprisingly, he doesn't hear the 'ring, ring' of his mobile phone, tucked out of sight underneath a sunbed.

Just like reaching for the suncream, stretching for the phone seems an unbearable chore; but Ann somehow manages to summon up the willpower to reach out a hand and answer the call.

Brendan Elwood is on the line — and, suddenly, the real world comes crashing in; invading this perfect blue haven.

The Stockport chairman is apologetic, polite, and asks Ann whether she is enjoying her holiday. But this isn't a social call. It is a call which will change David Jones' life; Brendan Elwood's life; and Stockport County's life. It's a call that will mean elation for Jones, and terrible heartache for the club.

Reveals Jones: "I climbed out of the pool, and took the phone off Ann. Brendan asked whether we were having a relaxing time, I said: 'Yes' and then he said: 'We've just had a phone call from Southampton.'

"I remember saying: 'Oh yeah, and who do they want?' — and the chairman replied, straight away: 'You.'"

Jones was probably silent for an instant; although the Premiership club's name spun around his head for what seemed like an eternity.

Southampton: the team County had stunned in the Coca-Cola Cup quarter-finals. The team that was now managerless, after Graeme Souness had struggled to keep them in the top flight — and then sensationally quit as soon as the season was over.

"I was a bit quiet; a bit taken aback," recalls Jones. "Brendan said he'd spoken to Southampton's chairman, Rupert Lowe, and had refused to give him permission to speak to me. But he was ringing now to give me permission to speak to them."

And that was how Stockport County lost the greatest manager they have known in 114 years of football. Jones was in paradise; County were in purgatory, and there was absolutely nothing they could do about it.

To his eternal credit, not even the chairman could begrudge Jones the promotion his talents so richly deserved. "Brendan said it was totally up to me," confirms Jones. "He wouldn't stand in my way. He knew it was something I'd always wanted, and he even wished me all the best there and then. I was on a high to be honest — although it was a colossal shock — and Ann was ecstatic. I was just very proud and honoured to be wanted by a Premiership club."

But the job wasn't in the bag just yet. Elwood's call came on Sunday afternoon; that same evening Jones telephoned the Southampton chairman.

"He virtually interviewed me over the phone," said Jones. "He wanted to know about me; my career; where I started; where I was born; what I did; what I'd done in management; what I'd done as a coach — things like that.

"He wanted to know what my philosophy was about playing. I said: 'I think you've seen that; I like to play good football,' and he remarked that the Saints' fans wouldn't accept anything less. I told him if he gave me the opportunity, I wouldn't let him down. The job wasn't mine then, but I had a very good feeling about it. You're never really sure, in a situation like that, but I just really got on well with him and I seemed to be talking the same language as him. He seemed a very straightforward man; he wanted honesty and that's what I gave him.

"He asked me what I thought about one or two of the Southampton players — and whether I'd seen them play. I said yes, of course, I'd seen them on the telly and watched them closely when we were due to play them in the Coca-Cola.

"He gave me a run down on their squad and told me what he thought was needed. It was just a very good conversation about football, about what I'd done at County, and how I'd gone about doing it."

Jones had flown to Majorca as manager of Stockport County; his plans for the new season in Division One already in place. The pre-season schedule had been drawn up; the trip to Portugal booked, and the players signed up.

He'd spent the first week of his well-earned holiday lapping up the sun — and the afterglow of promotion — and, as he stretched lazily on those sunbeds, his daydreams revolved around taking Stockport into the Premiership. Yet, in the time it takes to pick up a mobile phone, those dreams had been erased; replaced now by the prospect of leading one of the Premier League's famous clubs. "I knew instantly it was right," said Jones. "It's a Premiership club; it's a big club with a lot of ambition and it's where I've always wanted to be. I just never thought it would come so soon."

Rupert Lowe sent a two-man delegation out to Majorca the next day to meet Jones, and to fill him in with more details on the job. Even when they left, Jones still didn't know for sure whether he was the new manager of Southampton. He knew that Arsenal and England midfielder, David Platt, had been interviewed; and that David Webb, Terry Cooper and Alan Ball had all been linked with the vacancy. "Initially Rupert asked me to phone him at the end of the week to see if I had got the job," continued Jones. "But then I started thinking: 'If you've got to phone people then you're probably not wanted.'"

But the doubts were banished on the Wednesday morning. Jones was in his hotel room with Ann, getting ready for breakfast, when the phone went once again. "It was Rupert and I still didn't know what he was going to say for sure," recalls Jones. "But it was then that I got offered the job properly. I put my thumbs up to Ann, who was standing next to me, dying to know what was going on. When I put the phone down, she just said: 'Well done, you deserve it.'

"I couldn't tell anybody, because Southampton wanted to keep it under wraps until they'd cleared everything with Brendan. Rupert said he would phone him but I said: 'No, I want to contact Brendan first and tell him my decision.'"

The relationship between manager and chairman in football is notoriously fickle; and, more often than not, diabolical — usually ending in the dreaded vote of confidence. But Jones' relationship with Elwood was never in that mould — if Jones can form the same bond with his new chairman, he will be a lucky man.

It was important for the new Southampton manager to be the first to telephone Elwood. This was the man who had invested his trust in Jones; who had stood loyally by him during a disastrous start to the season, and who had been big enough not to stand in his way when the Premiership beckoned.

We all owe a debt somewhere along the line to individuals who somehow enter our lives and provide opportunities, and who open doors. Maybe they're teachers, maybe career advisors, maybe employers or even total strangers with a guiding word of advice — whoever they are, their influence can be monumental. Jones knows that Elwood will forever be one of those people in his life.

"I was looking forward to phoning him, although I knew it would be a very sad call," said Jones. "I have a very strong relationship with Brendan Elwood, and he had nothing but good blessings for me. I think he'd resigned himself to losing me, anyway. He told me that after his conversation with Rupert it was clear that Southampton really wanted me.

"You don't get an opportunity to break into the Premiership that often. I don't think Brendan thought in his wildest dreams there was anything he could do to keep me. It wasn't about money, it was about being in the best league in the world."

Jones and Elwood spoke for about 20 minutes and the County chairman agreed to contact his Southampton counterpart and thrash out the details of Jones' departure.

"I remember Ann saying it was a joyous occasion but also a very sad one — because really Stockport had given me this opportunity to go on to better things," said Jones. "It was like breaking away from a family — but you know you have to do that in life. Now I'm starting up a new family and that's the way it is. But the split between Brendan and me was very, very amicable — and that was important for me."

Jones was under strict orders to keep his appointment secret. But there was one person he had shared the news with ever since his first conversation with Southampton — his trusted right-hand man, John Sainty.

Sainty and Jones had worked together at County for the last six years.

There were no secrets between them, they worked out County's problems together, and they were the inseparable double act who had lifted the club into Division One. If Jones was going to Southampton, then Sainty was going with him — simple as that.

"I'd kept him in touch all the time," confirmed Jones. "When I was offered the job, I phoned Saint straight away. He's my right-hand man; he's the one I've worked with for six years, he's got a lot of good qualities and it was vital I took him with me. I told Rupert that right from the start.

"Saint's a great coach, a great administrator, a great buffer — he's just a great number two. He's totally trustworthy; he knows what I want and he can work within my boundaries without any problem.

"I suppose he could have been in with a shout for my job at County, except that he doesn't want to be a number one. He was delighted when I told him I'd got the job, and that I wanted him to join me — he never even spoke about money, he just left it all to me to sort out."

There were still more dramas ahead for Jones, however. The family were all together at Majorca airport on Thursday afternoon, waiting for their flight home, when his mobile phone rang once again.

"It was Rupert to say that there were one or two problems — namely County now wanted compensation," revealed Jones. "I was just praying the whole thing wasn't going to be scuppered. I immediately phoned Brendan and he said: 'Don't worry, we'll sort things out.' Then Rupert phoned back and said: 'Whatever happens, don't worry; you'll be Southampton's manager on Monday morning.'"

Jones went to Edgeley Park for the last time on Friday morning, where he met Elwood and made it clear nothing was going to stand in his way. "Brendan said there were one or two little snags," recalled Jones. "I said it was an opportunity I couldn't refuse: and, if County were going to stand in my way, then I would resign.

"But, thankfully, it never came to that. We were talking about lots of things — what I'd achieved — and I understood he didn't really want to see me go. But he also understood that he couldn't really stand in my way."

Elwood quizzed Jones over who he thought would be a good candidate to take over. Jones recommended Carlisle United boss, Mervyn Day; and Micky Wadsworth, who used to run the England Under-18 team and who was now at Scarborough.

And then came the moment when Jones had to tell the players; the men whose skills, willpower, devotion and endurance had got Stockport County promoted — and put Jones on his new Premier League platform.

Tony Dinning was already at the ground— having treatment after a hernia operation —and skipper Mike Flynn was being photographed in County's new kit for the 1997-98 season.

"I told Tony in front of Saint and he just said: 'Get away with yourself!'", said Jones. "Flynnie was made up, he really was pleased for me; although also disappointed because of the relationship I've got with him, I suppose."

Jones then started telephoning each and every player. "Paul Jones was gutted, Tom, Mazza, Brett, Mutchy, Sid Cowans — all the ones I could get through to at home — without exception they all wished me the best, and said I deserved it. That meant a lot."

Jim Gannon was also at the ground; and Jones' last duty as manager of Stockport County was to persuade the loyal centre back to sign a new contract that would keep him at Edgeley Park. "I told Jim the news just before I signed him up," said Jones. "I'm very close to 50 per cent of that squad. I told them to carry on with the good work they'd been doing. They've worked too hard and too long not to carry it on."

It was inevitable that news of Jones' appointment would start to leak out — anything involving a Premier League club finds a way of reaching the papers sooner rather than later.

"The phone calls at my home started at half ten in the morning on the Friday and didn't stop until eight at night," said Jones. "I didn't take any calls, Ann fielded them at home all day."

Jones kept far from the madding crowd the next day as well; going for a game of golf with his best friend, Phil Jones, at their local course, Formby Hall: "Everyone there had nothing but good wishes for me; although I couldn't tell them I had the job because it wasn't to be officially announced until the following Monday. It was just a case of: 'No comment!'

"But virtually everyone knew. I went to my niece's 18th birthday party on the Saturday night and everyone had seen it on Ceefax or Teletext, or read something in the papers. I kept joking 'no comment' — but they knew."

In fact, even Jones' children were saying: 'No comment' by the end of the weekend. His eldest daughter, Danielle, was home from college and working part-time in the local Kwik-Save supermarket to save money for a holiday. "Ainsdale's only a little village," he laughs, "and everyone knew she was my daughter— and all the shoppers were coming up to her and asking was it true? And even she kept saying: 'No comment, no comment!'"

Jones was up at six the next morning to catch the 8.30am flight from Manchester to Heathrow; where a driver was waiting to take him to Rupert Lowe's home in Gloucester. There, he met the Southampton directors and went over the finer details of his contract — and cracked open a bottle of champagne.

The next day, Monday, he was officially named as the new manager of Southampton at a press conference, and shown round the club's lavish training facilities. And, by then, the differences between Stockport and Southampton were starting to show.

Jones' contract with Southampton is 40 pages long — his deal with County was typed out on one sheet of A4 paper! And, when he started the 1996-97 season at Edgeley Park, he was on £50,000 a year — his new deal at The Dell is worth over three quarters of a million pounds over four years. "Looking at that, people might think I've gone for the money; but I'm not really money orientated," insisted Jones.

"It's good to have, but I'm ambitious to be in the best league in the world and people have got to understand that about me. Yes, the money's there — and that's a big bonus — but being in the Premiership is even bigger.

"And I could see the difference straight away. For example, Stockport have just acquired an absolutely superb training ground, but the one at Southampton is ten times better. It's Premiership standard; the quality of the pitches, the facilities, the way it's run from top to bottom, is all geared for the Premiership.

"At Stockport, we were at the bottom end — trying to achieve that in a round-about way. But everything's already on a bigger scale at Southampton."

The contrast is even more sharply underlined by just one glance at the fixture list for the new season. One minute Jones is making plans for County's opening games against Bradford and Bury; the next he's drooling at the prospect now facing him as manager of Southampton: "Our first matches are Bolton at home, Manchester United away, Arsenal at home and then Chelsea away. Talk about out of the frying pan and into the fire! But it's tremendous really — they all excite me, every one of them."

While the facilities at Southampton may be first class, Jones knows the club has spent too many years slugging it out at the wrong end of the table.

The glory days, when Lawrie McMenemy led them to an FA Cup final victory over Manchester United, are a dim and distant memory.

And their star player, Matthew Le Tissier, is a constant transfer target; and only agrees to remain at the club while they hang on to their Premiership status.

"I admire Le Tissier greatly as a player, and I look forward to working with him — I hope he feels the same way about me! He really is Mr Southampton and I hope he continues to be that way," said Jones.

"I think continuity has been their biggest problem. They'd had something like two managers in 20-odd years — and then, all of a sudden, they've had four in the last four years."

Jones insists he will tackle his new job in exactly the same way he approached his task at County — 'head-on': "The pressure is on me wherever I go. The first game of the season for Stockport would have been the same. They're all hard games; it's just I'm now in a league where you have to be spot on with everything you do. The first thing is to win over the players' confidence and then, hopefully, from day one the fans will support us."

Jones has been promised there is money in the kitty for new players, although how much he has yet to discover. "All I've got to do is identify a player I feel can do a job for Southampton; tell the chairman, and if we can afford him, we'll go for him. If the chairman says no, then I'll go looking elsewhere. I don't really want a budget.

"It was pretty much the same principle at County. I knew I had to work within a framework. Once we got into the First Division, I knew my limits would be around £150,000-£200,000 — now I don't know what the limits are."

And Jones doesn't flinch at the thought of suddenly dealing with highly-paid stars who earn more in a week than a County player does in three months. "Footballers are all the same, whatever level you're at," he insisted. "I've just got be myself; and if they don't like that then I've got to find players that do."

The name David Jones will be inscribed in the Stockport County book of legends for ever. His legacy was to give the club its greatest season to date: a cup run that thrilled the senses and produced moments that had previously belonged only in dreams; and a league campaign that led to the Holy Grail.

Jones produced a side that could play flowing, thrilling football, that could weave its way along the wings with instantaneous flicks and intricate passing movements. A side that kicked the long-ball game into touch, and left it there; a side that thought about its football, that used its brain instead of its brawn.

That sort of football hadn't been seen consistently at Edgeley Park for years. It brought the crowds back and it got the town talking about its team again. Even the rest of the country stood up and took notice as Blackburn, West Ham, Southampton and Middlesbrough were handed the shocks of their lives.

No true Stockport fan should begrudge Jones his promotion. The club has been fortunate that a man who is heading for the top stopped off along the way to give County a lift.

Jones should be remembered for the glories of season 1996-97; his achievements should not be sullied because he has now left the club. He leaves a hero — not a traitor.

"My strongest memories will be my relationship with the chairman; my relationship with the players; the staff; and everyone connected with the club — and, of course, my relationship with the supporters, who were absolutely superb," he said.

"I'll never forget the Coca-Cola Cup run — and the night we won promotion at Chesterfield. That game will always be with me; and I'll always be able to see the delight on everyone's faces that night.

"I've left Stockport County in a very healthy state. I'd like to think the fans will understand what's happened. I think the majority will realise I've gone to a league that's the best in the world and I don't think they would deny me that."

CHAPTER **9**
The Jones Files

THE PLAYERS: Paul Jones; Sean Connolly; Lee Todd; Tom Bennett; Mike Flynn; Jim Gannon; Matthew Bound; Kieron Durkan; Chris Marsden; Andy Mutch; Alun Armstrong; John Jeffers; Tony Dinning; Brett Angell; Gordon Cowans; Luis Cavaco; Ken Charlery; Kevin Cooper.

This is how David Jones really sees the men who made promotion possible for Stockport County; the men who embraced his philosophy and turned it into a winning formula.

It's not a guide to their vital statistics, their heights, weight, previous clubs, etc. It's simply a brief insight into what they're really like as human beings — whether they're jokers, loudmouths, womanisers, drinkers. It's the guide to Stockport County, warts and all....

THE PLAYERS
PAUL JONES: "Paul's our Keeper. He's nicknamed 'Jonah'. But he's called 'The Albatross' or 'Albie' by Joe Jakub, our youth team coach; because Joe's so small and Paul's so big. He rooms with Neil Edwards — 'Taff' — on away trips.

"He's definitely been accepted by the fans now. At the end of the last game of the season against Luton, he was throwing water at the fans behind the goal — and generally larking about with them. He's got to be popular with the fans — they still voted him Player of the Year!

"We got him for £60,000 from Wolves. He took over from local hero Neil Edwards, which was a hard thing to do. He had to come in win over the fans — and he did that, which shows a lot of character. He was the stalwart of the season for us — he commands his area, and keeps everything together.

"One save he made that sticks in my mind was one against Watford at home. It was a near-post corner, followed by a close-range header, and he just appeared from nowhere to clear it from under the bar. That was spectacular, but I think that his outstanding quality is that he does the 'bread and butter' work efficiently. I told the chairman that if your goalkeeper does that aspect well, he can give you 12-14 points a season.

"If he does have a weakness, it's his occasional lack of concentration. If he's finding things too easy, he can come for a cross a bit sloppy. So he needs to work on that a bit. Off the pitch, he's a gentle giant. He's a nice, honest bloke — he speaks his mind, but he goes about his business in a quiet way. We have no problems with him, whatsoever."

LEE TODD: "He plays at left back. He's known to the lads as 'Lizard'; but the staff call him 'The Slob'! He wears good clothes, but he always looks untidy — you could dress 'Toddy' in an Armani suit and he'd still look a tramp! The players call him 'The Lizard'. I think it's because he's a bit of a joker — always larking about. He's always at the hub of everything that's going on. He's forever giving out a lot of stick — and getting a lot back! He's a brilliant lad, though, really down to earth. Toddy's a fabulous person.

"He likes a pint — supporters always associate him with a pint in his hand. But don't let that fool you — he works very hard and he's got great ability. I genuinely believe that he should really be playing at a higher level.

The best game I've ever seen him play was against Everton in the FA Cup — where he marked Andrei Kanchelskis out of the game. He was magnificent — even Kanchelskis said to him as they came off the pitch: 'Todds' — that what he called him — 'you good player.' That always sticks in Toddy's mind!

"He reads the game quite well. People say that, because of his height, he'll always let you down — but he doesn't. He's a good tackler, always gives 100%. To improve his game he could work on his passing and distribution — especially his longer passing."

SEAN CONNOLLY: "Sean's at right back. He's actually qualified as a chartered physio. We had him here part-time while he was completing the university course a couple of years ago. Sean's been full-time with the club for three years now. He keeps his hand in during the week by helping out Roger Wylde, our physio. If Roger's got a heavy workload he'll muck in. The lads say he's useless! — but that's only a bit of mickey taking. He helps Roger out just to keep himself ticking over — his priority now is his football.

"His nickname is 'Eyebrows' — for obvious reasons! He's always at loggerheads with Toddy — Sean's a very well educated man, and he thinks Toddy is as thick as two short planks! There's always a lot of banter. He's had to handle a lot of mickey taking. He'll tell you himself that he contemplated packing the game in — football's a different world to university, the demands are totally different. He found it a bit strange to start with — a little hard to handle — but he's come to terms with it very well.

"His strengths are that he's a good reader of the game and a good passer. I think he's grown up an awful lot this year. I'd say the memorable moment for him this season was his goal against Middlesbrough. His weakness is that he must learn to take more responsibility and be a bit more forceful; but he's certainly another who could perform at a higher level. He's a very clever player."

MIKE FLYNN: "Flynnie's captain and plays at centre half. Rooms with Jonah sometimes, if Taff's not there. He's also known as 'The Ram' — because of his large forehead! He's a great lad, mucks in and everything, and he's always willing to do his bit for the community. He's just set up his own business — plant hire and security. He hires out the plant and then makes sure it's secure — what he's doing is looking to his future, trying to set his family up well.

"What can you say about Flynnie? He just gets better every season. His strengths are in his heading and tackling — and his strength in general. I'd say his weaknesses lie in his lack of awareness — which, at times, means he loses players — and his distribution. Saying that, though, his distribution has come on in leaps and bounds."

JIM GANNON: "'Jimbo' plays alongside Flynnie at the back. He's a bit of a loner. Bright lad — he's studying to be an accountant at Manchester College, so he does night school and goes in one day a week. He's been doing that for the last couple of seasons. Jimbo's always got his head in a book; sometimes on a coach journey he'll be doing his work — it's his release, I suppose. I don't have a problem with that, so long as he gives 90 minutes of football.

His strengths are that he always listens, and does the things that you ask. But he can be a bit strong-willed, and he always thinks he's right. He has to stop sometimes and step back a little. I've always got on with him, but maybe he's not the most liked person at the club — because of the way he always has to be right. But, at the end of the day, your not paid to be liked, you're paid to do a job — and that's what he does."

TOM BENNETT: "Benno's in midfield. He's a lovely lad — but the rest of them always take the mickey out of him. One example is over the fact that his wife has a hairdressing business in Scotland — and commutes there from their home in Chorley. The lads always kid-on that his missus has got another fella in Scotland! He takes it all in his stride, though. You always know when she's away, because he's first in and the last to leave the training ground!

"Benno's very cool, reads the game very well —and he never hides, even if he's having a bad time. He'll always be there, put his foot in and want the ball. When Tom plays, County play. The fans didn't take to him at first — but he's gradually won them over by the way he plays. He lacks a bit of pace, but County missed him last season when he broke his foot against Everton — and him being out injured might have been why we didn't make the play-offs. He's the sort of player who needs to know he's wanted — he needs that reassurance."

CHRIS MARSDEN: "Plays left midfield. Nicknamed 'Mazza'. He came into the football club with a 'big name'. He'd been at big clubs; and all of a sudden he getting the mickey taken out of him — there's no hiding place at this club! His girlfriend's just had a baby, so there was a lot of mickey taking over that. He was absolutely besotted with the whole thing — and we were telling him things like: 'When the waters break....' and he's saying: 'What do you mean, when the waters break?' — he hadn't got a clue! Sean's his best mate and he's known as Mazza's shadow — and we all wanted to know if he'd be videoing the birth! The pair of them are very close — they travel together from Sheffield all the time.

"We got him from Notts County on a free — they just wanted to unload him. I was warned not to take Mazza, because of his attitude and lack of discipline — but the 'hardman' stuff is just an image. He's a good lad and I've had nothing but good things from Mazza; OK, there's that loss of discipline now and again, but not too often. He's another player who wants to be wanted; to have someone believe in the way he played.

"He's not as tigerish as people think he is. He gets us going — like Tom, County play when he plays. His strength is his passing and his weakness is that he should control his temper. I think he should shoot a bit more — he's capable of scoring a lot more goals; he just doesn't believe in himself enough."

KIERON DURKAN: "Known as 'Kizza' — the nickname's followed him from Wrexham. Plays wide, left or right. Like Toddy, he's a bit of a joker. Kizza's not the brainiest in the world — but he works hard and is a very honest player. He's a great crosser of the ball, powerful. He needs to listen a lot more — and pick things up more quickly than he does. He works at it though — the demands that I put on him last year were a lot more than had ever been put on him before. He thought I was picking on him — but I told him that the time I wasn't picking on him, and didn't speak to him, was the time he should be worried. That would have meant that I didn't care about him. Potentially, if he put his mind to it, he could go a lot further than he has done.

"He likes golf and he likes going out with the lads — he's young and he likes a good time. When he went to Benidorm last year, a girl came round with some bunches of roses. He bit the head off one — and she gives him a right smack across the chops! So the lads were telling everyone that he'd been knocked out by a bird!

"He likes a laugh — as a single lad he attracts a fair amount of interest from women. And not all of them want to belt him, either!"

LUIS CAVACO: "Very, very clever young man. Luis speaks perfect English when he wants to — but not when he's getting a bollocking! He's adapted very quickly, a lot quicker than we thought he would.

"As a player he's very quick and very clever — he sees things early and whatever you tell him, he does. The better the players he plays with, the better he will become. His weakness is, perhaps, a lack of physical strength. He tires a bit towards the end of games; but, as he adapts to the demands of the English games, he's getting better in that respect. If he gets over his injury, he'll be a better person next season.

"He wasn't homesick at all when he came over, because he brought over his wife with him — and his parents — so he's settled in very quickly. He used to like his vodka, but it's too expensive over here — so Toddy's got him on the beer, and he'll have the odd pint of lager.

"Luis knows his way round, though. We were going to Rotherham on the coach and we got lost on the way. Luis found our way out! He knew where we were — and he was the only one who knew how to get us out of it! He'd travelled around the country with his wife — studying the maps and going to different towns."

JOHN JEFFERS: "Known as JJ. He's got brilliant ability. I got him on a free from Port Vale. Sadly, though, it looks like he might have to retire through injury. He's had a long-term groin problem — and it's caught up with him now.

"He's a scouser, as Kizza is — they room together and they're a right pair of scallywags. JJ's a great lad — and he's a bit of a joker. He's very, very clever — well educated — but he's got no common sense whatsoever. You'd think that, as a scouser, he'd be street-wise — but he's not at all.

"He's a lovely lad, though — a family man — and it'd be a great shame if he had to pack it in."

BRETT ANGELL: "Brett's a yokel — we call him 'The Farmer!' Him and Jonesy are a right pair of tractor drivers! He's as blind as a bat without his contact lenses. The lads take the mickey out of him about it. They point him in the right direction when they go out of the door to get on the pitch. He's a tremendous bloke though. He doesn't throw his weight around — but he'll speak his mind, he's not frightened to say anything. He's been around and knows what it's all about. Clever fella as well — well educated.

Cheers to a super season

"He's got a computer at home and spends a lot of time on the Internet. He loves a bet — he'll back anything, he'll bet on two flies. He studies the form on the Internet!

"His strengths are the fact that scores goals — he's got the knack of putting himself in the right areas at the right time. He works hard as well — harder than he's given credit for. His main weakness is, probably, his ball-control — that let's him down in certain areas. He never complains, though, just gets on with it."

ALUN ARMSTRONG: "Alan's a quiet, family man — but he could sleep for England! His favourite saying is: 'I'm f*****!' He's always sleeping — he can't sleep at nights, because he's always watching telly — so he sleeps everywhere else: on the coach, anywhere. He used to keep rabbits, but he doesn't anymore — I think he's totally consumed by his family.

"He's very quick, a lot quicker than people think. We definitely haven't seen the best of Alun Armstrong. The biggest thing that's helped him was Brett Angell coming in. Brett, and Andy Mutch, have taught Alun an awful lot about the game — about what he needs to do to get on. Bringing that experience into the club helped Alan tremendously.

"He's bit lazy and he needs to work harder in training. He also needs to realise what he's got. When he realises what he's got and what he can be, there'll be no holding him back."

ANDY MUTCH: "Mutchy' is an honest lad — I've known him a long time; I sold him while we were at Southport. He wants to stay in the game — wants to go into coaching or management. He's got a lot of ideas.

"Mutchy's an old man: he acts like an old man; he dresses like an old man; and he runs like an old man! Saying that, he's one of the biggest mickey-takers in the whole squad. If you do or say something wrong, he'll be the first to jump on it. The lads slaughter him on his dress-sense, but he comes straight back at them — he doesn't care.

"He been around, so he knows a lot about the game. He can score goals, will help others on the pitch as much as he can — and he's a pain in the arse! Never stops moaning, but I love the bones of him. He's getting older, so that's probably his biggest weakness. But he'll give everything he's got — he's a great old pro."

KEVIN COOPER: " The club haven't signed 'Coops' yet — but I hope they do. He's very quick and you can see he's been educated at a higher level. He can score goals, but he needs to work on his crossing.

"He's similar to Toddy — and I didn't think you'd ever find a bigger tramp than Toddy! Coops still wears tank-tops! He came in before a game once and had to have a bit of treatment. The lads were waiting in the changing-room, so they could take the mickey out of what they'd been told he was wearing. But when he came down, he was just wearing his undies! — he'd left all his clothes upstairs; because he knew they were waiting to hammer him.

"He's a loveable person, very polite. Like a lot of the lads, he's married with a baby. Perhaps, that's been one of the strengths of team, that they're nearly all family men."

KEN CHARLERY: "Ken's not been here that long — but he's already earned the nickname, 'Trigger', after the character in 'Only Fools And Horses'. You'll know why when I tell you that we were supposed to be meeting him at a motorway service station on the way to Bristol one day — obviously, we're heading south, and Ken was coming up from London. We're waiting for him for ages, but there's no sign of him whatsoever. So I phone him up on the mobile: 'Where are you Ken?' 'I'm at the service station,' he says. 'We've been here ten minutes, which side are you on?' 'I'm on the northbound,' replies Ken!

"You know those coffee-makers where you have to push the plungers down? Ken tried to unscrew it! — that's why we call him Trigger!

"The lads reckon that all those bomb alerts a few months ago, were down to him. He was always phoning in and saying: 'Gaffer, I can't get in, there's been a bomb alert and the motorway's closed.'

"Again, like the rest of the lads, he's a nice man — I think I got rid of all the bad apples. Ken's a very powerful player — I don't think the fans have seen the best of him yet. He hasn't scored the goals yet, but I'm sure he will — it'll come. His ball control lets him down sometimes — but, similar to Brett Angell, he'll give everything he's got. He been around, knows what it's all about — and I'm certain he'll be a big asset to County."

TONY DINNING: "Known as 'Dindo'. He's Jack the Lad — a typical Geordie lad. No-one can understand a word he says. He's a joker; like Toddy, he's always in there. He likes his golf — same as most of the lads. He's not married, likes a good night out and is a big hit with the women — people say he's good-looking, but I have my doubts about that!

"He likes a pint — but there's no harm in that. He's a strong player, a good passer of the ball — he's got a big future. He can play centre-half, or in midfield. He can even play in goal! Last season Neil Edwards got injured, at Carlisle, so I put Dindo in. So now he thinks he's a goalkeeper as well! We lost the game 2-0 — so he's bloody useless!

"If he's got a fault, it's that he sometimes thinks he's better than he actually is. He needs to work a bit harder on his defending qualities. But, saying that, I think he's got a big future in the game."

GORDON COWANS: "Known as 'Sid' — after 'Hissing Sid'. He was generally impressed with the whole set-up at Stockport. The biggest compliment he paid us was against Chesterfield at the end of the season. He said he's played in a lot of big games in his career, but the atmosphere, the way the lads handled themselves and how calm they were, was the best he'd ever seen.

"'Sid's a good pro. He came in — after being at big clubs and playing at big grounds, alongside big names — and mixed in straight away. He's not aloof in any way. He can still play, and still pass — you can see he's been a great player. He was a big asset to us when he came.

"He wants to move into to management, and I'm certain he'll do an excellent job."

MATTHEW BOUND: "'Boundy' plays at centre-half, but he's been unlucky with injury. Jimbo came in in his place and did well. Big, strong, powerful player. His weakness is that he lacks a bit of pace, but he never seems to get caught out — but the pace thing is probably why Southampton let him go.

"He's one of the best pro's you'll ever come across — he never moans, just gets on with it. Boundy's a bit of a Jack the Lad; he likes a good time. He lives in Manchester and likes the night life. That's not a problem — I've always found that if you treat your players like men, they'll act like men.

"When he first came to us, a couple of years back, he got attacked in a night-club. He'd had a drink and got involved; and all hell broke loose. He came and saw me and told me exactly what had happened. He was very honest about the whole thing — and I liked that."

There are one or two other players who featured now and again throughout the season. They haven't been mentioned here — but their contribution to County's glorious campaign has not been forgotten.

THE BACKROOM TEAM

David Jones likes to joke that his backroom staff could form one of the best five-a-side teams in the country — and he's not far wrong! With names like Gary Gillespie, Gordon Hill, Les Sealey and Roger Wylde to chose from — not to mention Jones himself — they'd certainly take some beating.

But it's what these men do off the pitch that is essential; each has performed a vital function in helping convey the Jones philosophy to the players. There may only be one manager; but management can never be a one-man job. Jones needed people around who held the same beliefs; and who could share the diversified workload that comes with running a football club successfully.

"People talk about getting the right players in, but it's doubly important that you have the right staff as well," said Jones. "The staff play a big, big part. If you have the right backroom team, then the players will be taught right and everything will be done properly."

So here they are, the president's men, each one hand-picked by Jones to fill a valuable behind-the-scenes role at Edgeley Park. And, in his own words, this is what Jones sees in them:

JOHN SAINTY: "He's my right-hand man, the one I trust the most. I share everything with him. He's the one I bounce ideas off; but, at end of the day, I make the decisions. I think very highly of his opinions — he's the elder statesman of our coaching staff because he's done it all, really.

"Saint's a very, very good coach. He started with Tottenham as a kid; but he played for Bournemouth, Reading, teams like that. He was the first-team coach for John Bond at Norwich and Manchester City — and then he had a spell as manager at Chester for a season; but he didn't take to it.

"We call him the 'quiet assassin' because everyone thinks he's quite laid-back — but in the dressing room, he's the assassin. If he thinks someone isn't doing something, he will say it. He speaks his mind — whether it's at half-time, or during the week. He's also got a very good sense of humour, and is very relaxed with the players — always ready to help them. But he's also very strong discipline-wise.

ROGER WYLDE: "He's the physio. It's important that you have a good physio, who really understands the injuries. Roger has a good background because he played. It's funny, because he knows nothing about football now! He couldn't tell you who manages what team or anything. He's completely gone away from that.

"He watches the game differently now. He doesn't watch the game for the football; he'll watch the players, and whether they've got a knock, or whether they're limping. He's not watching the match. He's spot on; he's a chartered physio, and he'll go a long way."

JOE JAKUB: "He's our youth coach. It's very important that you get the right person in that job and Joe is youth-oriented. He loves the kids, he's got to be their father, mother, uncle — everything to them. He's been different class."

GARY GILLESPIE: "Gary is a friend of mine, who was doing nothing. I got to know him during our playing days at Coventry. I bumped into him on the golf course and asked him what he was doing and he said: 'Nothing, Coventry don't want me, they pay me to stay away.' So I said: 'Why don't you come in and keep yourself fit; and do a little bit of coaching, because we are a member of staff down?' He doesn't get paid by us, we can't pay him while he's still strictly with Coventry.

"So Gary came in to help out — get himself fit — help with the pro's, and take the reserves, when we were doing the first team. He's done it all as a player; it was a case of seeing what he was like as a coach. I'd like to keep him — he likes to play, he plays the right way, he's similar to me.

"I think Gary wanted to get a manager's job. He might have realised now, however, that even though he's been a top player with a lot of clubs; he needs a grounding to, hopefully, go on. He's been in big games and that influences other players. If you're asking players to do something, and you can actually do it yourself, that's a big plus; and if you're playing five-a-side with the players and you're just as good as them — and you can still pass a ball and look comfortable on it — that goes a long way.

"You earn respect from the players like that. Here's a player who's played for Liverpool, played for Celtic — we call him the £2.5 million kit man! I always say it's a blue-nose getting his own back on a red-nose. He comes in; he mucks in with the kit, he picks them all up after the first team games and the reserve team games.

"At the Chesterfield game, he was very relaxed before the match; just giving a little bit of advice here and there — and you need that. He's also a good coach as well — not the finished article, because he's still learning."

LES SEALEY: "For a long time, the goalkeeper at County was just someone you fired balls at to save. But if you want to improve their awareness of angles and things like that, you need someone who knows that position.

"That's the one position that I wouldn't pretend I could coach in — because I spent half my career as a player trying to take the mickey out of goalkeepers in training; chipping them and stuff. When I did my coaching badge at Lilleshall, the one thing I did pick up was that goalkeeping is an art — and if you get people in who know what they're talking about, it'll not only help your first-team keeper but carry right through the club.

"Les used to come up once a week, on his day off when he was still with Orient. He didn't train; he'd come in and advise and things like that. When Jonesy came to the club he needed a run of games to build his confidence up. He's grown from strength to strength — and Les is part of that transformation."

GORDON HILL and **AUSTIN SPATE:** "They help out at the School of Excellence. Gordon runs his own soccer schools and we got involved with him when he phoned up, out of the blue, and said he was coaching in the area if we needed any help. He helps Joe Jakub out, along with Austin, who used to be with West Ham."